THE MAKING OF A LEGIONNAIRE

THE MAKING
OF A LEGIONNAIRE

My Life in the French Foreign Legion
Parachute Regiment

Bill Parris

WEIDENFELD & NICOLSON

London

Weidenfeld & Nicolson

The Orion Publishing Group Ltd
Orion House, 5 Upper Saint Martin's Lane, London WC2H 9EA

Copyright © William Parris and Susan Hill 2004
First published 2004

All rights reserved. No part of this book may be reproduced or
transmitted in any form or by any means electronic or mechanical
including photocopying recording or any information storage and
retrieval system without permission in writing from the Publisher.

The right of William Parris and Susan Hill to be identified as the
authors of this work has been asserted by them in accordance with
the Copyright, Designs and Patents Act 1988.

British Library Cataloguing-in-Publication Data
A catalogue record for this book is available from the British Library

ISBN 0 297 84616 7

Distributed in the United States by
Sterling Publishing Co. Inc
387 Park Avenue South, New York, NY 10016-8810

Printed and bound in Great Britain by
Clays Ltd, St Ives plc

ACKNOWLEDGEMENTS

THERE ARE A NUMBER OF PEOPLE TO whom I am indebted for making this project successful.

I would like to thank my agent, Andrew Lownie, for his belief that this could actually work, and for his boundless energy and commitment in making it so. Andrew introduced me to a wonderful person, Susan Hill, who was inspirational in helping me write this book. Susan's enthusiasm for this work was infectious and the book would not have happened had it not been for these two exceptional people.

When I first took ill I was told by a great friend, Neil Graham, 'You will discover who your true friends are now.' How right he was. Tommy Anderson, Brian and Jackie, John Fraser, Craig Freak, Rob Hind, Jimmy Howe and Jimmy Madden; many more, too many to mention but they know who they are. All good friends and true. They were there for me through some pretty bad times as well as the good and I owe them a debt of honour.

I would also like to thank Professor Neal, my consultant Mr Phillip Powell, Dr Pattman and the team on Ward Two at the Freeman

Hospital, Newcastle-upon-Tyne. Their skill and care made my suffering a little easier.

My thanks are also due to my publisher, Ian Drury, and his team at Weidenfeld & Nicolson for giving me the opportunity to see this work fulfilled.

Finally, but by no means least, I thank my loving wife Julie, and two outstanding boys, Jack and Glen, for whom this work was originally intended. You have all been the strength I have depended on to come through this illness. Without you I am nothing and but for you may not even have been here.

Bill Parris
DECEMBER 2003

CONTENTS

PREFACE

AS THE ROUNDS FIZZED AND ZIPPED over my head, I thought 'What the bloody hell am I doing here?' I was in a country I'd barely heard of, amidst a war about which I understood little and cared less and I was alone, separated from my unit and the comrades who had previously brought some sanity to this savage enterprise. Immobilized by fear, I cowered in the corner of a ramshackle shed which was being systematically demolished by machine-gun fire. I couldn't move, not a bloody muscle. The enemy had me in their sights and range; surely it was just a matter of minutes now?

Huge splinters of wood flew past me as more rounds devastated the rotted window frames. They fell to the ground, marking out a body shape, like one chalked around a corpse in an old detective film. I had a flash vision of my own corpse lying there.

I was covered in brick dust and the stench of cordite lacerated the air. The noise was horrendous; screaming and shouting, not only from commanders trying to regain some sort of order but also from the wounded and the dying that lay all around this dilapidated farmyard. I was aware of the constant baying of frightened animals as they stumbled about the yard trying to escape the noise and confusion, adding to the surreal atmosphere that prevailed. The African sun was blazing and I was rank with sweat – heat as well as physical exertion had drenched me. I lay now in a semi-foetal position; knees pulled tightly up to my chest as I tried to make myself as small as possible.

I knew where the gunfire was coming from, but every time I raised myself in an attempt to return it countless more rounds chewed up the already weakened brickwork of my battered shed. I thought it would collapse on me. I had become separated from my section whilst involved in a fearsome firefight with Tutsi rebels, who had rearmed and reorganized after years of exile in Uganda. They were marching on the capital of Rwanda to claim what they considered to be theirs. We were here to rescue civilians caught up in a vicious civil war. I was desperate to rejoin my section.

The small arms fire all around was ferocious and I had a big decision to make. I had to get back to the unit but I had lost all communication with them. I knew I was forward of them and to stand up and run back to our lines would leave me open to being slotted by my own guys as well as by the Tutsi fighters, whose fire was becoming ever fiercer.

With a sudden shattering of wood and a cloud of dust there stood, in what used to be the doorway of my shed, Steve Burns; friend, comrade and now white knight hero. Legion comrades are closer to each other than ordinary friends, closer even than brothers. The trust and empathy that Steve and I shared would have been a mystery to an outsider; to anyone who hadn't been through what we had together. Our trust in each other was absolute.

'What the fuck are you doing here?' he bellowed. At well over six foot and built like a rugby forward, Steve's physical presence was colossal and just one glare from his ice-blue eyes could make the toughest man stop and reconsider his plans. He dropped to the floor and grinned. 'You can't be trusted to do fuck all. Why am I always pulling you out of the shit?' My heart was racing, my breath came in gasps and I didn't answer for this was no time for banter. The bullets were still pounding the little outhouse to buggery and I didn't think it would stand up much longer. I struggled to my feet as if I was wearing roller-skates, slipping and sliding on the debris, unable to gain a good foothold. Suddenly, there was an unmistakable 'thud thud' from behind us. We both knew the sound of mortar rounds hitting the ground, and these were landing very close to us indeed.

Steve just looked at me and nodded, 'On three, OK?' No time for discussion or contingencies, this was our only opportunity. Chances would have to be taken. Did we want to be shot or hung? I certainly knew that I didn't want to be taken prisoner by the Tutsi. They did not have a reputation for being genial hosts. 'Three!' we shouted in unison and we burst from what had been the door of the shed, rifles blazing *à la* Butch Cassidy and then we ran like fuck towards our lines.

I had a brief thought of what grouse must feel like on the Glorious Twelfth. Around us, all sorts of weaponry, from the badly controlled machine-gun fire to wildly aimed rifle shots were ploughing the ground up. Clods of earth, some tufted with scorched grass, flew into the air. I was surprised that the fire was so ineffective, bearing in mind the close proximity of the enemy. They were only a few hundred metres away. An ineptly fired round can kill just as effectively as a properly aimed shot so I still had to be careful. With every second, I heard a whizzing sound, as a round passed precariously close to me, hissing like an angry snake. The round would smash into the ground or rock, peppering anything near by with debris.

We were both at full belt now, shouting and screaming loudly in the hope that our comrades would see and hear us, realize that we were on the same side and hold their fire. I could see a trench amidst the mayhem, about twenty yards away. Steve and I made a joint decision without even speaking; telepathically we both knew that trench could represent safety. We launched ourselves head first, like circus tumblers, into it. Me first, Steve very close behind. I took his considerable weight right on my chest and honestly thought my head would explode. Either that or my heart.

The front of the trench suddenly erupted as a heavy weapon zeroed in on us, its rounds churning the ground, showering the two of us with Africa's finest dirt. Our mini-battle had lasted only minutes although it seemed like hours and I was completely knackered. Any firefight, even a skirmish, has an intensity which can drain all your strength and energy. As fit as I thought I was, this was really tough. The heat of the day, the ferocity of the battle and general fatigue meant I was struggling to keep going. Great goblets of sweat were dripping down my face, across deep grime, and I wished I was somewhere, anywhere, else.

I became aware that the rounds going over our heads were coming from behind us. The section had successfully regrouped and was now laying down a very effective barrage of fire onto the enemy, who had now decided that they'd had enough and were withdrawing. Steve was just about to leap up in exultation, when I grabbed him by the crotch and hauled him back into the relative safety of the trench. We looked at each other and began laughing. Within seconds, we degenerated into helpless, almost hysterical, laughter, as above us the battle was in its final throes. We knew we were safe, for now anyway. Once we had settled, I peered out. It was an amazing sight; the destruction hard to comprehend. Dead bodies were scattered all around this smallholding. The smell of cordite and death remained in the air and stuck in my throat and the moans of the wounded and dying were piteous.

Later I began to think again of exactly what I was doing here and why – serving in the French Foreign Legion, in an African country I hardly knew and fighting in a war I cared even less about, largely ignorant of its aims. It was 1990 and I was twenty-nine years old. I wasn't there because of the wretched civilians I had come across or the Government that had called upon us to do their dirty work. Why then, and for whom? I had done it for my friends and comrades, and also the regiment which I was proud to be a part of. I had been in battle and not disgraced them or myself. I had been trained well. And it had all started because I was never satisfied with what was dished out. I always wanted a bit more.

INTRODUCTION

I AM UNWELL AND MAY NOT SEE MY sons grow up. This book is for them, just in case I can never tell them the stories, these true stories about what their Dad got up to once upon a time.

Like most of us I have a secret stash, a 'treasure box' which contains crucial evidence, fragments of my life: I want my boys to be able to piece every little thing together, somehow, someday. My wife Julie won't need any explanations: some of the items connect directly to her anyway, but Jack and Glen may be baffled unless they read this and learn something about those mysterious years before they were born, when I went AWOL from England. Whatever happens, I hope they will take some pride in what I did, just as my heart bursts with pride in them, and always will.

In the box are the tiny plastic bracelets slipped onto their wrists when they were born, the dried petals of the flower I wore on my lapel on the day I married their mother, a couple of medals, a blunt little knife I once used to cut into bread, coarse meat and cheese, shivering in rough terrain or weakened by dizzying heat elsewhere. And there are a few other things which may help them, one day, to understand.

What is missing is a simple white cap with a black peak. To my regret,

I impulsively and astonishingly just gave it away some years ago. I hope it is respected and treasured by the lucky guy who now has it. For my *képi blanc* was and remains my badge of honour – earned with toil and worn with pride. I wish I'd saved it for my sons, for the kepi was the classic, distinguishing item of my kit when I served for over five years in the French Foreign Legion. Maybe you'll remember from old *Beau Geste* movies that in the past there was a flap of white cotton fixed to the back, designed to protect a Legionnaire's neck from desert sun. I think the first of those films was a silent, made in 1926. The Legion was already the stuff of legend by the time Gary Cooper 'enlisted' and nearly seventy years later rather less dignified movies are still being made.

My reality was that I had been trained to kill if I must and there were times when I did face an enemy and force myself not to flinch when it was him or me in hand-to-hand combat. I even felt invincible as I hefted a rocket launcher to my shoulder and blew a peasant farmhouse in Africa to flaming smithereens. It became sickening, although nothing like as haunting as the memory of an orphaned child staring bewilderedly at the spattered slew of her mother's brains.

But the positives I brought home with me to Tyneside after those years outweigh any pain or guilt: I remember most of all the brotherhood and loyalty, friendship and trust, courage and decency of the much-misunderstood commando force I served with. It admits the displaced, sometimes even the dysfunctional, ruthlessly deselects those who cannot cut it in training and then dispatches the rest with the priceless gift of self-respect. That white hat was, even more than my boots and tunic, the part of my uniform which marked me. It was emblematic of what the Legion stands and stood for – honour and fidelity.

One day my sons may understand. In the meantime I take a blank sheet and begin to remember for them and if there is a little unfinished business to address here, I hope they will come to understand that as well.

LIKE MANY LITTLE BOYS I'D BEEN enraptured by the Legion legends – tales of honour and adventure, guilt and redemption, escape and excitement. But by the time I enlisted in the 1980s the Legion had changed and was continuing to evolve. The Legion's role in the French conflict with Algiers in the 1950s and early 1960s had already scotched much of the comic strip and cinematic Beau Geste fantasy and the brigade was now on the cusp of becoming the considerable force it is today, relied upon by governments all over the world to deal with many kinds of trouble. Mercenaries? It will be a while before that enduring assumption is also forgotten, I guess, but with wages of around £3 a week in my time I doubt if anyone could accuse us of being in it for the money.

Me? My childhood was troubled, my family life tense and my background altogether difficult. An early marriage had been a disaster. Years dominated by the RAF in one guise or another had taught me much – but I had yet to learn about self-discipline and trust. I'd drifted and failed, I felt rootless and lost. I needed a home. I eventually found it with the Legion. Much later I found real roots, a real home, deep personal commitments and a sort of peace. But I don't think I could have done so without those years in the Legion and the knowledge about friendship, brotherhood and grace under pressure that I acquired there, to borrow Ernest Hemingway's elegant phrase.

Thus my book is not only for my sons and Julie but for the extraordinary guys I served with. Some of them were heroes. Others were bastards. I'm grateful to them all: between them they made my life worth living and – much more importantly – have quietly helped to make this world a safer place for us all.

Try to set aside notions you may have formed about the Legion – those of bullies, thugs, reprobates, losers and damaged chaps seeking redemption: set them aside but don't altogether cast them away. There were good historical reasons for the glorious Beau Geste myth to have taken hold and something of the buccaneer still informs the force: there will always be charming and cultivated adventurers amidst the hoods and hoodlums. Simon Murray, whose classic text *Legionnaire* was first published in the 1980s, was one such. My book seeks to show how the Legion today is a crack fighting force called upon time and time again by governments which, for one reason or another, do not wish to mobilize soldiers paid for by their taxpayers. The Legion has always been up for the dirty work.

I want to explain the crucial role played by the Legion within pockets of tense and delicate, potentially explosive fields of battle or terrorism all over the world – sometimes the sort of incident or ambush that you might read about in a few newspaper paragraphs or hear of in a guarded news bulletin. If some ghastly and alarming situation has been defused at the very brink of crisis it may well be that the Legion was there and played a pivotal role. Brigades were in the Gulf in 1991. At the wire this highly-skilled and strenuously trained force is second to none.

So while it never really was the force of tough mercenaries, vagabonds, desperados and psychopaths of myth, however much those detached from action relish that mythology, it was desperation of sorts that led me to the Legion.

Becoming a soldier in the first place was almost a foregone. Before returning to Newcastle and joining the Police Force my father had been in the RAF. His clerical work held none of that flyboy glamour but he had postings all over Europe and I spent my childhood on various rather faceless bases. Even back in Tyneside the five of us lived in a police house which, despite my mother's best efforts, was never really a comfortable family home. Neat and clean, certainly, but somehow never warm. My younger brother Michael might disagree, but I doubt it. Our sister Mandy died some years ago. Dad was pointlessly competitive with us boys and a fierce disciplinarian who did not encourage us to aspire to much. He seemed to find it difficult to express affection. Perhaps that's why Michael – who is now irreproachably responsible and works as a nurse – went off the rails a bit when he was younger and I just squandered time and whatever abilities I had.

Football was the only thing that really engaged me, and I might have made a fist of that, having been offered trials for a couple of good clubs, but Dad didn't even take pride in this. After leaving school with a few O levels I took endless jobs on sites and in warehouses, often walking out in the middle of the day if I'd become too bored. I couldn't afford a place of my own so I stayed at home, feeling crushed and defeated. I suppose I could have studied and found a decent job, but Tyneside in the early eighties was in recession. The forces offered a logical escape route.

The RAF's equivalent of the Royal Marines is known as the Regiment, and that's where I wanted to be. It was reputed to be one of the toughest branches of the British forces, almost elite. I signed up as a gunner for six years in 1981, when I was twenty, and I finally began to grow up. Our training was more brutal than the norm – the runs longer, the backpacks heavier and the discipline stricter – but apart from the occasion when I considered joining the Legion while on weekend leave from very tedious duties at Greenham Common where the Americans on the shared base seemed to enjoy much better conditions than us, I loved it and signed up for another term. There were tours of West Germany, Northern Ireland – and there was a very good-looking woman …

Against the advice of friends I married her. Maybe it was hard on her with me being away for months at a time, but she was in the RAF too and must have known what she was doing. Anyway, she was soon doing it with other blokes and when I found out we split up. My request for a posting as far away from her as possible was declined so I applied for a PVR (Premature Voluntary Release).

I felt let down by my wife, my superiors, my friends, illogically, and by my family as usual. Yet hating any idea that I was a pitiable, disempowered failure and genuinely considering myself to be a free man now, I thought about the Legion again. I had no ties. I had to get away and by then I knew what I was good at even if I'd botched some other aspects of my life. I wasn't to know that my RAF paperwork had not been completed, so I remained an official absentee after I left for Paris in the early autumn of 1986.

EXTRAORDINARY CIRCUMSTANCES can bring out the best – or the worst – in all of us. Lightly-built women have been said to lift a car if their child is trapped beneath it, a man can fast for months if nourished by his principles. I packed almost nothing and just did a blind, maybe mindless, runner, pausing only to scribble a brief note for my parents. I had very little money left when I arrived in Paris and it all went on beer that evening. I had no idea when I'd next have a night out like this. In an increasingly maudlin haze I began to see, over the rims of many glasses, why people always seem to romanticize the city. However, well after midnight, without money for a hotel and very poor French, I had no choice but to make my way to Fort du Nogent, the French Foreign Legion's citadel.

All I knew was that it was in Vincennes, an easterly suburb some miles from the centre of the city. People whom I stopped for directions gave me baffled or pitying looks, possibly because of the state of me, possibly because they knew something I didn't about what I would find there.

I'd like to say I'd sobered-up by the time I reached the Fort. Certainly I remember with utter clarity the sight of the place – like a medieval film set by Disney – huge, its crenellations grimly defined against the bleak night sky. The tricolour fluttered above the ramparts as I walked towards a pair of heavy, buttressed gates. Beyond them lay unimaginable deprivations – my years with the Regiment in England would come to seem like the proverbial walk in the park – struggle, fear and pain. And also unimaginable friendships, exhilaration and self-discovery.

I would learn to survive by stealth in an equatorial forest, I would test my body to its limits and plumb physical and emotional resources I didn't realize I possessed. I would confront and conquer my deepest personal terror and in Rwanda I would stare death in the face during hand-to-hand combat. It was to be a hell of a journey.

I reached the main gates, paused before the hatch, the Judas gate, took one more breath of free night air and knocked. I was about to surrender my identity and change my name. My whole life, in fact, would be marked, changed forever.

CHAPTER ONE

THE JOURNEY BEGINS

I HAMMERED ON THOSE ENORMOUS doors and stood back, feeling slightly ridiculous. Almost immediately the hatch sprung open and I saw the face of my first Legionnaire and it was not a pretty sight. The lad wore his *képi blanc* smartly enough but underneath was a face only a mother could love. Half his right ear was gone, missing presumed bitten, and his nose seemed to spread across a face dotted with exceptionally bad acne scars. He had very hard and hostile eyes. He flicked his head in curt acknowledgement but did not speak.

'I want to join the Legion.' I couldn't think of anything else to say. Anyway, he so scared the shit out of me, I was surprised that I could speak at all.

'Passport,' he grunted. As I handed it over I wondered if I'd ever see it again and already felt as if a part of me had been taken away. That was presumptuous because I didn't yet know if I would be accepted. The Legion is, and can afford to be, very selective about whom it recruits these days. There is a strict elimination process even before training begins and far more people apply to join than are actually taken on. In the last five years or so this has applied to both sexes, as a small but increasingly significant number of women have applied to join. The sentry glanced at the passport, slammed the hatch shut and opened the Judas gate for me. Without looking backwards, I left one world and entered another.

I was shown into a small room just inside the gate, by now becoming nervous and unsure. My earlier confidence and alcohol-fuelled bravado was apparently left on the other side of the gate. As far as I was concerned though, there was no going back, not now. The room was cold, with a stone floor and bare save for a long bench running its entire width. The door was slammed; there was a lot of door slamming, I remember thinking, and I was alone. A few minutes later, the sentry returned and by various grunts and gestures indicated that he wanted my rucksack. The bag and its few contents were thrown to the floor and I got the impression that the guard expected a bit of swag for himself. I think he was quite upset that there wasn't anything worth pocketing. I was pleased I'd decided to travel light, but the glare I got from the sentry indicated only one of us was happy. I really capped it when he asked for any money I had and I obliged by showing him the empty insides of my pockets. That last beer had definitely been worth it.

He went out and once again I was left alone, in the dim light of a naked bulb. I remained standing, not daring to sit. A while later – I'm not sure exactly how long because by this time I had lost track of hours and minutes, not having a watch with me – another Legionnaire came into the room and motioned for me to follow him. I went to pick up my things but he shouted 'Non!' I never saw those things again.

I was taken to an administration block, ushered into a small office and once again left alone. I was beginning to think that these people didn't speak at all, but just barked and gesticulated at each other. Or was it that they just behaved like that with people like me, the potential new recruits? At least there were photos on the wall of this office and I passed some minutes looking at them. There were photos of a Legionnaire parachuting and a different picture of the same Legionnaire being pre-sented with some sort of medal. I took them to be of my host. The door opened behind me.

A huge beast of a man entered the office and almost filled it with his sheer physical presence. He was tall, tanned and immaculately dressed. I immediately sprang to my feet and he motioned for me to sit. He had stripes on his epaulettes, which in turn had gold braid on, so I presumed he held some considerable rank. I saw he had my passport in his hand and appeared to be studying it closely. I don't know what for; I had only ever been to Spain. Maybe it was only for effect.

'*Anglais?*' he eventually said. I just nodded, unsure of what to do or say. He must have taken that to mean I didn't speak French. 'So you want to join the Legion?' he continued in heavily accented English.

'Yes sir,' I replied. I didn't know if he was a sir, I just wanted to hedge my bets and not upset this guy. He did not correct me, so I guess I got it right. He leant into his desk and began pulling out various papers and then, to my astonishment, he started to talk about football. I couldn't believe it, the whole thing was surreal; here I was embarking on the greatest adventure of my life and I was talking about bloody football to a crack recruiting officer of the French Foreign Legion.

During this interview, he confirmed all I knew. He was at pains to tell me I was in for a hard time, to forget any ideas of glory and did I wish to reconsider? I had come this far and had left everything behind; my answer was both swift and brief: 'No'. I was going to sign a contract for five years and from now the Legion would be my family. After looking at my passport one more time, he took my breath away.

'Peter Parker will be your new name. Your date of birth is 12/06/60. OK? And I make you born in Leeds.' And that was it. I knew about the Legion changing people's identities at their request, if they didn't want to be found, but I hadn't asked to change any details. I thought it a bit sinister. Then I realized, one life ended and another began, 'Just like that', as Tommy Cooper might have said. From this day forth, I was Peter Parker from Leeds. He slammed the large ledger, similar to ones used by bookkeepers in old films. Taken completely at random, I could have ended up as anyone.

The officer bashed on, completing other various forms, all in the name of Parker, and eventually put them in front of me together with a pen. Clearly I was to sign them, and yes, you've guessed it, I signed in my original name! This was going to take some getting used to. That error was quickly put right, he shouted to someone outside the office and said, 'I will not see you again. Enjoy this life you have chosen and serve with honour and fidelity.' I didn't realize the importance of his words then, but I would come to do so and they would remain with me for the rest of my days.

I was shown to a dormitory, empty except for a row of half a dozen bunk beds and manky mattresses. No sheets or pillows. I was left alone and decided to explore what else there was. I found the showers, found where to pee, but where were the traps? Where could I have a dump? I looked round the tiny dorm and along the corridor – nothing. Those of you who have visited France are probably ahead of me by now.

For anyone else, let me explain. What I thought were showers, were in fact the traps. Yep, you squatted over the hole in the base and deposited the load there and God help you if you had the squits. Suddenly a cheerless police house on Tyneside or even my old barracks seemed sophistication personified.

As the night wore on, more lads were being shown into the dorm. All looked as sheepish and nervous as I had probably done. There were all sorts of different nationalities and no one could or would speak English. A few hours later, to my relief and joy, I could hear the dulcet-sounding tones of an Englishman. I hadn't really missed the sound of my own language until others had started filling up the room, chattering, and I didn't have anyone to talk to. This was great. As soon as he walked into the room, I leapt up and introduced myself to him, as Parker. Parris had gone to Paris and become … well, I suppose there was some linguistic logic at least.

OF COURSE I COULD NOT POSSIBLY know, as I grasped his enormous hand, how profoundly this guy would impact my life. I still think about the bastard every day and hope that he's OK, wherever he is. It turned out Steve had done a runner from the British Army and this was the first place he turned to. I never asked him why he was on the run and to this day he has never told me. There is an unwritten rule in the Legion that you do not ask another Legionnaire why he is there. If the information is volunteered, that's different, but you never ask.

Being the only two English lads at that time, it was obvious that we would stick together. We didn't know each other but we were both English, and that was all that mattered at the time. I didn't realize just how good a friend he was going to be, nor how close we would become. Steve was the original gentle giant and exuded charm, presence and quiet authority. Tall, strong and disgustingly good-looking, he stood out in any crowd. He was normally taciturn but there was something about him, masked by the pleasant façade, which indicated he could and would kick off if he needed to. Steve Burns was a man who could handle himself in any situation and even then I was sure I could learn plenty from him.

Steve had managed to keep hold of his wristwatch, so we knew it was almost six o'clock when we were taken to the cookhouse for food; the first sustenance we'd been offered all day incidentally, and my first meal since a baguette I'd grabbed during my bar crawl the day before – a world away already. We weren't marched over, which surprised both of us, and we just ambled across the yard. This gave me a chance to observe this place at last. The yard was in fact a small parade square, surrounded on all sides by two-storey buildings. It was darkening now and they were all lit up, bright, shining hives of activity. People rushing about, carrying those vital pieces of paper that any decent army depends on; trying to finish their work on time so that they could go for a beer. I saw the main gate, from which I had entered this mysterious world, and behind me our accommodation block where, I presumed, the administration was also carried out.

The place, even in this twilight, was immaculate. It was October, there were no leaves on the trees that bordered the square, yet not a leaf lay on the ground. In retrospect this simple observation seems emblematic of Legion insistence upon order and discipline.

We entered the empty cookhouse – not deemed worthy to eat with Legionnaires proper, I thought – and were shepherded to the servery. Plates full, we sat and ate in almost reverential silence. An orderly from admin placed a small bottle of wine next to each of us, an old Legion tradition at meals and I thought to myself, I like it here. That was until I saw what I was expected to eat. Suspicious-looking lumps of meat floated along with some sort of vegetables in a greasy soup. Maybe the wine was to disguise the taste of the mush that congealed before us. There was a plentiful supply of thickly cut bread which I grabbed to soak up the stew. It may have looked awful but it didn't taste too bad and with the wine and bread I was at least full.

After the meal we were taken to the stores and there our lowly position at this garrison and within this organization was hammered home to us. A pile of uniform, and I use the term loosely, was thrown at us. A khaki-coloured shirt with years of sweat and filth ingrained on the collar, a pair of truly battered trousers and a jacket that I wouldn't have done gardening in lay before me. There was no measuring, just a very bored-looking storeman who quickly sized us up, selected a piece of clothing from the shelves behind him and placed it on the pile. He had probably seen this rigmarole countless times before. Pasty-looking youths from every corner of Europe and beyond, all wanting to be what he already was. Instructions were shouted in French and, like sheep, Steve and I followed the others and dutifully stripped off our clothes. These were placed on the counter and, I suspect, went exactly the same way as my other things.

I started to dress. The first thing I noticed was the stink from the trousers. Not just musty from being stored, but rotten from not being washed. The jacket and shirt were the same. I glanced over at Steve and saw his gear was similarly terrible. We both grimaced but carried on regardless, each deciding that silence was the best road to go down at this stage. Don't attract attention to ourselves. My jacket was two sizes too small and the trousers three sizes too big. Far from looking like some sort of demigod Legionnaire, as I had fancifully imagined, I looked like an extra from a Charlie Chaplin film, and a badly dressed one at that. At least the boots I had been given fitted, even if I was at risk of contracting some sort of contagious foot fungus.

The last item issued to us was an overcoat. It immediately reminded me of Second World War films, where you see refugees or defeated and despondent captured troops being marched towards prisoner of war camps. The coats had neither buttons nor belts; they were oversized, mothy and scruffy. They made us look forlorn and wretched and I knew how those prisoners must have felt. I had a feeling that this was all done deliberately. It was almost a statement by the Legion to let us know exactly how far down the chain we were. We were simply unworthy of any decent kit. I think they were bringing us all down to the same level and slowly they would bring us up to an acceptable standard. We all started with absolutely nothing, save what they decreed to give us. The Legion owned us now.

INSTEAD OF GOING BACK TO THE DORM, we were taken to the kitchens. Even I didn't need a translator to know why we were there. The piles of stacked pots and pans all needed washing and we were the required labour. Actually, this experience was to stand Steve and me in good stead for the future. We learned early that when you worked in the kitchens, you ate first, ahead of everyone else, so there was always plenty. Secondly, you could help yourself, instead of being served by some numbskull who may have taken a dislike to you and therefore doles out less than your share. Thirdly, and most importantly, it was warm. Others bemoaned their luck at having to work there. While I didn't exactly relish the task, I certainly always made sure I got something out of any chore.

On leaving the kitchens, we formed a long extended line like a police search team, minus the dogs. On this occasion, it was not evidence we looked for, but rubbish. We had to pick up every scrap of litter, hence that absence of leaves on the ground, and anything else that shouldn't have been there. Anything that breeched and offended the high standards of order that the Legion demanded had to be removed. An idea of what I faced began forming in my mind.

Once back in the dorm, there was a fashion parade of sorts, and even with the language barrier and cultural differences, we were, for the present anyway, all one. We swapped items of kit but even so no one's uniform fitted correctly, we all stank the same and if this was the Legion's way of bringing everyone together to share the same early frustrations and irritations, the exercise definitely worked. We looked like a bunch of circus clowns – and even laughed about it – but the final humiliation was to come.

There wasn't any time to get used to the dorm. Two Legionnaires I hadn't seen before entered and ordered everyone out and into the courtyard. I had latched onto a French-speaking lad who seemed quite friendly; he turned out to be a cracking chap and a very good friend who often guided me through the early, difficult days. His name was Philippe, a name I would not forget. I wasn't keen at this stage to form any sort of friendship simply because I didn't yet know how long people were going to be around, me included. What I did know, however, was, I needed to be around someone who could at least understand French and translate back what was happening to us. The selfish streak coming out or the survival streak?

Philippe told us that we were en route on foot to Gare d'Austerlitz, to board the train that would take us onwards to Aubagne, the Legion recruiting centre in the South of France – for selection or rejection. It seemed that everyone I had seen at Fort du Nogent was travelling south. Any rejecting would be done at Aubagne. I was surprised though to see fellow badly-dressed convict types join us on the platform. They had, according to rumour, enlisted at another Legion *quartier* in the north of France, near Lille. You can join the Legion at any *quartier*, or by presenting yourself at a *gendarmerie* (police station) and they will take you to or set you on the right road to a Legion recruiting base. I couldn't believe that they would let us be seen in public dressed so shabbily. Our accompanying NCOs were in their much smarter barrack dress and it wouldn't take the brains of an Einstein to work out who and what we were.

We looked, and I felt, terrible. I noticed how civilians in the streets looked admiringly at the correctly dressed Legionnaires and at us in utter contempt. I did wonder if this was another ploy by the Legion to let us know exactly where we stood with them. The twelve of us looked like fugitive criminals being kept in line by these honourable soldiers of France. At least that was the way I felt, and by the bleak cast of the faces of my travelling companions, so did they.

We were piled into an old-fashioned train carriage. Not the modern TGV, that marvellous super-fast railway, for us. Oh no, we boarded a cattle train that would take about twelve hours to rumble through little towns on branch lines, not that we could see a lot out of the few filthy windows. The compartment was small and cramped; hardly room to stand, never mind sit. I squatted nonetheless and claimed my spot. One of us made a grave error and dared to ask for some food. He got a punch in the mouth from an accompanying Legionnaire guard for his trouble and the reality of my situation began to sink in. This was the first sign of any violence that I had seen towards recruits and it became a very quiet compartment that travelled through the night. I found it impossible to sleep and I noticed that the two NCOs slept in shifts. I wondered if this apparently mindless deprivation was imposed deliberately, and I knew deep down that of course it was. We were their property now, and we could only go where and when they said we could.

The stench in our carriage must have been disgusting as body heat and fumes from filthy clothing mingled all night, but despite the almost stifling warmth, I shivered and hoped that no one else noticed it.

CHAPTER TWO

SELECTION

THERE WAS A TRUCK TO MEET US IN Marseilles, an old American World War Two type vehicle, double wheeled at the rear and with a canvas covering over the wooden seats in the back. The back was open so that we could see where we had been but not where we were going. One NCO jumped in the front and the other in the back with us. They didn't seem to want to leave us on our own at any stage. I remember being ravenous, bleary eyed and absolutely knackered, for I hadn't managed more than a few minutes sleep on the journey down which had been completed in total silence after that incident on leaving Paris. The sheer brutality of the assault on our fellow recruit had rammed home the reality of the situation to all of us. It would have taken a brave or foolish man to break the silence that shrouded us. The drive to Aubagne passed in a blur.

Although the sun shone brightly, it was cold. Even the South of France can be brisk in October and everyone hunched into their oversized coats, each of us plunged in silent personal gloom, hands thrust deep into pockets, collars upturned and heads disappearing into the comparative warmth of our coats. Not for the last time, the glimmer of some school history lesson crossed my mind and I remembered something about tumbrels and the guillotine and prayers for deliverance.

The approach to the headquarters was completely different from that to the ancient fort in Paris. This was a thoroughly modern complex, not unlike a grass-surrounded low-rise army barracks you would expect to see in England. From the road, which ran past the main gate, the buildings and parade square could easily be seen. There was no sense of secrecy here.

Two Legionnaires in full ceremonial dress, white kepis sitting proudly on their shaven heads, met us. Their brightly coloured epaulettes exaggerated already broad shoulders and their immaculate uniforms appeared to be tailor-made as they stood on either side of the gate with their FAMAS rifles slung across their chests. They say first impressions count and I felt revived and inspired at the sight of them. After looking at such proud, formidable men, I really wanted to be in amongst them and be one of them. The image of those guys was to stay with me for a long time, and at times was the driving force behind my passing through the selection procedures. I was already well aware that the Legion fails more aspiring recruits than it keeps.

The truck stopped and a perfunctory check was carried out by one of the sentries. He went to the passenger side and spoke briefly to the NCO who had collected us; they laughed and then shook hands. The sentry signalled to the guardroom and the gates slid aside on well-oiled wheels and we were inside. Sentry duty is an integral part of Legion life wherever it is based. I was to perform my share and more over the years to come. It isn't always about affable exchanges with *confrères* in the sun: more often the duty involves a unique combination of boredom, vigilance and discomfort – perhaps in any army the discomfort is designed to counter tedium and ensure alertness.

The ancient transporter of warriors past chugged, coughed and spluttered up the incline by the guardroom, emitting enough fumes to charge a modern car, belching great clouds of black smoke from the rear and surely protesting at her latest task. We shuddered to a halt about one hundred metres from the gate, next to a building some distance from the rest of the barracks. This would be home for the next few days or weeks – depending on whether we were destined for deselection or to become numbered amongst the chosen few. I learned from Philippe, my new friend and our team translator, that this was where all the initial selection procedures were to be carried out. Philippe had been ahead of the game and asked some of the *bleus* (those waiting for selection) what lay in store for us. The man was worth his weight in gold. Forewarned is forearmed and knowledge is power. To know what to expect kept us one step ahead of the rest of the pack vying for places. Medicals, aptitude tests and interviews would be conducted here and if success-ful, the recruit would move on to basic training at Castelnaudary, a camp near the foothills of the Pyrenees and deep in the rugged French coun-tryside where ancient memories of wars and skirmishes with Moors and Cathars are still etched in every Romanesque village church and evoked in local legend.

Once in the block, we were allowed to discard the shabby gear that we had worn all the way down from Paris and were given clean tracksuits and new trainers. I wondered if all that terrible old kit was packed up again and returned to the Paris fort to dismay a new group of rookies. I immediately felt better and when I noticed a Legion badge on the chest of the jacket, I admit to feeling several inches taller: it was the first step towards belonging. We had virtually been reduced to tramps earlier; was this the start of the building-up process?

Steve and I stuck close together and made damn sure that the trusty Philippe was with us as well. We were herded into a large hall which appeared to be set out for an examination. Individual desks, with a piece of paper and a pencil on each one, were laid out in neat rows. I sat at a desk and for an innocent or naive moment I thought we had to fill out an application form. But all we were required to do was write our name, date of birth and country of origin.

Within a couple of minutes, more orders were barked out and although I couldn't tell exactly what was said, the meaning was entirely clear. We streamed upstairs and piled into dorms that would be our home for the days or weeks ahead. I had heard some of the commands a few times by now and they were becoming familiar to me. Orders such as '*Attention!*' are pretty much the same the world over; it was words like '*Manger*' meaning to eat which I would have to get to grips with quickly. '*Debout!*' ('Out!') and '*Allez!*' ('Quickly!'), accompanied by animated arm waving did not need much interpretation. With Philippe's translations, I was beginning to feel a bit more at home and aware of what was going on around me.

The room contained ten sets of bunk beds with a small cupboard next to them. Steve and I were quick to ensure that we shared a bunk. Both of us former squaddies and aware of the risks, neither of us wanted to be underneath a bed wetter. The room, unlike the dorm in the fort in Paris, was light and airy with windows from which we had a good view of the rest of the barracks. This was an awe-inspiring sight. Whitewashed buildings flanked an immaculately kept parade square. A huge French tricolour fluttered proudly in front of what I imagined to be the Commandant's office. Black tarmac roads, each lined with white-washed rocks linked together with white chain, all led to the square. There was a lot of white! Carefully tended flower beds all around created an illusion of dainty, almost suburban, order and civility. The sun brilliantly bathed this image with perfect light and for a moment I was a million miles away, lost in my own thoughts. But soon shouting from the corridors outside brought me crashing back to reality and we were on the move again.

We were off to the cookhouse, or *réfectoire*. The place was empty save for the lads behind the servery. As we made our way in single file I got a closer look at what was on offer. The food looked awful, truly awful, especially a great sludge of unrecognizable stew from which emanated a very dubious smell. Philippe did not help matters when he told us we were going to eat wild boar, a dish I now know to be regarded as a delicacy by many. However, back then, used to *cuisine Newcastle* and suspicious of any raw green stuff which could not be drowned in the gloop from the salad cream bottle, I was alarmed. I could see the head and trotters floating in a pool of greasy fluid. It was disgusting, I told a startled and more sophisticated Philippe. But like everyone else, I was really hungry and when you're hungry, you will eat anything. The only saving grace was the small bottle of wine, with which I managed to disguise the taste. I would probably rather have died than admit that I enjoyed it at all. It was beginning to sink in that I would have to adapt to a whole new culture, language and way of life; and I would have to adapt quickly.

When we had finished, I began to understand why all Legion barracks are so tidy. Once again we lined up and walked very slowly from the cookhouse back to our block. Close behind were NCOs and anybody who missed the tiniest piece of litter was summarily whacked over the head with a stick. Thank God, my eyesight was good. This task was called *corvée*, a word that would be indelibly etched in my vocabulary. To this day I find that I cannot walk through my garden without performing my own version of *corvée*, even if it does drive my wife Julie and the two boys absolutely mad.

Back at the block we snaked in a single line around the exam hall and as we reached the tables we were given various items. A packet of razors, some soap, socks and underwear, T-shirts with a Legion motif on the breast and finally a packet of cigarettes. I'd never smoked but I'd been here before and knew that in this cashless environment, those cigarettes would be like gold dust, a fantastic currency to barter with. Other items such as a towel and other essentials were issued and then it was back to the dorm to look at these gifts more closely. It felt like Christmas. As people began putting the things away, I noticed that some characters were eyeing up where certain stuff was being kept and I could smell trouble brewing.

It was dark outside now and I guess work had ended for the day around the camp. Everything appeared to have calmed down from the hectic events of the afternoon and we were called for evening *appel*, or roll-call, before turning in for the night. The different nationalities tended to stick together which is not surprising in view of the language barriers. Steve, the cosmopolitan Philippe and I sat together on a lower bunk and took the chance to reflect on the day's events and try to predict tomorrow's. We worked out that there must have been two hundred potential recruits here and the Legion only wanted forty for the next basic training course. The rest would be shown the door.

Some disembodied regular bellowed '*bonne nuit*' and the lights were extinguished. I was suddenly overwhelmed by fatigue and fell into a deep sleep almost at once. It felt like I had only been out for five minutes when all hell seemed to break loose. The mêlée was in the far corner of the room and because of the darkness I couldn't see who was involved; I was just aware of a mass of arms and legs thrashing together and an awful lot of shouting. Within a couple of minutes, order had been restored and an uneasy silence followed. Philippe told me that apparently one of our number had tried to use the cover of darkness to relieve another guy of the cigarettes we had earlier been given. This despicable stealth had obviously failed him and I went back to sleep, but not as soundly as before.

The next day started very much as the previous had ended, with a lot of shouting and us recruits running around like headless chickens. The time was 0600, it was cold and dark, except for the lights blazing from the blocks as other occupants stirred from their sleep, gathered their thoughts and rose to greet the new day. Ablutions completed, we formed up outside the block and marched, or rather shambled, for we were not yet trained men, to breakfast. It was not a continental breakfast in the hotel brochure sense of the phrase, far less the full English. There was a mug of cooling, thin coffee and some stale bread without butter or jam. I thought if an army marches on its stomach, then we should just about make the main gate. Sunday, we'd been promised, was different. On the sabbath, we would get a mug of hot chocolate and a pastry, *pain au chocolat* – big deal. Having said that, in the weeks and months ahead, I would really look forward to Sundays and that little treat even if I still sometimes thought wistfully of bacon and eggs. And I never quite lost my curiosity about the football scores back home.

These early days in Aubagne passed slowly, and as far as I could discern, without real direction. When a group of young men of differing nationalities is mixed together in an uncertain atmosphere like this, tensions can mount and trouble can erupt out of nothing. With one careless word or misread glance a situation can easily get out of hand. I found myself in the middle of an unlooked-for fracas one morning while we were waiting in the yard for the day's work detail. As usual with such episodes, it had started off innocuously enough. We were just milling about in small groups, when a French lad kept staring at our group and at me in particular. I didn't need Philippe's helpful translation to work out he had taken a dislike to me. The eyeballing lasted a few minutes and I had made my mind up that this guy wasn't going to get the better of me. He muttered something clearly offensive to his herd of muckers and they began to laugh. I mouthed 'Fuck off' in their direction and waited for things to happen. It didn't matter what I had actually said; my face and eyes let him know what the score was.

He sauntered over and I could feel everything in the yard come to a halt. All eyes were now upon this face off. I knew I couldn't back down now; my life would have been a complete misery for however long I was to remain here. We were toe to toe, eyeball to eyeball, so close I could smell his foul morning dog-breath and the stench of stale sweat that rose from his armpits. Behind my back, I had my right fist clenched tightly, ready to launch it upward to his chin if he moved to hit me. I didn't want to be the one that started the fight, but I certainly wasn't going to stand back and let him walk all over me. There was pure hatred between us and you could feel the malevolence in the air, it was powerful enough to cut. I can only think that this guy had a hatred of anything English. I still feel that it was just unlucky that he picked on me; it really could have been any of us English speakers. This, I knew, would have to be sorted, but at a place and time of my choosing, not his. It was a weird feeling for me because I had never hated anyone before; well, not like this, for no logical or even illogical reason. The feeling was totally alien to me, yet here I was, ready to fight with someone I didn't know, over nothing. I could sense Steve behind me, almost on my shoulder. I can only assume that I exuded the unstoppable and fearsome fury of the justly enraged because as I anticipated attack, this guy took a few steps back, smiled at me and nodded. Then he turned and walked away.

'You won that. No problem,' said an English voice I didn't recognize. I got a couple of slaps on the back and other comments I didn't understand. Philippe told me that most of the lads were impressed by what had happened. The French kid was a real bully and had given some of the other recruits a hard time over the last couple of days. Nobody had stood up to him and he was flexing his muscles, looking for trouble and showing off. I accepted the plaudits but I knew that this wasn't the end of it and I would have to keep an eye on chummy from now on. His smile had been as phoney as his accent – I already had him down as one of the Frenchmen who enlist as Swiss or Belgians because the Legion doesn't officially admit French nationals.

Philippe was a really ace bloke and invaluable to me, especially where his translator skills came in. It's perfectly possible that he sometimes acted the diplomat in his translations, but that didn't occur to me at the time. He wasn't particularly big but he had a certain steel and I got the feeling that although he may never come first in a test of strength or speed, he sure as hell wouldn't give up and would continue whatever contest he was engaged in until he dropped. Philippe had black hair, dark eyes and with his deeply tanned, weathered face, he had the appearance of a North African tribesman. I could picture him leading a caravan of camels across the Sahara desert, being pursued, indeed, by a Beau Geste Legionnaire character. The irony of that was not lost on me. I never delved into why Philippe had joined the Legion; the tradition of not asking another Legionnaire his reasons for joining forbade it. As our friendship and mutual respect for each other grew, I had the feeling that he would open up and tell me. Perhaps it would be over a beer or just a quiet moment one day.

On the sixth day at Aubagne, things started to move a bit quicker. We three, Philippe, Steve and I, decided that the best way to pass the time whilst waiting for the various tests we would take was to volunteer for every work party that was going, no matter the task. Being away from the yard meant that we avoided any more potential trouble and also that we would find out quickly which were the best jobs to go to. By volunteering it would also show our willingness to graft in any situation. If we couldn't work, the three of us would fantasize about future postings in glamorous locations around the world. Silly I know, but it kept us occupied. There had been no further trouble, about which I was pleased because although I knew I could face up to it if I must, I've never gone looking for that sort of action. This isn't to say I didn't feel edgy at times, watch my back and crane to hear mutters in the foyer if I thought they might concern me. I've sometimes read about how savage little girls can be in the playground when they choose to gang-up … let me tell you, little boys in the barracks can be just as petty, especially if one or more of them feels cheated.

One day I was in a group of ten, which included both Steve and

Philippe, and suddenly we were separated from the rest. At first I sank into a gloomy dread that this was the end of the road and we were being dismissed, deselected. Instead, we had been chosen to begin the next stage of the recruiting process.

Within the Legion there is a section called the *Deuxième Bureau*, or the Gestapo, as they are affectionately known. This branch of military intelligence works closely with Interpol and is responsible for the screening of potential recruits. If a rookie is trying to escape from a crime or misdemeanour it is at the Bureau's discretion whether he is handed over to the police or hidden amongst the Legion's ranks and left to the FFL's dubious mercies. The romantic notion still held by many people that the Legion hides criminals is seldom true today and retribution tends to follow crime just as surely as orange follows duck. Depending on the seriousness of the offence, if Interpol can prove that the perpetrator is in the ranks, then the Legion is obliged to hand him over. With the sheer number of people wanting to join the Legion, it can be selective, and consequently anyone who is too hot to handle or is a disruptive troublemaker will be refused at this early stage. The days are gone when you could turn up and be accepted, no matter what your history and background.

I was interviewed at least six times over a three-day period. The first question asked was 'Why? Why do you want to join the Legion?' There was no easy answer and I didn't want to appear to be either dreamy idealist or simpleton, a smart arse or to give the impression I was trying to evade the question. I gave answers I thought they wanted to hear: some bullshit about how I wanted to be part of the best, to gain experience and the sense of adventure my five years would bring. The interviewing officer and the Legionnaire who was translating began to laugh quietly and I thought I must have blown it. The translator told me the English lads still had this idea about the Legion being like *Beau Geste* films, that it was a romantic and magical place. He stifled his amusement and told me to forget that immediately, although this wasn't strictly necessary as I'd been pretty much making things up anyway. My five years, I was reminded, would be long and hard. There would be times when I would curse the day I had heard of the Legion and wished that I were back home in England, far away from this madness and misery. I was asked if I wanted to go away and think about it some more. I replied that I had thought enough and this was what I wanted to do. I also said I had a pretty good idea of what lay ahead and that any daft residual ideas about the Legion had been left far behind in Paris. That seemed to go down well and I was taken back to the yard.

Our numbers were already drastically reduced, the selection process having kicked in. They had introduced another sideshow, this time at the cookhouse. Before entering and being allowed to eat whatever gruel was being served, everybody had to stand in line underneath a bar suspended above us, about seven feet from the ground. It must have always been there; I just hadn't noticed it until now. Its purpose suddenly became clear. To gain access to the dining area, we each had to complete ten heaves or chin-ups to the bar. This involved jumping up to grip the bar and then hanging there completely still. On the duty Legionnaire's command we pulled ourselves up to the bar and lowered the required ten times. Success meant you got in to eat, failure meant you went to the back of the queue to have another go. Should you fail again, then to the back of the line you went. This went on until you either completed the task or you ran out of time and mealtime was over. And all for a bowl of muck, although if a man is ravenous he will eat pigswill and be grateful. In retrospect I wonder if those long-stewed casseroles of 'interesting' cuts of meat could be dished up in fancy London restaurants these days ... Whatever, those who failed went hungry. This was clearly another test and I didn't want to give them any excuse to send me away which was motivation enough for me, never mind the hunger.

Sometimes during the day, in the distance I could hear the deep-voiced singing of Legion songs accompanied by the slow, plodding march synonymous with the Legion. It is the march of a monarch as he surveys his people; it is a statement from the men marching, 'We are the best, we are supreme.' It is slow and deliberate and sends a shiver down the spine of those fortunate enough to witness the spectacle. I just wanted to be part of it so badly. I could see several people becoming very pissed off with this 'theatre' and they were flagging under the pressure anyway. To me this was all part of the process of weeding out the unsuitables and those obviously not cut out for this Legion life. I didn't gloat over those who didn't cut it, but I couldn't help reflecting that every man who 'failed' was one fewer in competition with me. Perhaps this was a selfish attitude but I really wanted to be a Legionnaire and some of these people were in the way. My way. And there are those of many political and philosophical persuasions who'll argue that enlightened self-interest accrues to the good of all. Bugger that retrospective reflective moment – I simply couldn't understand the whinges of some of the lads who were complaining about this new basic fitness test. We weren't, after all, joining an ordinary unit and most importantly, we wanted to join them. They didn't ask us to come here.

The Bureau subjected me to another bout of questioning the following day and I felt quite calm about it, keeping my answers much the same as I had in previous sessions. But I had become separated from Steve and Philippe who were both away on work parties. I knew Philippe had been struggling on the heave bars and I hoped this hadn't gone against him. Funny how if you like someone you make allowances ... I certainly hadn't thought of him as wimpy at all as he struggled: I knew he wanted this as badly as I did. Fingers crossed, *mon ami*.

At the evening meal we were once again all together and eager to recount the day's experiences. I was especially pleased to see Philippe as it meant he had successfully negotiated the bar. The numbers had been reduced further and we three felt that maybe, just maybe, we were going to be OK and pass. The feeling was reinforced after dinner. We were shepherded into the same hall where we had sat the tests earlier and at the front were five chairs. Standing behind each of them was a member of the admin staff we'd seen over the last few days and in their hands was a set of hair clippers. We were about to receive the trainee Legionnaire haircut, *la boule à zero*, a savage strimming from the clippers which had no guard on the blades, meaning that your hair was cut to the bone of your skull, leaving only a raw stubble. I couldn't say that we enjoyed this, delivered as it was without any soapy lotions to smooth the process, but we all knew that they only gave you this cut if you were going on to training. We had passed the first hurdle and I greeted the news with more relief than elation. I couldn't have faced returning home having failed. We may have looked rather like convicts now but somehow this was different from the scabby 'orphanage' impression that might have been rendered if we had been packed off as failures without the bone-crop.

From there, we went to the Commandant's office, where, in groups of six, we swore allegiance to the Legion. A tape recording started, first in French and then in English, stating that we were going to sign a five-year contract and once signed, there was no going back. The voice sounded robotic and distant. I still felt faintly bewildered – it was what I had aimed for and I was chuffed to have come this far, but to swear allegiance to a disembodied voice did seem a little odd. By now, however, I had come to respect the Legion's ways. This was it – the point of no return. They must have seen some potential in me, and I thanked God that I hadn't involved myself in any fighting. There would be plenty of time for that later.

Once the tape ended, we filed out into another office where the contracts lay upon wooden, school-type desks. The documents were written in French, not that it made any difference. You were simply expected to sign and be on your way. I hadn't seen Steve or Philippe for a while and was getting a little apprehensive but then they both entered the room, to my relief and joy. Their arrival confirmed it; we would be going on to basic training together. Fantastic! There were smiles and handshakes all round until a barked order fractured this little self-congratulatory group. We were to return at once to the block that had been base, collect our meagre possessions and then come back to the hall.

Some of the lads in the block were asking what was going on, but I think that they knew. Certainly I was in and they, unless they were lucky enough to be reconsidered, were out. No one said 'Good luck' and no one said 'Goodbye'. I didn't give a toss, bollocks to them, wasters the lot of them. I felt elated then and in retrospect I feel ashamed of myself for behaving like a cocky dick at that moment which must have been dismal for some of the others.

It was off to the stores next for us, with light hearts and light feet, for the issue of kit we would need for training at Castelnaudary, some few miles to the west. I saw my pal from the altercation in the yard and although he didn't look directly at me, I was still well aware that there was unfinished business and wasn't too pleased to realize he'd be heading towards the Pyrenees too.

In previous days things had seemed to be almost idle at times, pointlessly sluggish, but now the speed of events was breathtaking. Kit issue consisted of walking along a counter holding open a bag into which storemen, Legionnaires who were waiting for their discharge or those injured and waiting to return to their regiments, tipped items of clothing and equipment. At the end I had a sack full of kit but had no idea of whether all my gear was there or not. My bag, however, looked much the same as all the rest so I must have been kitted-out all right. All the canvas bags were labelled. I was getting quite used to being called Parker by now and left mine in a corner of the stores. Once again, we formed into a basic squad formation, and marched around the parade square to a large building. On the side of the building was a huge Legion banner with the words *Legio Patria Nostra*, the Legion is our Homeland, emblazoned on it ... Without having to be told, I somehow knew this was a special place. It had the ambience of a cathedral. A silence, observed only for the most revered places, was conversely almost shouting at me about how fortunate I was even to be allowed near this monument. This building was the Legion museum, a hallowed place, where centuries of courage and acts of supreme bravery performed by past Legionnaires were honoured, immortalized and remembered. I felt proud and humbled to be there.

When we were admitted a sergeant, respect and admiration for his task palpable, conducted the tour. He spoke in both French and English and in the careful way that an old man might talk to his young grandson. We all listened in respectful silence. He spoke of men and deeds he could only have heard or read of, but it was clear that he was in awe of the men who had taken part in those historic Legion actions. We saw battle honours, captured enemy regalia, photographs and medals awarded to past Legionnaires, obviously left to the museum in order to keep them in the family. The history of the Legion was unfolding before us, and it was awesome and thrilling: just to be in this glorious place added to my motivation to be even a tiny part of the Legion, to be spoken of in the same breath as these fearsome warriors.

Then we were shown the most special shrine – the articulated, severed wooden hand of *Capitaine* Danjou, displayed in a case within the Chapel of Remembrance. It was the only piece of his body that was recovered. This relic commemorates the Battle of Camerone Hacienda, 30 April 1863, when Danjou commanded a small detachment of sixty Legionnaires who fought off 2,000 Mexicans under a blazing sun for an entire day. Danjou was eventually killed and the five surviving Legionnaires, threatened by Mexican bayonets at their throats, were forced to surrender. This surrender was not complete, however, until the *caporal* in charge demanded and received permission for his men to retain their arms and receive medical attention. Danjou's hand (his real one had been lost in an earlier conflict in Crimea), was recovered and returned to the Legion. Camerone became an inspiring symbol of the Legion's fighting spirit and is still celebrated by Legion units around the world on its anniversary.

The message from Camerone is simple: a fight to the death against overwhelming odds is central to the Legion's tradition and each Legionnaire knows he will lay down his life should the brigade demand it. Soldiering means combat and combat could very well result in death. Why enlist if this simple truth is not understood? It was a marvellous piece of psychology: to show us this place just before we were due to leave for Castelnaudary and the beginning of a real basic training that would make the previous weeks seem tame. The great game, the great adventure, was about to begin.

CHAPTER THREE

BASIC TRAINING AT CASTELNAUDARY

RIGHT AFTER SUPPER AND THE VISIT to the Chapel we were shoehorned into the back of the truck that was transporting us to Castelnaudary. There was no room for benches, what with all our baggage and equipment as well as us men. There were thirty of us crammed into a space designed for fifteen. Some looked thin and weak and I wondered how they could possibly manage such a physical course. But then, I thought, if they want this as much as I do, they will overcome and be successful and I had a certain respect for them. The truck had little in the way of springs or suspension. Every bend or manoeuvre, apart from driving in a straight line, sent men crashing; every bump bounced us painfully around the slatted wooden floor. It was murder on the legs, the spine and our arms as we strained to keep hold of the canvas covering. The only relief came when we had to stop for traffic signals or at road junctions. The roads were quiet because of the late hour and we made good time hurtling through the cold, dark night. By the time we reached Castelnaudary, or Castel, as we would soon be calling the depot, I felt as if I had done fifteen rounds with a heavyweight boxer and was absolutely knackered.

Castelnaudary is a small medieval market town, near the Andorra principality, at the foot of the Pyrenees. The town consisted of only one main street with half a dozen cafés and bars, together with a few modest hotels. There wasn't much there, not that it mattered as we wouldn't see the town again for some time. I'd practically forgotten what it was like to mingle with ordinary shoppers and browse along a main street at my leisure, so I wasn't troubled by this. The Legion would be opening accounts for us within their own bank and most of our basic wages would be paid in direct. We would receive a nominal amount in cash each week from our section commander for the purchase of beer in the foyer and other small 'luxuries' like toothpaste and chocolate.

As we pulled into the barracks, the main gate ablaze with light from huge floodlights fixed high up on pylons, I was immediately struck by how new and big the place was. This was the home of the *4eme Régiment Étranger*, responsible for the training of all basic recruits and some promotion and specialist courses as well. It had only recently been built. After passing by the inevitable sentries, we disembarked behind our accommodation block. It was a great relief to get out of the truck and, lugging our kit, we filed inside. I had no idea of the time save to say it was late, deepest night. You could smell the newness; the still-drying paint and the oddly musty smell that only comes from carpets newly laid after months in storage. There were already other recruits in the large classroom which we were shunted into, bringing our total to sixty. We would form the *2ème Compagnie*. Standing behind desks and chairs, people began to whisper to each other and tried to guess what would happen next. The whispering had reached a level slightly above a murmur when a shouted '*Silence!*' settled everyone down.

'*Attention!*' echoed around the room as an officer and, I presumed, three NCOs entered the room, walking briskly and smartly to the front. At the officer's command we sat and were introduced to the training cadre instructors – Lt. Colomb, who would prove to be a tough but very fair officer; Sgt. Herchsfeld, a German who was even tougher and two *caporals*, one a Frenchman called Lasalles and the other a man from Northern Ireland, Martin Fennel. Their differing characters and styles of leadership would become very noticeable as our training evolved.

Things appeared chaotic at first, but it had all been planned, even down to who was roomed with whom. Steve had, however, somehow managed to blag his way into the room I had been allocated so at least I had someone to talk to. I was startled to find myself suddenly reflective. I had been away for several weeks and had only occasionally thought of home, such had been the intensity of events. But now I promised myself that I'd phone home the first chance I got off barracks. I didn't expect I'd get a particularly warm reception and it was with a heavy heart and a feeling of loneliness and isolation that I finally slept that night.

The following morning, after breakfast, we were issued more kit – webbing, helmets, rucksacks and other paraphernalia. This equipment was taken to the classroom and left there, whilst we formed up into smaller sections of twenty. I could see the layout of Castel better in the crisp, winter sunshine. The camp was still under construction in some parts and the roads around the work areas were mud-splattered, which constantly challenged the Legion ideal of an immaculate camp area. I noticed a work party on the far side who appeared to be washing the road down with brooms, hoses and buckets of water. Fennel saw me looking and told me in a faintly menacing way they were recruits on punishment, and would be out there until the roads were clean.

Four two-storey accommodation blocks edged a huge tarmac parade square. Each block contained a company of Legionnaires at various stages of training. The *2ème Compagnie*'s block was situated on the north-east corner of the square and further behind was the cookhouse and foyer, a shop where you could buy various small items, and a bar. As new recruits, we would not be allowed there for some time. Beyond that was a sports ground, complete with a 400-metre running track and even a small stand, football and rugby pitches together with a swimming pool. To the front of our block were the admin offices and further on, the infirmary. It was like a self-contained village.

Meanwhile, Sgt. Herchsfeld was attempting to teach us the basics of marching. The Legion has a unique style of marching; only eighty-eight paces per minute as opposed to 120 paces per minute favoured by other armed forces. It is remarkably difficult to walk at an unnatural pace, especially if one is attempting to keep to an exact rhythm with fellow marchers. I would come to realize that the very discipline required for this particular style of march was emblematic of Legion tradition and that, moreover, there could be something remarkably sinister and threatening about a column of men advancing slowly like this – almost quivering with caged and controlled purpose, energy and aggression – especially if the soldiers accompanied their steady approach with Legion songs sung low and true.

The results of this first lesson were hilarious for us but drove Herchsfeld to furious despair. I had half expected our inadequacies to be met with beatings or a similar punishment but Herchsfeld just shouted and threw his hands around. Some were marching too slowly, some too fast and some were so inept, they stood still, hoping for some miracle. Concentrating too much, rather than hitting a rhythm, can cause a man to make a complete arse of it altogether and fortunately it was never something I had much trouble with. Already I was beginning to feel a bit more like a soldier, rather less like the shabby renegade who'd left Paris. The marching lesson continued, behind our block and out of sight of everyone else. It remained a shambles, the whole company let down by the lads who hadn't got the hang of it right away. After about thirty minutes, Herchsfeld eventually gave up and we did receive our first punishment. Not a physical beating as I had expected, but almost worse – crawling on our bellies along the same road we had just been 'marching' along. Ten minutes of ripping the skin off our hands and knees on the tarmac resulted in a miraculous improvement in our group marching skills when we resumed.

Back in the classroom, we were each paired with another recruit. A French-speaking rookie is matched with someone who doesn't speak the language and is known as his *bonhomie*. It is the task of the *bonhomie* to ensure his comrade understands what is being said and what is happening, until such time as the other one is capable of comprehending for himself. In this respect and many others the Legion's training cadre is unparalleled with any other modern army. Each company of new recruits is a mix of nationalities, races, religions and languages. The instructors must hold together this undisciplined mass, ensuring that each recruit can speak and understand enough French to respond to commands. This was far more sophisticated than the bawlings of drill sergeant majors I had known before. There were more marching lessons after lunch. They continued well into the darkness that had enveloped Castel. This was to be no nine-to-five billet. After the evening meal, known as *la soupe*, whatever we were given, slop or solid, we were back in the classroom and seated beside our *bonhomie*. Mine was a squat, ugly little man named Henri. The squashed nose and numerous scars along his forehead indicated that he wasn't averse to standing up for himself. He was a good lad, slightly younger than me, at nineteen, and he made sure I didn't miss out on any information. After a relatively short time, I found myself quite liking him. He would endeavour to teach me to speak with a French accent rather than my natural rapid-fire Geordie inflections. I would get more respect from French speakers, he advised, if I tried to talk with an accent. These were wise words.

The training staff entered the room and we stood to attention, the noise deafening as we scraped the chairs on the bare floor. The atmosphere in the room became a little more relaxed when Lt. Colomb told us to sit and began to outline the planned sequence of events over the next months. There would be two weeks here at Castel consisting of fitness tests, basic weapon handling, marching and learning Legion songs. We were to be taught enough to make us capable of marching in time and used to handling our rifle, the FAMAS, and how to dress properly and at least look like soldiers, even if many of us weren't. The songs would be a pleasure to learn – their tones and harmonies, coupled with the menacing plod of the Legion march could be thrilling and inspirational, as well as alarming to an enemy, and I couldn't wait until we got it right. Once the fortnight was complete, those of us who had proved to be satisfactory would move as a company to a place at the foot of the Pyrenees called simply 'the Farm', where we would stay for about a month. During this time we would be tested with even tougher further training exercises, complete more physical tests, endure long, forced marches and, if successful, be awarded the *képi blanc*.

On hearing this, everyone started chattering in excited voices until Herchsfeld roared '*Silence!*' and the room calmed. Herchsfeld shouted an awful lot, as did most of the NCOs I had come across, but there was still no sign of the physical violence I had anticipated. I had really thought that a beating would punish any misdemeanour or mistake, however small, but even by then the Legion adhered to pretty much the same rules and regulations as the regular French army and it's probably even more restrained today. Legionnaires are exposed to the outside world a lot more than in the days of Simon Murray, when harsh and brutal punishments could be meted out on a whim, sometimes sadistically. However, even though I had not heard of or seen any beatings, I still didn't rule it out from ever happening.

That night before *appel*, there was a lot of movement within the block, as everyone had to ensure they were roomed with their *bonhomie*. Somehow, and I swear it was not contrived between us, Steve and I managed to share a room. There were ten of us in each room, which had a washing area set off at the end. Each section had its own showers and toilets further down the main corridor. There was no sign of

Philippe, however, and we agreed that we would seek him out when we could. We had not forgotten how good he had been to us in the early days.

The following morning, after the usual 0530 reveille, saw the start of the fitness tests. We split into groups of ten and had to complete a round robin course of running, climbing a rope without using feet, heaves to a bar, sit-ups, press-ups and a swimming test. We were told to complete each test individually, do as many of the exercises as possible in the allotted time, normally three minutes, but most important, to do our best. I didn't realize it at the time, but there was no pass or fail mark for these particular tests. As long as you tried your best, and didn't look as if you were doing the bare minimum, then the NCOs were happy. People were, however, being watched and the fit and strong recruits were being noted and future assignments planned.

By lunchtime, I was starving but instead of returning to the cookhouse, we sat in the middle of the running track and were given bread, a tin of sardines and a small bottle of wine. A picnic in the south of France! All it needed was a peach and some good cheese and I'd have been ready to drift off for the afternoon ... But the tests, interspersed with marching lessons, carried on for the rest of the day, with all the results being carefully noted down. At various stages during training we would have these same tests and you had to show an improvement each time.

After *la soupe*, it was back to the classroom for more French lessons. Even the NCOs joined in the laughter as some of us made complete fools of ourselves trying to learn the new language. I could feel the atmosphere changing as everyone's initial fear and nervousness began to fade. There were still little cliques but that was mainly down to the language barrier. The language you spoke dictated which clique you would be in, but during the next few days, the actual number of cliques shrank and those remaining grew larger as language barriers broke down and some of us became genuinely friendly. The lad I had trouble with in Aubagne was in the *2ème Compagnie* but not in my section. Although he never spoke to me, there was palpable tension between us and I knew another confrontation was inevitable.

These early days at Castel flew by. There was so much to take in and learn. We were taught rudiments of the history of the Legion, the formation and rank structure of the various regiments and little by little the true meaning of the Legion family began to emerge. The systematic organization of the Legion is its main strength and self-supportiveness is built into its systems. Everyone knows where they stand and what is expected from them. Fools are not suffered gladly, but a man in need or trouble can rely on a decent hearing. Discipline is strict and hard but fair. The days of extreme violence from officers and NCOs towards both recruits and men have all but gone. But I don't wish to sentimentalize the Legion because human nature can never be tamed – there will always be grudges and dislikes amongst men cooped together and even the most scrupulous NCO could occasionally dish out a punch or a kick after a misdemeanour. Summary justice, I believe. Sometimes that was more acceptable than punishment meted out by your officer, which might well result in jail or loss of pay, or both. The fear and threat of jail alone was enough to dampen many potentially explosive situations.

One night the section all convened in the room I shared with Steve and the others. Fennel was going to show us how to store kit in our lockers, a space roughly three feet wide, shelves and drawers to one side and a hanging area for your best dress to the other. We had no civilian clothes so there was plenty of room for everything. We were to discover that there is a Legion way of doing just about everything, even folding your underwear. Each piece of uniform had a certain way of being folded and a designated place in the locker. If you should get anything wrong, punishment was both swift and precise, as I found out to my cost one dark and wet morning. The shirt in my locker was not folded to the requisite twelve centimetres. Herchsfeld, the inspecting NCO, had a piece of wood measuring exactly twelve centimetres and when my shirt and this stick did not align he went ballistic. He emptied the entire contents of my locker onto the floor whilst screaming at me in a mixture of French, German and English. His face turned puce and I thought the veins on his forehead would burst. As I stooped to collect my kit, he trod on my hand and screwed his boot backwards and forwards on it, as if he were stubbing out a cigarette. I dare not let him know how much pain I was in. He then scooped up everything on the floor and hurled it out of the already open window. Someone sniggered at my misfortune, which only served to further enrage Herchsfeld and he proceeded to empty every locker in the room and every piece of kit followed mine out of the window onto the mud below.

Fennel told me later that it wouldn't have mattered if every locker in the room had been perfect, the end result would have been the same: all the kit out and onto the mud. Herchsfeld had decided that our room was the target for that inspection. Tomorrow it would be someone else. Nothing personal, that's just the way things were done. It was unusual for anyone in the room to miss out on Herchsfeld's locker arranging. He would simply choose a different locker for each inspection. I am sure he thought that we would put more effort into getting our lockers spot-on for the next visit. I hoped Herchsfeld would remember that it was my kit he launched, and move onto someone else next time.

Fennel was a difficult man to fathom. He was tall and well-built with a quiet, soft Southern Irish accent as opposed to the harsher tones of Belfast. He appeared to be very deep and when asked a question, he would reply with the fewest possible words and never freely engage in conversation. I initially thought it was because we were recruits and he didn't want to speak to us on any level other than strict Legion procedures dictated, but even after training and when we met up again years later, he was exactly the same: moody and distant. Fennel did, however, have a magnificent method of teaching us about our rifle, the French FAMAS. Should anyone not know, instantly, the name of any part of the rifle – for instance, when it was stripped down he might hold up the firing pin carrier – he would then proceed to either hit you with it or throw it at you with considerable force, ensuring, for he had an excellent aim, that the part hit you on the head. The effectiveness of that method can be judged by the fact that before we left for the Farm, we all knew every part of the FAMAS including its weight.

The FAMAS, like many engineering products known by their initials, doesn't sound quite as romantic when the full title is spelled out: Fusil Automatique, Manufacture d`Armes de St Étienne. Weighing about 3.5kg (7.7lb) the weapon is quite light. It is lovingly referred to as *le clairon*, the bugle, because of its distinctive shape. It has a bull-pup configuration with a relatively long barrel (488mm) making it an extremely accurate assault rifle. The weapon is very robust and able to withstand severe conditions such as water, mud, sand, dust and temperatures ranging from -40° to a blistering +51°. Even after firing over 15,000 rounds of ammunition, it is still accurate when other weapons would be firing all over the place. The rifle can be fired even if wearing thick gloves thanks to the ingenious design of a removable pistol grip. Firing single shot, three-round bursts or on fully automatic, the FAMAS is a remarkable weapon and its versatility is compounded by the universal sling attached, meaning that by altering the sling accordingly it can be fired by left- or right-handed soldiers.

Our shortcomings (some people just could not comprehend that marching is only walking smartly and were bashing into lads in front of them) were still evident at this early stage of training. We were in a foreign army and still struggling with a foreign language, after all. The punishment following these shortcomings was basically the same for every misdemeanour – to get us as dirty and tired as possible. Steve and I, with our army experience, tried to help those finding difficulty during training. We tried, with our limited French, to encourage the others without treading on the instructors' toes. We explained that this mindless hardship was normal for the Legion and was only intended to fuck us off. They wanted to see how we reacted under different types of pressure, who could take it and, more importantly, those who couldn't. I could see that several recruits were flagging.

In the main, however, we slowly improved. The marching was coming together now, it was certainly less chaotic, and my French was getting better, partly due to the singing which I enjoyed so much. I was a lot more confident, both outwardly and psychologically. Enormous emphasis was placed on singing and we really did put heart and soul into it; the NCOs appeared to be pleased with that. They liked effort.

Henri and I gradually became true comrades and had started to trust each other. He told me one night why he had joined the Legion. I didn't really want to know and feigned interest out of politeness, but his tale gripped me and I felt nothing but admiration for him at the end of his story. His stepfather had abused him since he had been small. I didn't want to know the actual details, though I could imagine the horror he endured. What was clear was his total hatred for the man. As he grew older, and realized what was happening, he began to stand up to the beast. Once the stepfather knew he couldn't get away with abusing Henri anymore, he turned his attention to Henri's younger brother. This he could not stand and one night whilst the stepfather slept, Henri beat him about the body with a hammer, left a note for his mother and joined the Legion. Henri correctly guessed that his stepfather would not report the assault and he felt no need to mention the incident at Aubagne. At no point did he seek comfort or commendation; it was, as Fennel would have said, just the way it was.

Since arrival at Castel, we had been paid our meagre wages – met by the French Government. We did not, however, receive it all. Only a small portion was given to us in cash, the rest being banked in a Legion account set up for each of us and which we could only access once posted to our respective regiments. The excitement about even those first few francs was tangible amongst the section. For many of us it was the first time for weeks that we had held money in our hands. We were allowed to the foyer to buy sweets, chocolate and other goodies. Almost ridiculous, that grown men such as we were so excited about pocket money. We would soon be leaving for the Farm and everyone was in good spirits, so perhaps this was another piece of psychology.

The plan was that we would return to Castel just before Christmas and I wondered how I would feel at that potentially difficult time. Christmas had always been a special time to me and I remember thinking that my response to it this year would be a measure of how far I had come. Maybe I'd get a sense of whether I had it in me to continue. This would be my first Christmas away from my family and I did feel pangs of guilt about my mother, who still didn't even know where I was. I knew she would miss me and I hoped I hadn't hurt her too much.

Our departure for the Farm was now imminent. I watched fully-fledged Legionnaires walking around the camp. Their aura of confidence, the determined look in their eyes and the obvious pride in themselves and their 'family' just made me want more than ever to be a part of it. We were told that on our return from the Farm we would be allowed into the foyer – the bar and relaxation area – after duties. This was indeed a land-mark and we were reminded that at that point we would also be able to write and receive letters from outside.

Only one recruit had departed from Castel. A German lad had been handed over to the police and taken away, never to be seen again. Rumour had it, and rumours are a vital form of communication in any army, that he was wanted back in Germany for an attempted murder. Another rumour had him being discharged because he had some disgusting sex-ually transmitted disease. I shall let you decide which one became legend.

CHAPTER FOUR

THE FARM

THOSE HEADY FEELINGS WE BRIEFLY enjoyed at Castel were beaten out of us by the truck ride to the Farm. I could feel the temperature dropping by degrees as we made our way towards the foothills of the Pyrenees. Nobody spoke of it, but I think we had all tried to picture the Farm and what awaited us there. I doubt if any of us imagined a fantasy farm, warm and cosily chaotic, with placid animals, an apple-cheeked farmer's wife and her beautiful daughter tending to delicious things in a rustic kitchen. But we may not have expected our farm to be quite so far removed from that idea.

The convoy of four trucks and two jeep-like vehicles snaked its way along narrow, tree-lined roads built for tractors and small cars, not lorries whose canvas was thrashed every few yards by overhanging branches. The sight which greeted us at the end of the road as we pulled into a cobbled yard was horrendous. It was as if major demolition had begun when a passing Legion officer told the occupants to cease work and then commandeered the site for the instruction of recruits. No rebuilding had been carried out and there appeared to have been no attempt to repair the damage already done. I was reminded of a badly run builders' yard as I surveyed my new home. From a distance everything looked OK, but as I neared the barn that would house us, I noticed cracked windows, window frames coming away from the walls and many tiles missing from the roof. As we neared the building, there was an explosion of flapping and fluttering as the resident squadron of nesting birds escaped the rafters. This was a regular occurrence and I soon learned not to look up as the birds departed each time we returned to the barn. Some of the troops couldn't resist the natural temptation to see what was causing the noise and paid for it with droppings in their faces. I guessed the barn and other buildings were about one hundred years old, but like everything else in the Legion, it looked twice that age. This was going to be home for at least a month and winter was already howling down the valley bringing rain and snow.

We would just learn the basics of soldiering whilst here at the Farm. Further specialist training would continue when we reached our various regiments. Everyone was starting from scratch. This included people like Steve and me, despite our army training. The idea was to bring everyone down to the same level, even down to the poor kit we were first issued and then through instruction, bring us all up to the same decent standard. We would certainly know how to handle a rifle and ammunition without endangering ourselves or anyone else nearby. We would all be of a high fitness level, have a basic idea of battle tactics and of looking after ourselves while out in the field. The instructors would train us to the point where we could be allowed to be seen in public in uniform without embarrassment and we would know how to march and sing. Most importantly, for me anyway, was that on our return to Castel, we would be allowed to wear our *képi blanc*. On completion of our final forced march, some seventy-five kilometres over the Pyrenees carrying a weight of about 45kg (99lb) plus rifle, we would be awarded the kepi by the Commanding Officer at a special ceremony. This was what I had striven for: my Holy Grail.

The rest of that first day was spent organizing everyone into accommodation, sorting supplies and kit and basically ensuring we were ready to begin the serious training next morning. Whatever we had been through up to now would soon fade into a memory of some rather gentle, pleasant interlude in the sun. I could already see that things would be tough here. Both levels of physical endurance and mental strength were to be tested. Facilities were worse than basic and it promised to be cold, very cold. Normally after a hard day training you could recover with a hot bath or shower but this would not be possible for us here, where there was no hot water for us recruits. We were to wash, shave and clean dirty kit in icy water. Everything had been designed to make life as difficult and harsh as possible. I had a feeling that this was going to sort the chaff from the section and I could already see a few disgruntled faces. What else did they expect?

A huge barn-like building was to be the centre of our world for the next month. All of us recruits, the fifty-nine that remained, would be housed in the large dormitory, a bed and single metal locker each the only furniture there. The stone walls were bare, without even a coat of plaster or paint to lift the austere atmosphere and chill of the room. It was the type of space that would be cold in the height of summer, never mind the depths of an Alpine winter like this. Leading from this bleak room was a corridor to the classroom and a kitchen/dining area. This cheerless place was to be the fount of all new knowledge for us. After a supper of a mug of coffee and maybe a piece of bread, we had evening *appel* and then it was time for head-down and lights out.

Since arriving at the Farm that day, we had been made to prepare the place for the start of training, which was rather like asking turkeys to vote for Christmas, as they say. We fetched and lugged and cleaned and scrubbed till hands and knees were raw and every muscle ached. Right now there was little evidence of the famed Legion camaraderie – cold and exhaustion had made most of us literally thin-lipped. Once

I had stripped off my uniform and climbed into the ridiculously light sleeping bag, I realized just how cold the night could become. My whole body seemed to freeze, starting at my shaven head and moving slowly and cruelly downwards. With the cold, my apprehensions about the forthcoming training and the noise of others talking echoing around the cavernous room, sleep was impossible. I could manage ten minute stretches at the most and it was after one of those wonderful dips into unconsciousness that the lights were switched on, accompanied by the deafening din of a stick being bashed inside a metal bucket. Together with Herchsfeld's shouting it was a pretty effective alarm call.

Morning ablutions got the day off to a stinging start. After Herchsfeld's melodious awakening, we were told to dress only in boots and trousers. Then we were ordered to take our helmets, shaving gear and towel to a wall-mounted tap outside. Helmets were half filled with cold water for outdoor washing and shaving. I was surprised the water didn't ice over as I was sure it was below freezing out there. This was the beginning of the toughening-up process. My shaving gear consisted of a bar of foul-smelling soap (only the Legion could make a soap that smelled so disgusting) and one of those hateful yellow disposable Bic razors, making the procedure somewhat akin to shaving with a samurai sword. Fennel stood in front of the section and demonstrated how to shave. He went through the whole rigmarole from rinsing his face to lathering up and then which direction to scrape the razor on our faces. The difference was, his water was steaming hot and as he started his shaving instructions I experienced feelings of jealousy that I would have doubted myself capable of. When I saw the clouds of steam rising up from Fennel's bowl of water, I just wanted to hold my face over it, even for just a few seconds. It was torture watching the hot air rise from his wash bowl and almost sparkle in the freezing air as it lofted upwards. I was soon shocked out of my steamy fantasy as I swept the icy water onto my face and began the harrowing task of self-abuse. My face was scraped to ribbons and looked like I had used barbed wire instead of a razor.

I soon learned that we would only be shown this art once, as we would with all instruction, be it care of kit or cleaning or anything. There is, remember, a Legion way of doing everything and it was expected that once you had been shown how to perform a task, that was the way you would do it in the future, no arguments, no negotiation. God help you if you didn't complete it properly or worse still, claim you didn't know how to do it at all. I once saw at the Farm a recruit being reprimanded at inspection for not shaving one morning. The kid's face already looked like a pizza, with scabs and spots and other foreign objects growing on it. Anyway, rather than run a razor over his pustules, he simply washed with soap and water and then lied to Herchsfeld that he had shaved. A monstrous mistake. I thought he would be kicked all over the square. But no, Herchsfeld, in a disturbingly quiet voice, told him to go to the barn, collect a razor and return immediately. Once back on the square, the poor unfortunate was told to shave. Without water and without soap. It was a bloody and terrible sight. I had never seen anything before to match it for sheer brutality and it squares up to quite a few of the horrors I've seen since. I can assure you that every man in our company shaved perfectly from that day on.

Despite the spartan accommodation and eating facilities, standards of discipline, cleanliness and tidiness at the Farm remained the same as those which pertained at Castel, apart from certain 'generous' concessions. For example, all stone floors would be swept and washed at least once a day but they did not have to gleam as a linoleum floor in barracks would. The rooms were inspected twice daily and any slovenly work was summarily punished. That inevitably meant the perpetrators getting filthy by crawling across the muddiest section of ground currently available. Actually, getting us muddy and covered in black, smelly God knows

what was a favourite sport of the instructors. It meant that any free time
we had, and that was precious little, had to be spent in cleaning kit in
order to be ready for the next inspection. It was a very effective way of
keeping us going all the time.

Here at the Farm we got our first taste of the most boring and tedious
of assignments – guard duty – even though it was hard to imagine that
any mountain bandit would be stupid enough to attempt entry to this
freezing 'fortress'. Each section of the company provided six men each
night to mount a guard. Two would guard the kitchen area, so any proposed raid for a midnight feast was impossible. Two patrolled inside the
buildings and two were outside. When on guard you prayed that you
would be with another English speaker, so that you could at least while
away the hours with idle chit-chat. Anyone caught outside the dorm
after lights out had to have a bloody good reason for being there. Our
orders were to waken the duty NCO and immediately report any irreg-
ular occurrences. However, being on duty did not excuse you from
training the following day. You were expected to work as normal, even if
you were exhausted. It was the same for everyone, no exceptions,
although some coped less well than others and they suffered on the
future marches. Some of the recruits were not yet physically fit and to go
without their beauty sleep and then endure a tough day's training was a
bit too much. They were, however, encouraged along with several hefty
sticks to the head by the instructors.

The early days at the Farm were well structured and followed the
same pattern. After breakfast – the usual mug of coffee and bread which
appeared to be the Legion's staple diet – and inspection, we would spend
some time trying to perfect our marching, singing and French speaking. These were basics and we had to get them right before we could go
on to the next stage. Mistakes were made and punished with physical
exercise, either apparently mindless running, jumping or crawling, but
there was a hidden agenda within these punishments as our physical

fitness was improving drastically. The morning lessons were followed by lunch and the afternoon was spent on weapons training, tactics and even more French lessons.

Firing a rifle is much more than just pointing the barrel at a target, pulling the trigger and checking your target to see if you have hit the centre. The secret is in learning how to breathe and relax correctly. Lying in the prone position, which is on your belly, left leg extended and the right leg bent at the knee and pulled upwards towards your chest, gives you a solid base from which to take aim. The FAMAS is supported and balanced on the bones of your elbows and the butt of the rifle firmly held into the shoulder. If you attempt to control the rifle by using the muscles in your arms only, you will find that the barrel of the weapon wavers and moves in small circles and therefore you won't be able to hit a cow's arse at ten metres. Once you have lined the target with the foresight, you begin to apply pressure to the trigger slowly, careful not to disturb the position of the sight. Should you snatch at the trigger or pull too quickly, the barrel of the FAMAS will jump, knocking your aim off. So, you become comfortable, breathe and relax; line your sight to the target, exhale your breath slowly, apply firm but careful pressure on the trigger ... then *Bang*! Enemy terminated ... hopefully. It really is an art and takes a lot of practice and concentration to perfect.

We became more familiar with our rifles and learnt more about their versatility. There is a clever device which stops gas escaping after firing a round. This device is closed, keeping the expunged gas in the chamber. The FAMAS can then be converted into a grenade launcher. Smoke, tear gas, anti-tank or anti-personnel grenades can then be fired with tremendous accuracy. When firing the weapon as a grenade launcher in the standing position, the butt of the weapon has to be held firmly into the shoulder or else the recoil could quite easily knock you over. This happened on a couple of occasions to members of my section, causing great hilarity amongst the instructors. There is nothing as ungainly as a soldier being dumped on his arse and his rifle lying a few feet away because he couldn't control the recoil.

At night we would be taken out to some dense woodland and ordered to sit in one large group. A *caporal* would disappear into the thick undergrowth and light a cigarette, demonstrating how clearly visible you would be to an enemy sniper. Herchsfeld then went on to tell us how much further noise travelled at night and that even the slightest movement of equipment would send out a signal as to your position. Although I had seen all these lessons before in England, I still enjoyed this part of the training; it was like a refresher course. Afterwards we could expect an order to dig a trench in under an hour, in the pitch-black. There was no instructional purpose to this exercise; it was impossible to complete anyway. No, it was just to piss us off, making us all hot and sweaty just before *extinction des feux*, lights out. Again, during these lessons any shortcomings were punished by some form of exercise.

I enjoyed the French classes very much. They were not like school lessons, as such, where you conjugated verbs parrot fashion and learned *plume de ma tante* stuff – we learned to speak everyday, idiomatic French. We were taught how to ask for basic items, how to communicate at a local level. Having a *bonhomie* was a great boon and with Henri's help and advice I became quite competent, even on occasion impressing Philippe. The days were so full here that sometimes it was hard to draw breath. Only very occasionally did I have the chance to talk to Steve at any length. He was still full of himself and by all accounts thoroughly enjoying his time, despite all the pissing about. All part of the game, was his attitude, it isn't personal. He really was the sort of bloke you wanted on your side when things are tough.

At the end of the first week, we had tests to see how we had progressed, again with all the results being noted. This was not just to see how much we had improved, but would also dictate to which regiment we would be posted and thus how much we would earn. Not only was the 2ème REP, the parachute regiment, the most desirable and presti-gious of the Legion regiments, it was also, because of jump pay, one of the better paid units. Another of the better paid postings was the *13ème Demi-Brigade Legion Étrangère*, based in Djibouti, Africa. A posting to this unit, with its enhanced pay, was unusual for anyone recently out of train-ing. You had to prove yourself first and take your place in quite a long queue. Which posting you received depended on how you had per-formed during instruction and on your Commanding Officer's report, combined with your preference. Nobody wanted to go to the infantry based in France where you would be at the bottom of the pile when the money was dished out. During the written tests I saw much scratching of heads and thought that some of these lads wouldn't be earning a lot.

On Sunday evening we were told that our first forced march would take place the next day. We would only be carrying weapons and one man would carry a rucksack containing a sleeping bag, food and other essentials in case of an emergency. The weight of the rucksack would be shared amongst everyone during the march. We were not told how far the distance was nor for how long we would be out; they just said to do our best and keep up with the NCO in charge of the group. Each group would have between twelve and fifteen *engagés* and would all set off on different routes. We would all, however, experience part of each of the different routes at some stage. Doubtless this had been going on for years but it must have been a nightmare in the first place to devise fifteen sep-arate, yet intersecting routes of equal toughness. Anyway, if you kept up with the NCO, then you were not doing anything wrong. Simple logic, but I felt we were being just like sheep, following a leader but with no idea where we were going or why or for how long. By then, however, I knew better than to ask stupid questions and did exactly as I was told. We could always debate the subject later, not that it would do any good.

I received some bad news after *la soupe*. I had been picked for guard duty that night. Bollocks and double bollocks. First forced march and I was going to be up all night. Knackered before I started. Never mind, it would have to be a case of head down, arse up and off we go. Whinging wasn't going to change anything.

The guard duty was dull and dreary. We had a briefing before starting about what was expected from us. Basically, it was a fire watch combined with a security watch on the food site. Because we were using such high levels of energy during the day and not really replacing that spent energy with food at mealtimes, everyone was hungry most of the time. The temptation was overwhelming at times to sneak into the kitchen and help yourself, but the guards on duty ensured that this fantasy did not become reality. It was the first time the issue had been raised, but on this watch we were also a deterrent for anyone wanting to run away.

Desertion is the most despised crime a Legionnaire can commit and the one he least wants to fail in. Desertion is thought so odious that anyone caught trying to desert or captured while on the run is subjected to merciless treatment both by his captors and then in jail serving the inevitable sentence dispensed to him. We were also informed that if anyone did desert during our tour of duty, then we would all be held responsible and therefore charged with aiding the deserter. I found out later that this was completely untrue, although it had the desired effect on me and my mates. I spent my whole time with eyes like a hawk and hearing better than a bat.

To even attempt to get away from the Farm was absolute madness anyway, although two lads did try later, in the middle of nowhere in the middle of winter, with no money and no idea where to go or how to get there. Their idea was verging on the suicidal. While the Legion has modernized in many ways, the punishments for desertion then still dated back to the brutal early days. It was the most important thing *not* to do. Yet these two foolish lads still tried their luck.

Next morning, after inspection and when it was still cold, dark and damp we formed up on the parade square in groups and awaited the order to move off. Herchsfeld was leading the group that I was in, so I knew we were in for a hard day. He didn't disappoint me. We set off at a cracking pace, not quite a run but not a parade march either; it was something in between, almost like a trot. The FAMAS rifle is not particularly heavy, but after carrying it for a few hours, my arms felt like they were hanging around my ankles. Just to break the monotony of the march, Herchsfeld would order us to lift our rifles above our heads, arms reaching up to the leaden skies and we would march like that for a few hundred metres. It is surprising how heavy the rifle felt after doing that a number of times. There was a reason for us doing this, as ever with the Legion. It was to build up our upper body strength. A couple of hours passed marching through thick forest, the fresh smell of pine a welcome relief from the stench of sweaty feet in the barn, and we halted in the middle of a stunningly beautiful valley. At this stage the terrain was friendly and not too severe. Even in the winter gloom it was a wonderful sight: snow-covered mountain peaks, lined with glossy green fir trees like a Christmas card illustration.

It was with this splendid scene in the background that Herchsfeld decided to give us a lesson in reaction to enemy fire. In groups of four, we would walk in a straight line, Herchsfeld would initiate gunfire and we would react. Down, find cover, fire, roll over, fire again, up and sprint forward, down, roll over, fire again, crawl forward (always forward), up, down, up, down. I was completely shattered after repeating this a few times. Herchsfeld was impossible to please; nothing we did was ever good enough for him, so he made us do it again and again. The area was well worn and I thought of the hundreds of other Legionnaires who had passed through here. It was perfect for training; plenty of rolling, undulating ground that afforded us loads of cover as we practised a fighting advance. The section had been split into smaller battle groups mainly so that Herchsfeld could keep his eagle eyes on us and make sure that everyone was working hard enough. Of course, we were hot and flustered and sweaty when at last he told us to stop and while we waited for the others to go through the beasting we had just endured, the bitingly cold wind scythed its way through our uniforms, cutting into the skin and bones. We went from boiling hot to freezing again in seconds. The coarse, wet wool of our uniforms clung to our bodies, emphasizing the chill even more. I had never realized that being so cold could cause so much pain, real physical pain. I couldn't ever remember being so cold, but worse was to come in the days ahead.

Most British squaddies will tell you that when they embark on a 'yomp', they are told how long it will be, where they are going, the purpose of the march and what is expected of them once they reach their destination. Here, it was just head down, arse up and march. No idea of length, no idea of purpose and no idea what to do if it went tits up and we were in trouble. By that I mean if the instructor for some reason was injured or he himself got lost, there was no emergency plan, which I found very strange. It certainly didn't smack of professional soldiering to me.

We returned to the Farm as dusk fell in the late afternoon, having preferred to munch on the bread and cheese we had for lunch on the move rather than stop and sit down, thereby risking hypothermia or piles, or both. On our return, we were told the march had only been thirty-five kilometres; just enough to break us in gently, a smiling Fennel informed us, that sick bastard.

The boots we'd been issued were of a strange design, one I'd certainly never seen before. They were called 'Rangers', American by design I think, and they reached halfway up the calf. The boot was laced to a point just above the ankle and then a large flap of leather, bound by two buckles, completed the boot. Mine were ill-fitting, resulting in blisters on both heels. It was pointless complaining, so I had to accept that my feet would end up in a mess after each march. Forget discipline and the virtues of stoicism, this was sheer self-defeating craziness when you think about it. My feet were as much a tool of the trade as my rifle. I looked after my rifle meticulously, so surely the same care and attention should be applied to my feet? But I knew that if I complained, there would be trouble. Thanks to Steve's fantastic first aid, we managed to repair the damage done to them that day, and he gave me great advice on how to treat my feet in future. Bursting the blisters and treating the wound before it got infected would save countless tears in the days and weeks to come. It was, however, these ill-fitting boots coupled with my reluctance to complain that very nearly crippled me a few days later and could quite easily have ended my Legion career before it had really started.

It was to be our third march; the second had passed off without incident and thankfully without injury, and now we were all carrying rucksacks, weighing about 18kg (40lb), as well as our rifles. The distance had also increased and was now up to sixty-five kilometres – about forty miles. The previous night had been the coldest yet. Absolutely perishing and impossible to sleep, the discomfort was so intense. In a vain attempt to conquer the cold, at least psychologically, I tried to think of all the warm and sunny places I had ever been in my life, but as a lad whose experience of balmy climes was restricted to one trip to Spain this didn't take long and the cold soon seeped back into my brain and resumed its tyranny. Despite the small practical problem of size, I even thought, briefly, of getting someone to climb into my sleeping bag, or me into theirs, in order to share what body heat we had. I had heard of people, strong and brave people I convinced myself, doing just that in emergencies and surviving. I quickly dismissed the thought. Can you imagine me trying to convince any of the monsters in my section to climb into a sleeping bag with me and spend the night cuddled up under the pretence of keeping warm? What would have happened to me if my bad French or their misinterpretation meant they got the wrong message entirely? I would have been massacred. I shudder now, even at the mere thought of it. Stupid boy.

Anyway, after such a wretched night I was knackered in the morning as we formed up ready to move out. I knew that I hadn't been as thorough as I should have been in checking my gear before we actually got to the square. I find it odd, almost spooky, how often we know we're on a self-destruct, even as we do something we think we'll get away with. It's like those letters you half read and prepare to chuck, hesitate and then discard. Part of your brain knew it would turn out to be a vital piece of paperwork which could have saved you a lot of trouble down the line.

That morning was cold, dark and damp as usual. It was the sort of weather you often get in the Lake District on a dizzyingly dismal autumnal afternoon, emphatically not the weather I expected in the south of France. But in my defence, a lot of people have this odd notion that the south of France is blazingly sunny and at least warm all year round. Again, we hadn't any idea of the distance to be covered that day and as we were forming up on the square, Steve again gave me the benefit of his army experience: 'Don't think about the distance; don't try to work out how far you've done or how far you have to go. Just put your head down, get your arse and rucksack up and walk.' He had noticed that we weren't issued any rations, so we couldn't be out that long, could we? Herchsfeld was in charge of my group and he would do all the navigation and issue the orders. Steve was right, wasn't he? All we had to do was walk.

Suddenly, Herchsfeld was up and away. No order to move, he simply took off and I guessed we were expected to follow. He set off at a fast pace again and after only a couple of hundred metres, the group was already strung out. After about 500 metres, Herchsfeld came to a halt in order for the stragglers to catch up. In that relatively short time, I had gone from freezing cold to boiling hot and now that we'd stopped, I would be cold again. The sweat I had built up froze onto my skin, making my clothes damp and allowing the wind to bite through. Herchsfeld, though, was boiling. Boiling mad I mean. He was furious that we hadn't been watching and paying attention to him back at the square. Our summary punishment was thirty press-ups and they weren't as easy to complete as it might sound. The rucksacks on our backs, probably badly packed as we hadn't been shown as yet how to load them properly, kept slipping off our backs and the FAMAS rifles that we had slung around our necks smashed into our faces as we pushed up and down.

The rucksacks were, in my opinion, badly designed. They only had two shoulder straps, and no belt to secure it to your waist, meaning that with the slightest imbalance or wobble the sack would slip off your back. Herchsfeld, in the meantime, was walking up and down the line of grunting *volontaires*, occasionally standing on someone's hands if he decided that not enough welly was being put in. All the NCOs really liked to see a lot of effort in any task given. To give you an example, take a simple chore like washing a shirt. An inspecting NCO would rather see a recruit on parade with a soaking wet shirt, showing the lad had made at least some effort, than to hear lame excuses about lack of time or facilities.

Back to the march, and I could feel my right boot becoming loose. I said to myself that once these press-ups were finished, I would tighten it up knowing that if I didn't, I would really suffer later. Such was Herchsfeld's anger though, he didn't even wait for everyone to complete their press-ups before he was away off again. This time everyone went with him. I didn't want to be left behind, so I took off as well. It was a monumental mistake, for about one kilometre later the lace on my right boot snapped completely. I shouted to Herchsfeld and asked if we could stop so I could replace it. He looked witheringly at my face, then at my boot, said 'Non!' and turned away to continue the march.

I would have to finish, and I didn't know how much further it would be, with a boot that had no lace, held together by two buckles just above the ankle. Even after just a few metres, I knew this was really going to hurt. We were still going at a hectic pace and my foot was sliding around inside the boot however hard I tried to grip with my toes. As the march continued, I could feel blisters forming and I was already in considerable pain. I managed to tell Steve about the state I was in and a pained, shocked expression appeared on his face. He dropped back behind me and began talking, telling the most stupid and unfunny jokes, trying to keep me going.

Humour can get you through bad moments such as these I was enduring now. Steve was a natural comedian, a master of taking a simple everyday occurrence with ordinary people, and turning it into a riotously funny sketch. He had an annoying habit, though: when telling a tale, he always began in the same way. He would gather us in close, like some gang of conspirators plotting a devilish scheme and in a hushed voice as if it was a state secret, he would say, 'It was a cold night (or day, dependent on how the story was to be told) but not as cold as the night (or day) before,' and then launch into a story in which the weather had absolutely no bearing on the outcome. I once asked him why he always did 'the hushed conspirator bit', and he replied, 'Well, it sets the scene and gets everyone interested.' Despite the master-storyteller's efforts that day, I was beginning to fall behind the group. Six kilometres or so further on, I was in desperate trouble. The pain and discomfort had reached such a level I could hardly place my right foot on the ground. Herchsfeld noticed this and called the group to a halt. He half jogged to the rear of the line and waited for me to catch up. I hobbled to where he stood, hands on hips like a mother waiting for the weakest of her kin. I had already decided that I would not collapse but stand my ground. I dare not let him see how much I hurt.

'Are you in trouble Anglais? Hey, in pain?' he snarled at me. '*Toujours, Serjeant!*' I shouted loudly in reply. Always, Sergeant.

'OK, fix the boot,' and he went back to the head of the group. A huge surge of relief swept over me and I felt tears pricking the back of my eyes. I don't know if they were tears of pain, relief or frustration or a little bit of everything. Steve again came over to help me. 'Don't take it off Pete, you'll never get it back on,' he advised. 'We can sort your foot out later, but for Christ's sake, leave the boot on.' I replaced the useless piece of twine, probably over-tightened everything and we set off again. It felt as if someone had put small, sharp pieces of granite inside my boot and every time my foot hit the deck, little pieces of red-hot shrapnel embedded themselves into the broken skin of my foot. As the march continued I tried to think of anything nice that had or could happen to me. Anything to try and erase the intensity of the pain. It didn't work, as the pain easily suppressed any other feelings or thoughts. I wasn't sure if the wet inside my boots was sweat, blood or fluid from the burst blisters. This was hard. Harder than a big bag of hard things and I was really suffering.

Throughout that seemingly endless day, Steve kept up his attempts to encourage me, never letting me slip into self-pity. He made me laugh, got me angry and called me worthless before saying it was the bravest thing he had ever seen. Without him, I would surely have given up. God alone knows what the repercussions would have been had that happened. Six long and tortured hours later, we reached the top of a hill and down below, not too far away, was the Farm. I cannot express the depths of relief, almost ecstasy, I felt at that moment. The ghastly dump was my El Dorado. I could feel a surge of strength within me as adrenaline flooded my body. I could never have imagined that I could feel such happiness at the sight of the place.

My joy, however, was brutally cut short by that fiend, Herchsfeld. He stopped us at the crest of the hill and told us we were to have a lesson on battlefield tactics. He was going to teach us how to approach the crest of a hill without being spotted by a potential enemy. My heart sank. He looked me directly in the eye as he spoke and I got the impression this little charade was for my benefit, to delay me from sorting out my shattered foot. I may have been wrong but I don't think so. The lesson lasted only forty-five minutes and I don't think anyone in the group actually got anything out of it. As a lesson in tactics, it was crap. As a lesson in how to fuck off recruits, it was a masterclass.

I do not expect any sympathy here concerning that march. The point in relating the episode is to explain that Herchsfeld was teaching everyone a lesson; I was the unfortunate fall guy on this occasion, but it really could have been anyone. I was a perfect example of someone not checking their kit properly, the delaying effect that this can potentially have on the rest of the section and possibly other units dependent on the success of our task. What would have happened if I had been carrying a vital piece of equipment or was needed to complete a mission which may have had a direct impact on other soldiers' lives? My negligence could mean our mission was unsuccessful, thereby jeopardizing other missions and costing lives. If you are told to be somewhere at 0500 hours, it is no good arriving at 0505 hours. Another unit may have had a plan that depended on your prompt arrival at 0500 hours. A dramatic scenario, I agree, considering this was a training exercise, but wars are won by being thorough in training, and while that may not guarantee success in battle, fortune favours the prepared and disciplined soldier.

I wasn't the only one who was suffering after the march. Remember that, before enlisting, ninety per cent of the section had probably never walked further than the local chippy, or whatever the Eastern European equivalent is. To send us off on a beasting of such intensity as the one we had just completed was to my mind pure folly, even though we'd completed two lesser marches earlier at the Farm. A lot of the lads were neither physically or mentally up to it. We had, and I class both Steve and I in this description, only been soldiers for a few weeks. Some of the others had walked in off the street not having done any proper physical training for years. Before joining the British forces, you are warned well in advance of your first day of the physical fitness required. You have an idea as to what is expected from you. A cup of tea was the heaviest thing some of these lads had lifted in their life. Still, no good whining; for now we were all in this together, for better or worse.

There was to be one more fuck around before I could get to the relative sanctuary of the dorm and begin to sort out my throbbing feet. It was only a fuck around to me because we had to clean our weapons before putting them into the armoury. I can see that it all had direction, everything we did was for a reason. We would be grateful for these lessons in the future when our own and our comrades' lives depended on how good we were under the most severe pressure. I knew that, under duress, it would be reassuring to grab a firearm that had been properly cleaned and stored. But believe me, if I'd had a round in my weapon there and then, I could quite calmly have slotted Herchsfeld. It is said that a good instructor can measure his success by how many of his pupils want to kill him.

I sat on my bed for a good few minutes trying to muster the strength and the courage to take my boots off. I could only guess what sort of gruesome sight would greet me. The boots came off with remarkable ease but I could see dark, vivid stains on my standard issue green socks and I also knew that removing them was when the pain would really kick in. To prepare myself, I tried to liken it to stripping off an Elastoplast. You know, where it has been placed over a particularly hairy part of your anatomy and is just ripped off; you feel nothing for a few seconds, then the pain starts at the area you've just scalped and *then* hits every nerve in your body, sending emergency signals to the brain in the micro-seconds before a scream must be stifled.

'Now this is for your own good, Pete,' said Steve, as he gripped my sock just above the ankle, and looking me directly in the eye, the bastard pulled my sock off in one sweeping movement. He told me later that he had never heard a scream quite like the one I released – apparently it assaulted everyone's ears within a very large radius. My anguished cry brought Fennel rushing into the dorm, perhaps wondering if someone was being tortured. He came to the side of the bed where I lay, whimpering in self-pity, looked at the exposed foot and said, ominously, 'Get that sorted for tomorrow,' and left. Tomorrow? I had to go through the whole thing again, of that I was certain. What fresh hell would that bring? When the other sock was removed, it didn't seem as painful as the first. I don't think my brain could have accepted any more pain and refused to believe that my body was once again being subjected to that horror. Steve and Henri half carried, half dragged me to the shower area and sat me down. Then with extraordinarily gentle skill and care they washed the blood and fluid and dirt away from my feet. The pain had subsided considerably and I managed to hobble back to my bed where some great news awaited me. For that evening's French and singing lessons we could dress in *tenue de sport* – tracksuit and trainers – so my feet had a few more hours to recover before the next day's anguish.

CHAPTER FIVE

THE KEPI MARCH

IT IS IMPORTANT TO UNDERSTAND that the instructors were not trying to create elite soldiers of us at this point. They were merely steering us towards being more military, more professional in general attitude. This included learning to prepare yourself and your kit properly. Discipline had to be instilled immediately by whatever methods necessary but as yet we were only being taught the very basics. The real job of training would begin when we were posted to our various regiments. Rightly or wrongly, I had made it known that I wanted to go to the REP and I wanted them to know just how badly I wanted it.

Despite the apparent horror of the marches, characters were beginning to emerge from within the section as the language barriers came down. Inevitably, all the English-speaking lads stuck together again, as did the French speakers, the Germans and so on. I definitely formed the opinion that the other Europeans were wary of us English: we only numbered half a dozen but the others believed us to be somewhat deranged. They called us the *Mafia Anglais* or *les hooligans*, a name derived from our noble football supporters, I think.

We were told that evening that our rank, and how we would

be known for the next few weeks, was *Engagé Volontaire*. We were also told that every company had its own song, which was its signature or hallmark. Although we would learn many other songs, it was the company song that you burst a lung for and sung with added enthusiasm and gusto. Ours was called 'La Lune est Claire'. It tells the tale of a Legionnaire and his girlfriend – when the Legion calls for him to go to battle, he leaves. Although he loves Jeanine dearly, his love of the Legion is stronger and he leaves to go and fight, explaining there is nothing he can do about it. Although Jeanine wasn't a faithless woman, my recent experience with women had left me wary of treacherous liaisons and I rather identified with it. I was by now drawn inextricably deeper into this Legion world, feeling that I really belonged there. The others mainly seemed to feel the same and none of us – whether or not we were nursing recently broken hearts – appeared to miss the company of women much. We were too busy and there was no free time to think of them. Perhaps it was too ball-freezingly cold for that, anyway.

The pain I felt in my feet only a few hours ago had all but disappeared, a genuine case of mind over matter. We were being built up to believe that anything was possible if your mind was set correctly. Everything was now very military: I could already see nearly all of the section improving in many ways. The singing was better, as was the marching and even communicating in French had marginally improved. There were, however, a couple of lads who were clearly unhappy – a Dutch boy who I didn't really know and an English kid from Bristol, who I made every effort to ignore. For some hunchy reason I didn't like him or his attitude and I felt that if I was to associate with him, I could be identified as another malcontent. In short this kid was a gob-shite. I guessed him to be about twenty years old, but by Christ, what he had done in those twenty years was world-class, phenomenal. You name it, he'd done it, been there and either designed or stolen the T-shirt. I had caught him out in so many lies that it was no longer funny and I sensed that he wasn't cut out for this. He was also a coward.

Philippe told me that the Dutch lad was sure he had made a mistake in joining up and was desperate to get out. Everyone could see how miserable he was and few were unsympathetic. It is truly painful to see another human suffer right in front of your eyes. Most of us felt that he should be away from here, it was obviously not for him and his continued presence here could drag us all down. Misery is contagious and spreads quickly. He had been advised by us to stick it out here at the Farm for the few weeks that remained and upon our return to Castel, be honest, explain his situation and see what developed. Maybe they would send him *civil*. It's not unknown and the Legion is far too wise to keep hopelessly unmotivated soldiers. Brian, the kid from Bristol, also wanted to get out but he wasn't prepared to wait the few weeks. He apparently collared the Dutch kid after *la soupe* and cajoled him into leaving with him that night, making a run for it into Spain. The idea was crassly stupid and impractical but Brian didn't have the bollocks to do it on his own. They had no maps, no food and only a basic idea of where they actually were. I reminded him he was likely to drop the guard in deep shit by these actions. It was freezing cold and snowing. Steve also joined in the collective attempt to get him to change his mind. But nothing doing – the selfish bastard was hell-bent on his Great Escape whatever we said. We were caught in a ghastly dilemma. Did we let them go or – cruel to be kind – inform Herchsfeld of the plan? After a last attempt was made to deter them Steve said, 'Well, just get on with it. You stand no chance.'

As I've said, it was virtually impossible to sleep in the barn. The cold worked its way into your bones and lay there, leaving you in a perpetual state of pain, like really bad toothache which throbbed through your whole body. All that night there was a lot of movement in our room. The guards made their hourly walk through, shining torches into our faces and stomping on the floor like jack-booted Nazis. *Just wait until it's my turn, you shit*. I think everyone thought like that because the bloody noise was the same every night. We were all longing for revenge against the previous night's silence wreckers. I must have drifted off at some point because I was woken by the clattering of a dustbin being bashed with a hammer and ordered out for routine *appel* and ablutions. That time of the morning is very confusing with all the comings and goings, and so it wasn't until *appel* and just before *le petit déjeuner*, breakfast, that Fennel noticed we were two *engagés* short. They had done it. They must have used the cover of the guard changing and disappeared sometime during the night. Fennel handled the situation with remarkable aplomb. He completed the roll-call, sent us off for breakfast and obviously reported back to Herchsfeld and Lt. Colomb.

The incident was mentioned only once, at the parade before we separated for instruction that morning. Colomb spoke calmly, stating that they would not get far, that they would be caught and punished. He was right; they were caught fairly quickly, which came as no surprise, and sent to *La Tolle*, the jail, where they were severely punished as we learned when we returned to Castel.

Their tale became one of legend and rumour, both of which keep most armies going. The two had left in the dead of night, bypassing the guard – which led to those guys being punished. It would have been even worse for them if the deserters had not been returned to the Farm before being carted off to jail. The runaways had, either by good luck or skill, and I prefer to believe the former, arrived in a town called Carcassonne, at the foot of the Pyrenees. With their distinctive haircuts and uniform, combined with their dishevelled appearance, it was not long before they attracted the attention of the local *gendarmerie* and were subsequently arrested. They were collected by the *Police Militaire* and suffered quite a beating before they were dragged back to the Farm.

What happened next was purely for our benefit, as a brutal example was made of them. With their *sac à dos* heavily laden, they were forced to run up and down a hill to the rear of the barn. The hill's incline was about sixty degrees and it stretched for over 700 metres. Up and down they went for over four hours; they were simply crawling at the end. Every hour or so, a different group of us would return to the Farm from lessons to watch this spectacle. Once the instructors had enjoyed their fun, the two were carted off back to camp. According to rumour, the two deserters were seen around Castel, barefoot and enduring all kinds of abuse. They were on permanent *corvée* and the jailer wasted no time in telling any passer-by exactly what his charges had done. They suffered beatings from other Legionnaires who were in jail for lesser offences and their life must have been a living hell. Once the sixty days' punishment had been completed, with no time off for good behaviour, they were taken into downtown Castel and dumped. No money, no food and no idea what to do next. I saw them once while on guard duty at Castel as the jail was next to the guardhouse. The sight of two such broken young men was shocking.

My feet healed quite miraculously considering they had no real medical treatment. The lasting consequence of that hellish march was that I can put my hand on my heart and tell you there was no better prepared Legionnaire than I when it came to marches. I always had spare laces for a start. Instruction carried on at a cracking pace, probably to keep everyone occupied, and by the third week at the Farm we had turned into something resembling Legionnaires. We could now belt out 'La Lune est Claire' whilst marching and, I swear to God, I saw Herchsfeld smirking in self-congratulation one day as he presented us to Lt. Colomb. 'Look at my work,' he could have been saying, 'I have turned a rabble into this. Not perfect but not bad.'

The final march, the kepi march, was only a few days away. There was an air of expectancy around the Farm. The atmosphere between us, the *volontaires* and the instructors, was almost relaxed and it was during this hiatus of anticipation and reduced pressure that I very nearly blew all my hard work.

The lad, called Galle, who had taken a dislike to me back at Aubagne had decided that now he was fitter and stronger it would be a good time to finish the business he had started. We were milling about the square one morning, waiting for Fennel to give us instruction in weapon handling. The sun was actually shining and it was slightly warmer than it had been. Everyone was feeling pretty good. I saw a group form around the French kid and I knew instinctively that something was going to kick off and that it would involve me. I quietly let Steve know what was happening and he asked if I needed any help. I told him no, this was to be one on one but if anything changed, please feel free to join in.

Sure enough, Galle's little group looked over and started laughing. I had already decided enough was enough, and I walked over to them. '*J'ai en vraiment plein les couilles. Allez!*' I have had enough of this. Come on!

He grinned inanely at me, really winding me up. '*Parlez Français. Parlez Français,*' he sneered. I swung my right fist and caught him squarely on the solar plexus and as I was so close, I felt a rush of air as the contents of his lungs exploded out through a goldfish mouth. Without thinking I immediately launched my left fist hard at where I thought his face should have been. Only it wasn't his face I punched, but his very hard steel helmet. My first punch had nearly doubled him up and he was raising his head in an attempt to suck in air when my fist and his helmet clashed. Steve later told me how hilarious the next few moments were. Galle fell to the floor wheezing and gasping like some kind of chronic asthmatic as I screamed out in pain and fell to my knees, cradling my hand. No one went to Galle's aid, while a few people gathered around me, patting and slapping my back which only served to increase the intense pain I felt. I looked at my hand and knew instantly that I had broken it, for it had already swollen like a soufflé and had begun to show bruising.

The commotion had caused Fennel and Herchsfeld to appear on the scene. They didn't ask for any explanation but simply lifted Galle to his feet, said something I neither heard nor understood and sent him on his way. Herchsfeld lifted my hand, looked at it and then sent me with Fennel to the instructor's quarters. He asked me, in English, if I was in pain. 'Just a lot, Corporal, just a lot,' I replied. Lt. Colomb appeared and he had a quick look: '*Oh, putain de merde!*' Fucking hell! He gave Fennel the first aid pack. Fennel took out a syringe, said 'Morphine', and injected this wondrous substance into my rear end. Within a few seconds I was floating on air in a fantastic world many miles from this one. Then he told me I would be immediately taken back to Castel, to the Infirmary for treatment, and I began to panic. That meant a plaster cast at least and I wouldn't be allowed to do the kepi march. Shit! I didn't want to be re-coursed and have to start all over again after coming so far. Fennel said not to worry right now but to see what happened at the Infirmary. I wasn't convinced.

It was Fennel who drove me back to Castel on one of the admin runs the instructors often did, about thirty miles as I recall. My hand hurt like hell whenever the painkillers wore off and Fennel had already warned me that I wasn't getting another shot of 'the good stuff'. He told me that I had done all right so far and that I wouldn't necessarily be re-coursed. I really wanted to do the march, though, I wanted that kepi and to have earned it, not to have it given to me. Continuing in his alarmingly matey and jovial mode, Fennel said that the instructors had been watching my and Galle's little performance with interest. He laughed and said I had a good right but my follow through was crap, adding that if Galle had any bollocks, he should have done me good and proper when I was injured. He was indiscreet enough to murmur that they too thought Galle was a shit and he deserved everything he got. He was certainly going to be quieter now. 'These things sort themselves out,' said Fennel obliquely. He volunteered little fragments of wisdom like that on many occasions and when he did so you knew that conversation was over.

Entering the Infirmary was like entering a different world, not like Planet Morphine but almost better – a world of cleanliness, white sheets and comfortable beds. I was shown into a small room which contained four beds and looked out onto the huge parade square. I emptied the little bag I had with me containing wash kit and other essentials into the locker beside the bed and looked happily around me. Aah: pillows, crisp white sheets and soft blankets. Maybe the pain and discomfort would be worth it for a night here. A short while later, I was summoned to a treatment room, along the highly polished corridor. A doctor asked a variety of questions which were translated for me by a medical orderly who happened to be Canadian. After basic enquiries the doctor looked at my hand and said that I would need an X-ray. For that I would be taken to the civilian hospital in town. I was once again pumped full of painkillers and then left in my room, alone. I was still at the stage of being frightened to upset anyone, so instead of collapsing onto the bed, despite every muscle and sinew in my body begging me to do just that, I stood in the centre of the room and waited. In fact, I waited until the next morning. I had long given up hope of anyone coming for me, so I took a chance, stripped off and climbed between clean sheets for the first time in weeks. It felt absolutely fantastic. I did think of the lads at the Farm, oh, for at least twenty seconds, and then fell into a wonderful, deep sleep.

The sound of others moving around the building woke me and I was up, washed and dressed before an orderly came and led me to a communal area where I had breakfast. I thought I was in the wrong room. A large table was laid with bread, brioche, cheese and various cold meats. A large pot of coffee was bubbling away in the corner, waves of delicious caffeine smells overcoming the normal clinical odour associated with this type of place. There was no shouting here and everything was

THE MAKING OF A LEGIONNAIRE

nice and relaxed. Although it was great, I didn't want to get too used to such luxury. It would make returning to the Farm all the more harder.

Shortly after breakfast, the Canadian orderly came for me and drove me the short distance into town. It may sound juvenile but I sat in the front of the jeep that took me into Castelnaudary and I looked in wonder at the countryside and buildings as we passed them. It made a great change to see where I was going, rather than where I had already been, so used was I to looking out from the rear of a truck. We drove past Le Quartier Lepasset, the old Legion training HQ, during the short journey. My stay in the hospital didn't last long. I was fast-tracked into casualty, X-rayed and discharged in about thirty minutes. The doctor I saw there confirmed I had broken a couple of metacarpi – bones in the hand – and my hand needed to be set in plaster. This was done back at our Infirmary by an *infirmier*, a Legionnaire learning to be a medic on detachment from his regiment. The process was very quick, very efficient, when it eventually took place. I stupidly thought that I would have the cast applied that morning, once I had returned to the Infirmary, but it was over forty-eight hours from the initial incident before the plaster was finally put onto my hand, and that was an experience I never want to repeat.

The Canadian, who had taken care of me since my arrival, had been designated to apply the cast. We got talking as he prepared the bandages, the type with plaster already impregnated. 'Just add water' could be their slogan. He told me he was here from the 2ème REP, the parachute regiment, to train as a medic. He said that the pay was much better there and that a lot of English lads were in the regiment. He also mentioned the *Mafia Anglaise*. The more he told me, the more I wanted to be posted there. He was like a recruiting officer and made it sound fantastic. They were always on the go, always the first to be called in. They were simply the best, and it confirmed my wish to join them. The fact that I was terrified of heights and had been since I was small did not deter me. I had so much self-confidence by now that I felt I could achieve anything as long as I set my mind to it.

The Canadian then told me this was the first plaster he had ever put on, so I would have to bear with him. Bear with him! I nearly punched him with my good fist. This was a bad psychological move because even with the best will in the world, no one wants to be a medical experiment: I wouldn't even want my breakfast cooked by someone on their first day at catering college and this was my bloody hand. I was no medical man but I sure as hell knew that when you put a plaster cast on any part of the body, a protective layer of cotton wool is put over the skin before the plaster is applied. This bloke was putting the plaster bandages straight onto my skin. I could feel the bandage constricting as it dried and my fingers swelling as the blood supply was cut off. I pulled my hand away and asked if he wanted to put something on my hand first. I could see it register on his face and he agreed. God only knows what would have happened if I had let him carry on. Some training here, but no supervision.

The doctor saw me that afternoon and said I must stay in the Infirmary for a few days until the cast dried completely. I knew the kepi march was imminent and I desperately wanted to be there. When I said this to the doctor, he looked at me in bewilderment. Why, he asked, would anyone give up the chance of a nice, clean, warm bed for the spartan, cold billets up at the Farm? Despite what I'd been told, I was pretty sure that if I missed the march I'd have to complete the entire Farm hell all over again – most probably without my mates. Besides, I didn't want to go through on the nod just because of this wretched hand, even if this had indeed been suggested. I repeated that I needed to be there. He shook his head and told the orderly that I could go the next day, provided the cast had set. He left the room muttering something about the 'crazy *Anglais*'. The Canadian thanked me for not telling anyone about the cock-up with the plaster. I replied that everyone has to learn, and anyway, I reckoned that I might need him one day when he was fully trained and I needed preferential patching-up.

It is amazing what a couple of nights in lovely, warm surroundings can do for morale. I returned to the Farm refreshed and ready to face anything. The cast would be awkward, that's all. The section was out on instruction but Colomb was there. He welcomed me back and asked if there was anything I had to say about my injury. I told him it had been an accident and everything was OK and that seemed to satisfy him but his last words to me before I was dismissed were: 'No more, OK, it is finished. *D'accord?*' I could hardly argue as I never knew why the bad blood between me and Galle had existed in the first place. I saluted and left. I remember thinking that the instructors must have eyes and ears everywhere. They always seemed to know what was going on.

The day of the final march, the kepi march, arrived. We were all tense with excitement. Colomb once again asked if I was OK to do this and I replied there was no way I was going to miss it. After all, I'd only busted my hand, not a foot. What difference would it make? It was a particularly cold and horrible morning and as we formed up on the square into smaller groups of ten, the rain began. Not the fine mizzle we get in northern Europe, not even a burst of hail. No, this was like small, metal pellets relentlessly driven into your face by a bitingly cold wind. Each rucksack, or *sac à dos*, was weighed to check that we all carried exactly 45kg. We were issued water and rations; and for the fiftieth time I checked my boots and laces. I had been able to buy another couple of pairs of laces while back at Castel and these were safely in my pocket. The little matter of changing them one-handed was not something I paused to fret about.

I wasn't in the same group as Steve or Philippe and I thought the best way to accomplish this march – and remember that in this context 'marching' was not the Legionnaire's dignified slow plod, but a long cross-country scramble – was head down and arse up. I had a head full of things to think about en route and I hoped they'd take my mind off the march. And then we were off, Fennel at the front. The distance was about seventy-five kilometres, to be completed within two days.

It was deceptive at the beginning. Even the distance didn't sound too taxing after all the training. We quickly left the confines of the Farm and walked across meadows rampant with flowers whose names I could only guess at. The rain had eased off for the time being and the sun won, briefly, its battle with the clouds and shone upon us, radiating a little warmth and creating a false dawn. Way above us ranged the mountains, hard, sharp, granite grey peaks upon which snow lay, glinting in the winter sunshine. The pace was brisk but not fast and for a short while you could almost imagine you were on a holiday jog. But within minutes the ground turned mean, along with the weather. Sunshine faded into a murky half-light and we were lashed by both rain and snow. From lush green meadows, we marched up an unforgiving mountain side. The gradient increased with every step and breathing became laboured as oxygen was sapped anew with every metre we climbed. This was now very tough going. Fields full of geraniums and Pyrenees lilies might as well have been a world away as icy rain drove into my face and my mind became a blur of wet and cold. No matter how hard I tried, I could concentrate on nothing but the pain I was now in. The cold seemed to have made a direct hit onto the fractures in my hand, pain like that of constant and relentless toothache. I noticed that Fennel rarely looked at his map so he must have done this countless times. My chest was heaving and my lungs were screaming out for the little oxygen there was. I was thinking this couldn't last forever, I couldn't (I hoped) die from this, although I longed to be struck down dead. Such thoughts drove me on.

We were high in the mountains and panted up to a shabby old hut. Fennel halted us and ordered everyone inside. There, amazed, I saw a raging fire in the centre of the room along with a supply of bread, ham, cheese and, believe it or not, bottles of Kronenbourg. He told us to eat,

drink and sort ourselves out, we had thirty minutes. As ever Legion planning and stop-watch timing was in evidence. I was checking my feet
when Fennel came over and asked why I wasn't eating. I reminded him
about my previous experience. Although the physical wounds had healed
on my feet, I could still remember and feel the pain from the earlier
march; I showed him pockets crammed with scoff and said I could always
throw food down my neck on the march but I couldn't check my feet
then. He nodded.

This hut had been used by the Legion over many years for replenishing sections on marches and also to pick up any *volontaire* who just
couldn't continue. A truck was parked nearby but out of sight in case it
gave anyone ideas about chucking it. My feet were actually fine, but I
felt much better having dry socks on. We had actually completed about
sixteen kilometres but I didn't know that. Fennel told a few of us about
the history of the hut. The route we were following was an old
smugglers' trail, anything from tobacco to alcohol, and it dated back
centuries. It had also been used during World War Two by escaping
Allied prisoners of war en route to Spain. All pretty useless information
but it underlined the changing attitude of the instructors towards us
volontaires. We were now being spoken to as men, not donkeys, and
with something approaching respect.

After the break we had to up the pace as the earlier weather had
slowed us down considerably. Snow was by now falling heavily and I
dreaded having to stop, as we had to, for the stragglers to catch up. My
momentum wavered during such pauses. I was sweating a lot and
shivered uncontrollably whenever we halted. We continued marching
through the afternoon and into the evening. It was difficult to tell when
night fell as the cloud had descended and the weather really closed in.
We marched for another few hours blindly stumbling along mountain
tracks until Fennel told us we had reached the halfway point and we
tumbled gratefully into another ramshackle hut for the night. At least

it was dry, out of the wind, and there was food ready again. There were still duties to be carried out though, guard and *corvée,* as standards had to be maintained.

My cast was giving me some concern. I hadn't been able to protect it from the elements and consequently it was wet and had lost a great deal of firmness. I wasn't going to say anything as we would be back at the Farm tomorrow and probably in blessed Castel a day or so later. It could wait until then.

The weather hadn't improved by the morning and at first light we set off again, going as fast as the weather would allow. The exertion required was considerable and every muscle in my body was screaming in protest. It must have been the same for the others. But when you think your body cannot possibly take any more punishment it is quite surprising that by pushing on you go through a pain barrier and can carry on. After a good few hours of half running, half marching, I saw the Farm in the distance. It was over, almost literally downhill, now. Fennel told us, as we neared the outbuildings, that we had done well and despite the atrocious weather, completed the march within the given time. We had passed. It may sound strange, but I didn't feel elated or jubilant then. I just felt as if the job had been done. I was, however, really excited about the kepi ceremony to be held later.

The noise of excited chattering could be heard from the square as Fennel dismissed us – we were the last group back. Inside everyone had their own tales of the march and was keen to tell anyone who would listen. It sounded like an aviary. All of us were in fantastic spirits. I sought out Steve and Philippe to find out how they had got on. They had covered similar distances, in similar conditions but obviously in different directions. They too, had stopped at old shacks and had been fed like us. Steve had found the lack of oxygen as he climbed up the mountains a massive problem, but had found inner strength and driven himself on: he couldn't have stood the piss-take had he not completed the march. He said the pace and distance had surprised him, in that he thought we should have gradually built up to the march. Instead, after a couple of warm-ups, we were thrown in at the deep end. The kid I'd had the trouble with before, the hand-breaker, had been in Steve's group, and had apparently been overly nice to Steve, even asking how I was. Now, there's a thing. I didn't offer to shake.

Just before midnight we were summoned on to the parade square. Huge barrels were equally spaced and burning brightly in the pitch-black night. The section formed up in front of Lt. Colomb for *La Remise du Képi Blanc*, to receive the *Képi Blanc*. It was eerie as we stood in silence, the burning, crackling oil barrels making the only noise. Colomb welcomed us to the Legion family. We had worked well, he said, but there was more to do. We stood proud and strong in the flickering darkness whilst we recited *Le Code d'Honneur* which we had been practising for weeks. We wore our kepis with as much pride and honour as any Legionnaire, anywhere in the world. The countryside reverberated to 'La Lune est Claire' and we sang our hearts out, pure joy overcoming memories of mistakes. Lt. Colomb presented us with our *4ème Régiment Étranger* pins which we would wear on the lapels of our uniforms. We were now part of the Legion.

After the formalities, we went back to the dining area and drank and ate and sang more songs. It was a night I will never forget, so emotional and proud was I. Physical strains seemed to have been spirited away. We had a company photograph taken, kepis sitting proudly on our heads, and epaulettes worn for the first time. Colomb insisted I knelt beside him in the front rank for the photo and further insisted that my battered plaster was clearly visible. His Legionnaires could clearly conquer pain and discomfort to ensure orders were carried out. The phrase 'his Legionnaires' may sound patronizing to an outsider but a Legion officer does indeed regard every man in his command as his. His glory, his disappointments, his family.

I think I felt a tear prickle at the back of my eye, but I am sure it was caused by the wind that suddenly blew into my face.

La Lune est claire, la ville dort,
J'ai rendez-vous avec celle qui j'adore.
Mais la Légion s'en va, oui s'en va,
part au baroud, baroud.
Jeanine je reviendrai
sans aucun doute.

The Moon is clear, the town is sleeping,
I have a rendezvous with the one I love.
But the Legion is leaving, yes is leaving,
off to a gallant last fight, gallant last fight.
Jeanine I shall return
without any doubt.

CHAPTER SIX

RETURN TO CASTEL AND CHRISTMAS

IF WE THOUGHT WE'D DONE IT ALL at the Farm, then we had a hell of a shock when we returned to Castel. Far from being awarded privileges and swanking around like some cocky elite, we were restored to our proper place with training which continued to be relentless and hectic. But the month at the Farm had certainly toughened everyone up and we thought nothing now of a thirty- or forty-kilometre trek, fully laden, across steep hillsides. Our marching, singing and weapon handling had improved immeasurably – I suppose it is a testament to the excellence of our instructors that we almost took this for granted and didn't quite realize how much better and harder we were. As far as the pecking order around the *quartier* went, we would remain the lowest form of life until another batch of recruits came in and took our place. The Farm meant nothing here, after all every man had done it.

The NCOs kept up the pressure. Kit inspection was followed by room inspection which was followed by latrine inspection. Then there was always a run and a session of circuit training, press-ups, pull-ups and rope climbing, and then more French and singing lessons. There was still a lot to learn.

Now that we could handle our weapons competently and were not likely to kill or injure anyone we were allowed onto the firing ranges, where we spent many days. We fired from one hundred metres to 500 metres, the effective range of the FAMAS. We fired from a standing and a kneeling position, from the prone position and using the tried and trusted 'shotgun' method. This was particularly useful when fighting in built-up areas where you couldn't take proper aim, or where you have been ambushed or come across an enemy soldier at a very close distance. To fire effectively and also put the enemy on the back foot, the weapon is placed in the centre of your body and facing your enemy you let off a short, sharp burst of fire. As long as you are facing the enemy square on, you should, at the very least, wound him, which will give you time to suss out what is going on. I had heard that some instructors placed photos of nude women, legs wide apart, on the centre of a target in order to sharpen one's aim, but this dubious technique was not employed with us.

When we were not firing on the ranges, the NCOs ensured we were kept otherwise busy. Rifle cleanliness is paramount in the Legion, as it is in all professional armies, and ours never seemed to be clean enough at inspection. The instructors devised many punishing and complex ways of reminding us to clean our rifles properly. Quite often you could hear the squeal of an injured *engagé* when the rifle part he produced for inspection was launched at his head, scoring a direct hit eight out of ten throws. I had seen one *caporal* actually throw the concerned part away into some bushes nearby. Quite funny until the *caporal* realized that the part couldn't be found. The whole section ended up on their hands and knees in a fingertip search to locate the missing part.

They also punished us if our shooting was particularly bad and in the early days it often was. A favourite penance was issued on the 200-metre range. If the firing had been deemed poor, once completed, we had to crawl on our bellies to the target, patch them up and crawl back.

It may not seem much of a sweat to someone who hasn't had to drag themselves on their stomachs over that sort of distance, but anyone who has done it will know that it is exhausting. Added to that, our uniform would now be particularly filthy and require a great deal of attention back at the block. This, then, was indeed a very effective staggered punishment. Two for the price of one, really.

We spent hours on the ranges, day and night, and most of us became decently proficient shots. Some of the section, however, could not grasp the names of various parts of the FAMAS and Fennel was still a marksman when it came to launching the said part at an unfortunate dunce. He had more direct hits than misses. You had to know the very intimate details of your weapon. How each part felt in the dark, how it all fitted together and why each part was as vital as the next. The weapons might have to be cleaned four or five times while on the range, with an inspection after every one. Should we fail to perform this task adequately, and someone invariably did, the duty punishment was called *La Marche du Canard*. This humiliation meant squatting on the haunches, arse about six inches from the ground, and waddling over a designated distance, quacking like a duck. It was an immense strain on the thighs, never mind how much your pride was wounded. This sort of treatment went on for weeks.

One evening before *appel* we were surprised and delighted that the next day was to be a holiday from training. Cue excited chatter and anticipation all round. Then Herchsfeld dampened our spirits by telling us that we would still be working, but not here at Castel. Instead, we would be going to the Legion retirement home at a place called Puyloubier, near Aix-en-Provence. Here was the Domaine Capitaine Danjou, where many former Legionnaires saw out retirement and their final days. Many had no homes or family to return to, indeed the Legion for many had been their only family. Some of the section was cursing after *appel*, having looked forward, even if for only a few seconds, to a break. Me, I was very curious about the place and what I would find when we got there. I was not disappointed, although some of my comrades were, oddly. By talking and listening to these veterans, *les anciens*, I learned an awful lot about the Legion and its history.

We travelled by truck to Puyloubier, the temperature there almost sub-tropical compared to that we had endured recently. Lt. Colomb had already briefed us that we were to perform domestic duties at the home, but also to talk to the resident *anciens*.

'Learn about the Legion's battles, their victories and defeats,' said Colomb quietly, but with respect and passion. 'They are your victories and defeats also. Speak to the men who have fought, veterans who have survived horror in the battlefield and who have built the Legion's fearsome reputation, for these men are also our family now, they are still Legionnaires and your comrades,' he added. It was an inspiring speech.

The hills surrounding Domaine Capitaine Danjou were covered in vines and tall, wrought-iron gates opened onto a tree-shaded courtyard where we disembarked the truck. There was a huge manorial building which housed the administrative offices and all around the vineyard clearing fires sent plumes of smoke straight up into the clouds and still, chill morning air. After a harvest, the bare vines were burnt leaving a compost of ashes ready for the next season. A mood of tranquillity per-meated the place, but this was not a retirement home where sedated invalids sat dribbling in front of a flickering television set all day long. Although some had suffered horrific wounds as a result of their service and were in some way disabled, most were still active and contributed very effectively to the day-to-day running of Puyloubier – which is simply a working vineyard run by former Legionnaires. This is the place the wine served at meals at the various Legion installations comes from – the wine itself has been classified as a Cotes du Rhone. Other work carried out at Puyloubier varies from wood carving to leather work, sold at Legion posts all over the world. That day the yard was full of pigs, geese, chickens and other animals destined, I feared, for the kitchen and the dining table.

There were about 180 former Legionnaires at the home, although inevitably, at their age, the number could fluctuate from week to week. Everything they need is provided for them and few have links with the outside world, save for an occasional visit from an old comrade. The Legion is their family and all families look after their own. It was certainly a place of comfort for these *anciens* but most definitely not a place I could ever see myself in. I hoped, that when I had completed my time, however long that may be, I would have something to return to England for. Unless circumstances changed dramatically, this would be a place for me to visit and then leave.

Halfway through the morning, as I mooched around an old barn, I heard Steve shouting for me. He told me an *ancien* had heard him speaking English and struck up a conversation with him. The old man had only been talking to him for a few minutes when Steve decided that I should hear what the old geezer had to say. When Steve asked him to wait, the guy said to bring all the English back with him. Actually it would only be Steve and me, there being no other English with us. I went into a dingy room that had a damp and musty smell as if it never got any fresh air. Sitting in the corner in a wheelchair was a man, who even if he was ninety, looked a lot older. Decades of harsh, outdoor living were etched into a deeply creased face and long, bony fingers stretched out to shake my hand. Despite his gnarled features and the fact he was in a wheelchair, the old man's grip was firm and strong, without being the knuckle-crunching challenge of some handshakes.

He introduced himself as Karl and politely asked for our names. Karl began by telling us he joined the Legion in 1946, after serving with the Fallschirmjager, the German paratroops. Karl said that once Germany had surrendered the year before, he and others in his unit believed that the Allies would be after retribution. He and his pals high-tailed it to France and the Legion, who accepted him and others of like mind. He was at pains to tell us that he was an honourable soldier and always had been. We nodded. We could understand how, with shocking stories of the concentration camps in wide circulation, every German soldier must have feared he would be held partially responsible for such atrocities. There were tears in Karl's eyes as he told us how he had lost his wife and children during an air raid, but he held no bitterness towards either British or American people. '*C'est la guerre*,' he said.

Steve and I sat spellbound as he regaled us with tales of the Legion as it was in his day. He spoke of the horrors of the desert marches when it really was 'march or die'. When he told us of how the *fellagha* rebels in Algeria had captured Legionnaires and tortured them, I thought I would be violently ill. Some were found lying in the desert sun, their tongues cut out and skin eaten by the creatures of the desert. Two Legionnaires had been found in a house, just outside of Algiers city. They were naked and covered in their own blood; they couldn't tell their rescuers of their ordeal because their tongues, too, had been removed. The Legionnaires babbled like demented lunatics failing miserably to tell their comrades that they had also been castrated. They died shortly after being discovered. Karl told us that later that day, on his Commanding Officer's orders, they returned to the village, took away two men and shot them in front of their families and friends.

Karl became distressed as he recalled how fellow human beings can treat each other. Actually, in his time, quite a number of former Waffen SS officers ended up in the Legion and I doubt if they were all as decent as Karl. Even during my Legion service German Legionnaires were thought to be unkind, for example, to Romanies and I can't say I didn't notice.

'But everything changes,' he continued. I don't know if he meant for better or worse. He told us of famous battles in Dien Bien Phu, Algeria and other places. His English, although heavily accented, was very good and both Steve and I genuinely warmed to this frail old man. I think Karl could have talked for hours but we heard a commotion outside and realized everyone was being called to parade. As I stood up to leave, he took my good hand and gripped it so tightly this time that I feared it would break and I would have both hands in plaster. Then he said the most peculiar and almost spooky thing: 'Enjoy this life you have chosen. Serve with honour and be proud.' It was almost exactly word for word the same speech the officer in Paris had said to me before I left his office. I suppose I already had some small reason to be proud because of the 300 or so rookies who make it through the Fort's selection process over the course of a year only twenty or so make it as far as Castelnaudary, and fewer still survive the Farm.

We had a lunch of bread, cheese, ham and wine. After that we went to the cemetery and were shown the graves of famous characters in Legion history such as General Rollet, the 'Father of the Legion', and a certain Legionnaire Zimmerman, killed in the early days of French involvement in Algeria. Their bodies had been exhumed when the Legion left Algeria in 1962 and were reburied at Puyloubier. There are plaques commemorating all other Legionnaires who have fallen in combat. I had seen that the pensioners looked forward to the visits of new recruits. Most old people grab the chance to tell their stories, whether they concern battles or not, and these old men had few such opportunities. I felt that the privilege had been all mine.

I wondered afterwards how these men who had been active all their adult lives could settle into an institutionalized life like that. They must, I felt, although I hoped I was wrong, be terribly lonely despite being surrounded by so many comrades. Some turned to drink, I was told. They drank to forget places like Dien Bien Phu. I wonder if some of them are still in Dien Bien Phu and cannot forget. I would not, however, forget

Karl and to this day, if I concentrate hard enough, I can still see him in his wheelchair, smell that musty room and hear him say: 'Serve with honour and be proud.'

BACK AT CASTEL, THINGS WERE definitely changing. We could write and receive letters now and go to the foyer at the weekend to buy goodies and beer. Sadly for some perhaps, marriage was not yet permitted. Only after five years' service may a Legionnaire embrace this blissful state. Christmas was coming and we had heard how important the festivities are to the Legion and what we could expect. It all made me do some uncharacteristic soul-searching about my family in England and how I would deal with letters or telephone calls. Would they even want to hear from me? It had only been a matter of months but everything about Tyneside seemed so long ago and far away. A lot to think about, then. I was distracted from too much introspection when great excitement abounded at the news that on New Year's Day we would be allowed out into Castel in uniform, *tenue de sortie*, with some cash from our accounts. It would be a gloriously free day and my *confrères* were already planning to hit the bars hard. Some did.

Christmas with the Legion, as elsewhere, is a very special time. All Legionnaires, regardless of rank or marital status, must be on the *quartier* on Christmas Day. The Legion is your home and that is where you should be on 25 December. The rule includes all ranks, sergeants and above. Preparations start early and that year each section was to come up with a comedy sketch to be performed in front of the whole company, and make *la crèche*, a model made of paper, wood, plastic or anything else we could lay our hands on. It was to depict a scene to entwine biblical and Legion lore, including a voice-over by one of the section. Then there would be a regimental competition to see which section had the best entry. Competition was fervent and plans were taken very seriously – we might as well have been groups of small boys instead of crack troops. Anyway, our lot wanted to win this for Colomb.

Otherwise the days at Castel settled into a structured routine. At exactly 0600 the section was wakened and assembled in the corridor outside their respective rooms for morning *appel*. A quick wash and thorough shave, and then we changed into *tenue de sport*. Our rooms had to be tidied and beds made. Legion beds are not made in the normal way nor do they follow the 'bed-block' fashion – where the blankets are folded into layers and enveloped by another blanket forming a block – of the British forces. The bed is completely stripped and the blankets folded to an exact size and then placed in a neat stack at the foot end of the bed. The *couverture*, the counterpane, sits underneath, again folded to the same size as the blankets. The sheets must first be folded and then rolled into a tubular shape and laid on top of the pile of blankets, forming a cross. This ritual is carried out at every barracks in the Legion, every morning, regardless of whether one is in training or not. The room is then dusted and swept, while the washing area is cleaned and mopped. At first this seemed pedantic and mindless – but we got used to it.

0630 was *Corvée Quartier*, words still indelibly etched in my mind and doubtless those of thousands of Legionnaires. A straight line was formed to sweep around our building to pick up discarded cigarette butts and other minor garbage. Sick parade was also held now and if wishing to go on the sick list you had to report to the *caporal chef* in the company office where it would be decided if you were ill enough to go to the Infirmary or were slacking. We had heard stories concerning those who had reported sick only to be sent away by the *caporal chef* and punished. Rumours of beatings were enough to ensure that only those who were genuinely ill actually reported sick. After sick parade, a couple of Legionnaires would check the room to ensure it was properly tidy.

At 0700 *reassemblement* was assembly by section, unless it was a Monday, when we formed as a regiment. Our *caporal du jour*, NCO of the day, would hand us over to the most senior officer present and then we set off on a regimental 'cattle drive', or run – a breezy little six to eight kilometres. After a gentle warm up of a kilometre or so, the run gathered pace and at the end a series of press-ups, sit-ups and pull-ups were expected of everybody. 0830 and back at the block for a shower and change into *tenue verte*, green combats, which we usually wore for the rest of the day. After a quick breakfast of baguette and pâté we were set up for the day.

At 0930 we usually attended a lecture. I always enjoyed these and not just because it was good to sit down and use the brain rather than physical muscle. Since returning from the Farm many of the lectures concerned the different regiments and postings we could expect. Then came a short break outside, during which many of my comrades had their first cigarette of the day. Smoking was not permitted within the blocks. Then we'd have a French lesson before lunch. For some reason we always had to polish our boots before we had our midday meal and perhaps there'd be time for a quick aperitif before we ate our simple but perfectly OK repast. Did anyone have to read that again, thinking, 'This is supposed to be the Legion, not the bloody Guards. Aperitifs before lunch! Mine's a gin and tonic…'? The term here is used to describe an exercise session before any meal and sadly not a nice little tincture before lunch. It would normally mean more pull-ups, press-ups etc. for about fifteen minutes, just to get the appetite keen, in case we weren't already ravenous.

At 1230 the section would form up ready to march across for lunch. We'd always march and sing our way to the *réfectoire* and there was normally another section doing the same thing, so concentration to keep in tune and step was vital. We all wanted to be among the first in line so as to ensure we got our fair share but so did all the other companies and most times we would all arrive together. There wasn't a great deal of room on the road outside and the NCOs did well to keep everything in order. Fifteen minutes later we'd be standing in a long and orderly line from the door to the servery and one's initial thought might be 'I could be here for ages' or 'I hope there's still some left for me'. The *caporal* at the head of the queue controlled things and at the head chef's command of '*Quartre!*', four Legionnaires would walk to the servery and take a dish of food. Since each table was already laid out with cutlery and plates, only wine or beer need be collected too. It was a very efficient way of feeding a large number of hungry troops and indeed, hundreds of Legionnaires can be served in minutes, without any rampaging scrum or disorderly elbowing. Once finished, you left your plates on the table to be cleared by those on *corvée*. I half looked forward to the time when this duty would befall me – I'd have eaten first and maybe served myself with some of the better cuts of meat.

The quality of food in the Legion varies greatly from *quartier* to *quartier*. In some places, normally where there are staff officers, the food could match that in any civilian restaurant. In others, remembering Aubagne, it could be pretty disgusting. Whichever, there never seemed to be quite enough. Young men doing very physical work need a lot to eat but I suppose that constant hunger was also part of our training and kept us on edge. I looked forward to the trips to the foyer but in retrospect I'm glad I wasn't ever that keen on chocolate and other sweets as I might have squandered a lot of dosh on these quick fixes – they wouldn't have done much more than put on weight which would have to have been sweated off later.

Lunch wasn't a leisurely affair, and by 1300 hours we marched back to *le batiment*, our building, to carry out *corvée* again. The rooms were swept and we spent more time polishing dress boots which were to be worn for the first time when we undertook *le guarde*, on the main gate, soon. Next, at exactly 1400, the section assembled and the sergeant briefed us on the afternoon's programme. This might mean going to the Infirmary for tests. These could be blood and urine tests, chest X-rays and a talk with the medics, so that carefully observed and monitored health records would be *in situ* for reference once we left Castel. After my ritzy little break with a smashed hand I already felt that I knew my way around the place and, when there, took the chance to get my plaster checked out.

Drill was a given on any day. At 1530 there were further lessons. *Droit à droit*, or right turn. *Gauche à gauche*, left. *Demi-tour à droit*, the about turn. Just how perfect could a simple squaddie get? There was also *la présentation* to practise, a formality that was conducted by any subordinate rank speaking to a higher office. It was a simple task but one that had to be spot-on every time.

At ten minutes before five in the afternoon the company assembled for *le repas du soir*, the evening meal or *la soupe*. Again we sang and again we had a little aperitif beforehand. The food was wolfed down and by 1800 hours we were ready for *les chants de la Légion*, when we sang for some hours. Soon all would be memorized. We also practised *Le Code d'Honneur*, the Legion Code of Honour. There were short breaks for smoking outside during which smugly virtuous non-smokers like me just took the fragrant night air and enjoyed a little pause.

Not all the songs were sung in French, some were rendered in German and others in English. We were taught to sing in a very deep, low register, but good and loud. It involved many hours of practice and careful tuition. Lt. Colomb would take us for these singing lessons. I do not know a great deal about classical music but I realized that Colomb had an exceptional voice and an obvious love for these songs. Whenever he lead us in singing we were somehow inspired and when an entire section's voices are on song there is no sound like it, whatever Welsh Guards, or certain Highland regiments, might claim. The sight of forty Legionnaires singing in tune and marching with slow purpose, their kepis immaculately white and with the red epaulettes on their shoulders seeming to bristle with contained strength truly is a force, awesome to behold. No wonder Field Marshal Viscount Alanbrooke, Knight of the Garter, Distinguished Service Order and Chief of the Imperial Staff (1941–46) wrote in his diaries:

Out of the fast fading light and through the falling snow came a sight I shall never forget. The grandest assembly of real fighting men that I have ever seen, marching with their heads up as if they owned the world, lean, hard-looking men, carrying their arms admirably and marching with perfect precision.

It was this which we now had to live up to. Colomb, Herchsfeld and Fennel wouldn't allow anyone unworthy to follow in such footsteps.

At 2100 it was time for *appel du soir*, always carried out by a sergeant. If he was happy with our turn-out and the state of our rooms, he would bellow: *'Bonne nuit,'* to which we replied, *'Bonne nuit, Sergent'* and it should have been time to turn in for the night. However, this was an army like any other, and how many sergeants are ever happy with the first inspection? Occasionally we were still shouting *'Bonne nuit'* at three or four in the morning, only to have to rise a couple of hours later and do it all over again.

La présentation, the presentation, is a very important tradition in the Legion – a courtesy extended to anyone of senior rank that you engage with at any level. Until I attained any rank, I would have to observe it when talking to virtually everyone bar other *engagés*. The presentation is also said when pay is received or when entering a room occupied by a Legionnaire of senior rank. Imagine this scene: I had been called to Lt. Colomb's office for some reason – nothing of any startling significance. I knock on his door, wait, and then enter when bid. I approach his desk, salute and remove my beret. This is all done in slow, deliberate movements, every move a flourish, and then I intone:

'Engagé Volontaire Parker,
Trois mois de service,
Deuxième Compagnie,
Section de Lt. Colomb,
À vos ordres, mon Lieutenant!'

This translates as 'Recruit Parker, three months' service, 2nd Company, Lt. Colomb's section, *at your service!*', the last words almost shouted. *À vos ordres* would be changed to whoever's details were appropriate, i.e. a sergeant or *caporal chef*. This ritual was followed throughout my Legion career, more often when addressing someone I was unfamiliar with or maybe a couple of ranks above me. It was best practice to begin with the *présentation* if meeting someone for the first time. If they didn't require it to be said, they would soon let you know. Once I had served time and was established in a regiment, it could be shortened to something like, *'Légionnaire Parker, à vos ordres, Sergent'*. The reply would normally be, *'Oui, q'est-ce que tu veux?,'* a simple and direct 'Yes, what do you want?'

God might help you if you attempted to short cut the Legion way of doing things anywhere along the line, but He generally batted for the other side.

All soldiers throughout the world know that once you have learned your service number, or *matricule*, you never forget it, even if it is an endless series of digits in French. Even to a French speaker it would have been quite a task at first and to me and others like Steve it seemed nigh on impossible. Take a number such as 173662. Nice and easy to say in English. In French, however, it is another matter. Cent soixante-treize, six cent soixante-deux. Try it, especially after a couple of beers. A similar number was given for the issue of your FAMAS when drawing it from the armoury, or *le magasin*. Both these numbers had to be committed to memory and be recalled instantly upon request. A swift kick up the arse and a 'stick' aided some memories, the stick being a sharp slap to the back of your head or neck. It shocks more than hurts and you don't need many to realize it is easier and less painful to learn your numbers.

This place was tough but not vicious, no fiercer physically than any of the front line regiments in the British Army. If it seemed harder at times it was largely to do with the language barrier and even that was lowered every day as our French improved. I won't lie and claim I never saw a beating. The one on the train from Paris was merely the first. But nearly all the recipients deserved them for lying or dropping others in the shit or just being a twat. Most beatings came from other disgruntled recruits, not from NCOs. The unnecessary brutality that Simon Murray recorded in his classic book *Legionnaire* is pretty much a thing of the past. Today's Legion is modern and becoming ever more in line with other French Army units and thus subject to military law. The Legion is much more in the public eye and is consequently aware of being watched. For many, however, there comes a moment in the Legion when you must stand up for yourself. Mine came at the Farm. No one wants to be walked over. Yes, the Legion is tough and there are unwritten rules that we all accepted and lived by. Respect had to earned – as in any other walk of life – it could not be demanded. Most people learn this in life, if they are lucky. The Legion was just a particularly expert teacher.

The preparations for Christmas took on ever more urgency as the day approached. The French and Germans were rehearsing a comedy turn which I couldn't wait to see, given that neither set of lads was renowned for their sense of humour. The English speakers, and I include Philippe here, made steady progress with *la Crèche*. We had made a manger based on one of the old shepherd and smuggler huts we had used while at the Farm. I somehow remembered how to make papier mâché and from that, constructed models of the central characters. Joseph and Mary and even the shepherds looked OK but the animals …Well, what a disaster! If you can imagine, Joseph was twice the size of the cow I had made, and Mary's face didn't look much different from the donkey's that stood beside the crib, which contained a seriously deformed image of the baby Jesus. However, it's the taking part that counts and it did serve to cheer Steve up.

He was feeling a bit low. He'd received a letter from a girl he had been seeing just before he left England and he didn't know how she had got his address. Mind you, he showed me the envelope one day. It just had his name and 'Foreign Legion, Paris, France' written on it. Anyway, he hadn't realized how she felt about him. As far as he was concerned, they'd seen each other half a dozen times, there was nothing serious going on and definitely no talk of love. It was not, however, the same for her. Michelle, apparently, hadn't told Steve how she felt because she didn't want to frighten him off. So, Michelle doesn't tell Steve how she feels, and he legs it to the Legion – a classic misunderstanding, perhaps. In the letter, Michelle bravely told Steve how she felt and how his disappearance had hurt her and would he please contact her, even if just to say he was OK?

This really affected Steve, who became especially taciturn. When he asked me for advice I was at a loss what to say. Christmas can be a particularly bad time for making emotional decisions, so I advised him to leave everything until the New Year. We were going into town then, so maybe he could phone her and come to a decision. I got the impression that Steve's 'couldn't care less' attitude was nothing but a front because something in the letter had obviously bothered him. I really feared he was going to do a runner. If she wants you now, I said, she will feel the same in a couple of weeks. He eventually agreed with me and no more was said. Steve still hadn't told me why he had left England, so it was difficult to gauge how to advise him properly. If New Year's Day hadn't already promised to be interesting, it certainly did now. I would have to keep an eye on Steve till then. I'd never seen him like this before. ·

On Christmas Eve everything was set for a fantastic feast, that night being celebrated in the Legion more than Christmas Day. I had had to take some things over to the *réfectoire* earlier and the place looked fantastic. Long tables were already heaped with wonderful food, with more to come from the kitchens, to be served to us by the NCOs and officers. In the corner were about eight *crèches* illuminated by what looked like a million candles. The whole room looked warm, friendly and magnificently out of character. If anything was going to prevent me from missing home and hearth this was it – just this sight made me feel deeply content. I left to return to my room and dress in best uniform. It was our *tenue de sortie*, a smart green jacket, buttons shining, immaculately pressed trousers and polished shoes. The finishing touch ... well, that was wearing the *képi*. Later, despite the dress code, the atmosphere was relaxed and informal. The French and Germans made last-minute alterations to their sketch and Fennel scurried about with strangely touching concern for everyone's comfort and spirits.

We had marched over to the *réfectoire*, singing with the lightest hearts, and filed in to find the room already packed and the drinking well underway. When we were seated Herchsfeld was suddenly there, placing a large bottle of wine at each place setting. In further role reversal Fennel and Lasalles, the other *caporal*, ferried jugs of beer from a makeshift bar to the tables. They were natural barmen – fast, cheerful and keen to anticipate any need. It almost looked as if there was a competition between the instructors to get their company drunk first. We threw alcohol down our throats enthusiastically, doing our best to win this competition for our instructors.

Then we ate. I had never seen food like that before, and to this day I would wager that a Legion feast matches or beats any gourmet extravaganza in the world. Who would've thought it was prepared here in our own kitchens? Whole roast chickens, legs of lamb and sides of beef were carved for us. Bowls of potatoes, vegetables and salads, then plates of patisserie as only the French can create, together with pies and pastries, fruit and cheeses ... Perhaps the most astonishing thing of all was that our stomachs, so taut by now from continuous exercise and used to only basic rations, could accommodate it all.

About midnight, the mountains of food having been devoured by a cloud of locusts – because surely men alone could not have cleared those tables – each company commander called for silence. It was now time for gifts. In Legion tradition, each officer in charge personally gave every man a present. These ranged from radios, watches, electric razors and tracksuits (only Legion ones though, as civilian kit was prohibited), all funded by profits from the foyer, a great example of cash being recycled. It was a wonderful moment when each Legionnaire approached his officer – there was no salute on this occasion – and was wished *bon Noël*, his hand shaken with genuine warmth and affection. I was presented with two books. The first, a pictorial history of the Legion and the second, poignantly, a book about the 2ème REP and I thought I saw a smile in Colomb's eye. The only trouble was, they were both in French and I couldn't really read them! I thought about asking Philippe to read me a bedtime story.

After the presentation of gifts, all the Germans massed at the front of the room and sang 'Stille Nacht', voices deeply harmonious and the room silent in respect and admiration. Then the *Chef du Corps* attempted to speak to each Legionnaire. Fennel introduced me to him and he asked if I was enjoying my time in the Legion, what did I want to go on to do and which regiment did I hope to be posted to? He smiled when I replied '2ème REP', wished me well and said *bon Noël* before moving on.

We didn't win *la Crèche*, but Colomb was delighted with the effort and took it home with him the next day to show to his other family. Where all the booze came from I have no idea, but the singing and drinking carried on well into the early hours. People fell over, others were sick, some fell asleep where they sat but there was not one fight or even a hint of trouble. It was hard to believe, nearly 400 young men of different nationalities, cultures and beliefs, full to the gunnels with alcohol and far from home, but all behaved like brothers. I can't write with authority on much more because by now I was absolutely battered with the drink. I can't even remember anything about the comedy sketch my French and German comrades presented, although I gathered afterwards that it had gone down very well with plenty of laughs. All I can positively remember is waking up later on Christmas morning, still in uniform although minus kepi and jacket, having somehow found my way to bed and thanking the Almighty for the drunkard's homing pigeon instinct.

At 1000, after the luxury of a lie-in, Fennel crashed into the room and told us with sadistic pleasure that in an hour we were to run as a company for ten kilometres with our *sac à dos*. This was certainly one way of dispatching our monumental hangovers. The pace was mercifully easy and the run was not too difficult, just enough to blow away the cobwebs. After a shower we marched to lunch and were told to take the rest of the day off. That involved little groups pooling cash and buying beer to drink in the foyer. We managed to buy two crates and had a thoroughly great afternoon and evening, drinking and singing and thus did Christmas continue.

There were just a few weeks between Christmas and the end of our basic training, which would culminate in a final march or field exercise called *le Raid*. Before that we would have to complete the obligatory 192 hours of guard duty here at Castel, spend a week at a French army camp to practise small arms firing, a week at Canurae in the Pyrenees for more marching and be introduced to *la piste du combat*, the assault course. So there was a lot of work ahead. During one evening in the foyer, Fennel came over and invited himself into our group of mainly English speakers. He didn't bring any beer for himself but helped himself to ours, not that anyone had the bollocks to discourage him. He spoke quietly to me and said I had made a good impression so far and was already being spoken of by Colomb as being suitable for promotion to *caporal*. That gave me a great lift. Fennel told me that he himself had only been in the Legion for eighteen months and had been promoted quickly. There is a fast track route called *Caporal Fut Fut*, an accelerated promotion course. If your commander recommends you, your course report is excellent and you have a good grasp of French, you can reach *caporal* within a year. I got the message.

When the plaster was removed a couple of days after Christmas I was relieved to find my hand had healed perfectly. I was soon among the first to be selected, along with Steve, for guard duty. This is not particularly arduous but the preparation for it and the monotony of the watch requires a great deal of effort. Although I never thought of it as such when stood on guard, mind-numbingly bored, the duty is actually perceived as being an honour and privilege. I suppose we were the front line defence of the *quartier* and the face of the Legion to people passing by, and occasionally stopping to photograph us in all our finery. Those of us on the first guard were taken off the normal training programme the day before our duty started and spent the whole day polishing boots and ironing uniform. We dressed in *tenue de garde*, brown trousers and jacket, *épaulette de tradition*, the large red epaulettes, the *képi blanc*, naturally, and the *centurion bleu*. This is a wide, six-foot-long sash worn underneath our combat belts around the waist. It takes two people to put it on correctly. One holds it out straight and the other puts the side of the band to his side and revolves his body until the band is wrapped snug around his waist. The blue sash has a kind of tail which is folded over the band at the front of the body to give a smart finish. The sergeant, or *chef du poste*, is ultimately responsible for everything being correct and he checks that every Legionnaire's turn-out is perfect. Should anybody's *tenue* not be up to scratch, then the sergeant, the *caporal* and the Legionnaire could all end up in jail, so inspections were taken very seriously.

The Legion does not normally bother with sartorial bullshit *à la* British Army: highly bulled-up boots with polished soles, for Chrissakes. Indeed the working dress is rarely ironed; we washed and dried it daily, leaving our locker layout as near to perfect as the instructors would allow, and as long as it was clean, then that was OK. But when it came to *le garde* everything had to be immaculate. Each group of guards has another Legionnaire attached to them for the duration, to assist with dressing correctly, fetching and carrying food and generally almost pampering those on guard duty.

Duty would commence at 0600 when the previous night's guard was replaced. This is a ceremonial procedure which lasts about ten minutes. Sometimes the *Chef du Corps* will oversee the change and speaks with everyone taking up their new posts, the conversation informal, the questions simple and easy to understand. Used to small communication problems, he may even ask the questions in English. You work – and standing at rigid attention *is* work, believe me – for two hours on and then have four hours off. This is not as cushy as it may sound, for you are not allowed to sit down in case you crease your trousers. There is plenty of coffee available during your time off, but beware the wrath of the devil should you spill a drop on your uniform. You can leaf through magazines but there's little else to do, so it gets boring. The two hours on are tedious in a different way. One of the two on guard will have their FAMAS slung across their chest in the traditional manner. Again, the rifle doesn't appear to be a heavy weapon, but after two hours standing motionless, it seems like lead. The only relief comes when the order 'Gardez-vous!' and 'Présentation armes!' are given as a sergeant or higher rank passes through the gates. The second man on duty, unarmed and operating the barrier, has the luxury of being able to move around a little more.

There are no clocks on view and the wearing of watches is forbidden. For two hours you are on show and must remain absolutely still. You are the face of the Legion and you must exemplify perfect discipline. A strong bladder is a must as toilet breaks are forbidden during your two hour stint. Going to the loo waits until you are on a break. Not even the laws of nature can interrupt *le garde*. The time passes hideously slowly but you develop an ability to judge when the two hours have passed. Sometimes, however, you become convinced that your relief is late and you have been dicked for extra duty. Believe me, they are never late.

Another very important duty of the guard is the raising and lowering of the flag in the Place Darnée, accompanied by *le clairon*, a bugler. The ceremony is held at the beginning and end of each and every day. The flag must be smoothly lowered and raised in precise tandem with the bugle's refrain. The process closes just as the bugler plays his last note. En route from the guardhouse to the Place Darnée, the sergeant will threaten to shoot you if the procedure is mistimed.

When the working day in the *quartier* is complete, normally around 2000, the guard may be dispatched back to the block and change into combat gear, the normal and comfortable working dress, which is a great relief. Then the guard patrols with baton in hand and checks the ID of everyone passing through the gates. When morning arrives, the handing-over ceremony takes place, and you return to your section. There is no time off for working through the night. Your pals in the section organize some breakfast for you and then it is another routine day. A second section is on guard at the same time, like an immediate reaction force. They wear combats throughout the entire tour of duty and apart from a couple of practice call-outs, they will spend the time resting, watching television or reading. Equal amounts of time on both duties will be spent during the requisite hours of guard.

At Castel the jail is attached to the guardhouse and it was during the post-Christmas tour of guard duty that I saw for the first time since the Farm the two lads who had run off. They looked very sheepish as they collected our dirty plates after lunch. The sergeant mocked and laughed at them, encouraging us to do the same but they looked so wretched I couldn't join in with the piss-taking. They walked like pathetic old men, stooped and hunched, as if all their pride and self-respect had been beaten out of them. Ostracized completely, they were ordered not to look at us; they were not worthy. I certainly wasn't going to risk speaking to them, for fear of repercussions. Both Steve and I had tried to stop them, and we couldn't do any more to help. They each received sixty days jail for their attempted escape. After that, if they wished, they could go *civil* and leave. In reality they had little choice as the Legion didn't want them and it was possible that they could easily spread discontent through the rest of the section if they stayed. It would be better all round if they just went home. It would be their responsibility to get home though, as the Legion would kick them out without a single Franc in their pockets. I never saw either of them again.

ALTHOUGH WE WERE STILL RECRUITS, we were treated very differently at the French Army camp, near the town of Pau, in south-eastern France. The regular army were wary of us simply because we were Legionnaires. Myth and legend had preceded us, and discretion being the better part of valour, they gave us a wide berth, particularly whenever alcohol was around. We were there only a short time; then they could have their camp back. It was a peculiar feeling, knowing that a fellow soldier automatically feared you simply because of the unit you were in. Peculiar, but in a perverse way, bloody great.

We were there for training in small arms. The food was great and plentiful and three large foyers sold everything from designer clothes to gastronomic luxuries. The regular army troops kept their distance from us and there was little fraternization. Day after day we fired countless rounds through the FAMAS, various armour-piercing rockets, grenades and the mortar. We shot at night, tracer rounds zipping down the range, their trajectory illuminated by a ghost-like, green and red lustre, as it powered towards the target. Sometimes the tracer broke away from the round and deviated in an obscure direction, small fragments of phosphorous providing a surreal fireworks display before burning themselves out. We were taught how to use small amounts of explosive, firing charges in a controlled environment, giving the instructors nasty moments when a charge misfired or didn't fire at all. The week was intense with relentless instruction about the weapons we would use on a daily basis in our regiments. Some days the range resembled a wild west shoot-out as we Legionnaires went literally ballistic in our enthusiasm to get through as much ammunition as possible. The ammo supply seemed limitless. The only drawback was the tedium of weapon cleaning. Not at the end of the day, but all bloody day. Fire, clean, fire, clean, instilling into us the vital necessity to keep your weapon immaculately clean at all times.

BACK AT CASTEL, WE HAD MORE LECTURES on the different regiments and their roles. Steve and I had already decided to apply for 2ème REP. Philippe wasn't sure what he wanted to do, believing himself to not be fit enough for the REP. We decided to work on him over the next couple of weeks because it would be great if we could stick together, the Three Musketeers.

We had arrived back at Castel on the afternoon of New Year's Eve and once all the weapons and equipment had been handed in, it was time for *la soupe*. Then Lt. Colomb gathered us all into the classroom to give us advice on our forthcoming *quartier libre*, time off in town. For a bunch of young men who'd had plenty of nights on the tiles in our respective previous lives, we were strangely excitable about the prospect of a night out, as hyper as children anticipating an outing unsupervised by parents or teachers.

Colomb said he was pleased with us so far. He was satisfied with the commitment and effort shown at the Farm, and very happy with our conduct at Christmas. We drank a lot, he said, but behaved as Legionnaires should. Had there been even the slightest trouble this excursion into town would have been cancelled. We were warned that any drunkenness, fighting or disrespect to the citizens of Castelnaudary would be dealt with severely, meaning jail for probably two weeks. 'Go and enjoy yourselves but remember who you are and who you represent', he finished.

That evening I grabbed Steve and asked him how he intended to deal with Michelle. He said he honestly didn't know but would phone and take it from there. I had also decided to phone home and I was more worried about that than about anything I had encountered since the Judas gate in Paris. However, there was another agenda and we drew up a small shopping list before we went out. Little things that make life just a little bit easier. Stupid things like paintbrushes which were brilliant for cleaning the little nooks and crannies on the FAMAS, decent soap and razor blades that didn't take off four layers of skin when you shaved. Philippe lofted a bombshell when he overheard our plans. It is bloody New Year's bloody Day. Most, if not all, the shops will be closed and we'd be lucky to find any bar or café open. Bastard, shit! I couldn't believe it. I was devastated, deflated and I felt like a six-year-old child who has just been told Santa Claus doesn't actually exist. I could taste the beer already; I just imagined that it would taste better served by a twenty-something blonde beauty, rather than a forty-year-old, hairy-arsed Legionnaire. I was still plunged in gloom when Fennel entered the room and asked if we wanted to know where to get a decent drink tomorrow? I looked him in the eye and wailed, 'Are you taking the piss? Its New Year's Day. Everywhere will be closed.' He gave the sly grin of a man who knows something you don't. 'Every New Year's Day recruits go into town and get pissed. The bar owners know this and open up every year. They make a fortune from you lot,' he replied. If I was that way inclined, I would have kissed him. I soon calmed down – only the bars would be open, not the shops. Well, that was good enough for me.

After lunch on New Year's Day, we formed up outside Colomb's office, went through the presentation and were given the equivalent of forty pounds, a considerable sum, to spend as we wished. Dressed in *tenue de sortie*, we boarded a lorry to be transported to *Quartier Lepasset*, the old Legion depot, where we were dropped and would be collected six hours later. As I left Lepasset, dressed in uniform and kepi, I felt about a hundred foot tall, fucking fantastic.

Fennel was spot-on, as if you could doubt him, and the bars were indeed open, expecting us almost. We piled into the first one we came across, claimed a table for our little group and ordered our first Kronenbourg. The cosy, café-like bar, its small tables covered in check cloths, was obviously the first bar en route from the drop-off point, because within minutes the bar looked like a foyer, such was the number of Legionnaires there. The noise was incredible, all of us chattering like caged budgerigars and each man trying to be heard above everyone else. Without warning, the twittering subsided and silence enveloped the bar, starting at the door and sweeping through the place. The personage who caused this transformation of atmosphere stood silent and immense in the doorway, a colossus of a man dressed in combats with a black kepi upon his head, denoting he was at least a sergeant. On his right arm, just above the elbow, he wore a black band with the letters PM projecting both authority and respect. Behind him, baton in hand, stood a Legionnaire. These were the *Police Militaire* and they were simply letting us know that they too were in town. Any misconduct at all and it was the jail for you. He didn't speak, only glared around, clocking each face. The silence was palpable. After a few seconds he turned on his heel and left, without having uttered a single word. Whispering and hushed voices soon evolved into feverish chatter again but we'd taken the point.

We downed the first few beers very quickly; too quickly, as lack of food and general fatigue mixed with the alcohol made me feel a little light-headed. I could feel the early sensations of drunkenness approaching and told Steve I was off to phone England. He came with me. Surprisingly, the first phone box we came to was empty. Again, I was surprised when my father answered the phone and asked if I was OK. He went on to enquire whether this was really what I wanted. I believe that he had read stories of elaborate escape attempts and was asking if I wanted him to mount such an operation to free me. Did I want him to come and bring me home? No. I knew the answer even before the question had been finished. I spoke to my mother next. She cried and then I spoke to my father again. By now he was obviously angry because Mam was crying. This had to be cut short. It wasn't doing any of us any good. I said I was short of change and that I would write if they wanted me to. Of course they did, I was their son. And that was that. I came off the phone quite upset. I hadn't known what to expect and the sound of my mother crying because of what I had put her through made me feel like a really selfish shit. I was at my lowest point since this adventure had begun.

Once Steve had finished his call, I guessed, both of us would end up very, very pissed. The way I felt at that moment, I couldn't have cared less if they jailed me for ever. Funny how a good day can suddenly turn, very quickly, into a bad one.

Steve came away from the phone feeling no better than me. Michelle had been delighted to hear from Steve. Instead of getting the brush off, as he had expected, the lass was genuinely pleased to hear from him. The usual idle chit-chat had ended with Steve promising faithfully that he would keep in touch. Instead of being deliriously happy, he turned somewhat despondent. Maybe he'd said encouraging things to her which he already regretted. We decided to find another bar, one less thronged with buoyant Legionnaires and we sat by ourselves in self-inflicted melancholy. With a few more demi-beers we managed to convince each other that our domestic situations could be somehow rectified. Then, as we couldn't do anything about it now and this was the first day out for months and we had no idea when the next one would be, we thought we'd just go for it. We went for it all right and as the time to be collected neared we were both utterly bladdered. We had intended to get some decent food down us while on this jolly, but the phone calls had put paid to appetite and we just went to get as pissed as possible. It was a waste of a day, really. We nearly fell out of the last bar, missing the vital last step between doorway and pavement and attracted the gaze of a passing PM patrol. They looked at us, and we looked back, glassily, I expect. Our faces must have aroused some feelings of sympathy, as they simply shrugged and pointed us in the direction of Lepasset.

The mood in the truck back to the *quartier*, fuelled by copious amounts of Kronenbourg, was noisy and triumphant. Several of the guys had claimed that they'd been successful with women during the course of the day. These boasts were drowned in a cacophony of cat calls and jeers. For one thing there hadn't been many women out in town and those that were ... well, I wouldn't have touched them with Herchsfeld's dick, never mind my own. It certainly wasn't like the old days when the Legion ran their own brothels in garrison towns like Castel. They were called bordellos: the Legion recruited the girls there and the Medical Officer would examine them on a weekly basis should they develop any anti-social diseases. It was considered good practice, the Legion controlled where the men went and kept the risk of infection down. I would love to know what today's politically correct bandwagon would have to say about that.

There were also claims of fights with the local youths but again, these were pure fantasy. The *Police Militaire* would have been on the scene of any trouble within seconds and the perpetrators arrested immediately – and as far as I could see everyone was present in the truck. In any case, the locals had seen all this before and simply kept away when Legionnaires got their first pass-out. Experience told them the town would be full of testosterone-filled youths with more money than sense. They would lie low and resume normal life the day after. I just wanted to get back to the block, sleep the drink off and return to training as quickly as possible, trying to put my disastrous phone call as far back in my mind as it could go. I would write a detailed letter home and I hoped that my next call wouldn't leave me or my parents feeling quite so bad. The day had not gone well.

WE WERE ALL FOCUSSED NOW ON *le Raid*. We were very fit, strong and confident. We marched well and sang as if our lives depended on it. I felt like one of the Legionnaires that had impressed me so much back in Aubagne. I made my intention to go to the REP official and I hoped my performance in training matched my ambition. *Le Raid* was going to be vital for me. We would be tested on field craft, weapon handling, first aid and tactics. I was ready for it.

CHAPTER SEVEN

FINAL EXERCISE: LE RAID

WE HAD ABSOLUTELY NO CONTROL over our lives. We were basically told when and where to eat, drink and shit. Everything had a patina, at least, of order and had to be done in the Legion way. This was a training course where there was no pass or fail. Doing well and impressing the instructors simply meant you had first pick of the regiments and postings but personal choice wasn't guaranteed. The poor performers went to make up the numbers of infantry and engineer regiments. They may sound grand but the reality was they got all the shit jobs; the jobs nobody wanted. Some found the course harsh as they struggled to adjust to the disciplined, military life and the language. With Steve and Philippe as close friends, both savvy in different ways, I was very lucky.

Any aches and pains that had previously let me know how unfit I had been before I joined, were now a memory. My arms, legs and chest were solid muscle and with a new self-confidence I felt as if I could conquer anything. I was a completely different person from the reticent young man that had stood awestruck outside Fort du Nogent only a few months ago. I might have had that assurance which is sometimes mistaken for arrogance.

Hunger had been a constant problem throughout training. Bad as the food was, I always cleared my plate and still left the *réfectoire* feeling just as hungry as when I had gone in. I spent what meagre wages I had on snacks from the foyer. Keeping food in your locker, however, was definitely frowned upon, as only issue kit was to be kept there. With the final march and exercise fast approaching, Steve and I tried to think of ways in which we could hide extra rations to take with us. We would be using huge amounts of energy during the march and this would have to be replaced somehow. It is amazing how much a man can eat when forcing his body to endure extreme punishment.

There was a broom cupboard just off the corridor in the block. Although this tiny room was inspected along with the rest of the block, it was given only a cursory once-over. There were boxes of cleaning gear, soap and bleach and we thought the instructors would never notice an extra box piled on top of all the others. The Gang of Three – Steve, Philippe and me – decided to store war rations, our emergency supply, there. Over a remarkably short time we managed to build up a substantial stash of energy-supplying scoff: chocolate, peanuts and anything with sugar in it. One evening, however, disaster struck with a horrible, helpless inevitability and there was absolutely bugger all any of us could do about it. A German lad, known to me only as Hans, had been tidying the cupboard as part of his block duties when he stumbled across our cache of contraband. His shouting brought everyone out into the corridor to see what was going on. I think the last time a man could have shouted with so much joy must have been when some Neanderthal discovered the wheel or how to make fire. Hans, with a grin as wide as the Rhine, clutched the booty so closely to his chest that the chocolate was in danger of melting. He began dishing it out to his own pals, just as we three and Fennel all arrived on the scene. What were we to do? Claim the box was ours and incur the wrath of both Herchsfeld and Fennel, or stand back and watch as our hard-earned survival rations were devoured by this pack of parasites and gannets? I was fucking boiling as I had to stand back and witness the annihilation of our box of swag. The bastard never even offered us any. Fennel sauntered past us as we stood there fuming and as he passed me he whispered: 'Things like that shouldn't be left lying around. Anyone could help themselves.' Had the shit known all along that the box was there? Later that evening, when everything had settled down, I asked Hans who had given him the task of cleaning the cupboard, bearing in mind that his room was not responsible for that particular job. He looked at me as if I was potty and said, 'Fennel did, who else? He told me to make sure I did a thorough job.' The incident was never mentioned again, Fennel obviously thinking we had been punished enough. To watch those grinning apes, their mouths smeared with chocolate, my fucking chocolate bought with my fucking money, was all the punishment I needed.

The day of *le Raid*. This exercise would be the culmination of everything we had been taught, the final test, and how well we performed would decide which regiment we would be posted to. It was the middle of February, almost five months since I knocked on the Judas gate at Fort du Nogent, and it seemed like a lifetime ago. I had to stop and catch my breath when I thought about all that had happened to me since then. I felt unrecognizable from the pasty youth I was when I now saw in the mirror every morning the strong and confident young man I'd become. I'd wanted to become strong and confident, both in mind and manner and it looked like I'd made it. I'd challenged myself and had come through so far unscathed. But only time would tell. I was fully aware that there were more severe, more punishing challenges to come, but I felt ready, both physically and mentally, to face them. I only wished my parents could be proud of me, although I knew that this was a painful fantasy.

We loaded up the *camion*, the truck, and set off for Perpignan, a town near the Mediterranean coast, in the south-west. The weather was anything but Mediterranean and I knew this was going to be tough. The sun was forcing its way through bleak clouds as we disembarked from the truck, but no heat radiated from it and my breath formed clouds around me as I exhaled. The hand I had recently fractured was already throbbing in the cold and damp. I had to remind myself again that it was my feet that I should be concerned about.

As the crow flies, it was about one hundred kilometres back to Castel, but the route we were to take was a dog-leg; heading west before crossing the River Aude and then taking a northerly route which added a further sixty or seventy kilometres to the march. We were to complete this in three days, being tested along the way in various military evaluations.

In groups of ten and with an NCO at the head, my group once again led by Fennel, we began the long, hard climb up into the Pyrenees. This was daunting terrain at the best of times and these were emphatically not the best of times. The weather seemed to get nastier by the minute. I'm well aware that some people actually spend good money and come to this place for enjoyment and pleasure … yet there are those who've called *me* mad. At least I was being paid some paltry wages for this torture. The *sac à dos,* better packed this time, lay heavily and awkwardly upon my back, sliding across and back again, rubbing and leaving welts which eventually turned from raw sores to crusty scabs.

Fennel was like a mountain goat, bounding up the side of the first hill, unhindered by any burden on his back. I attempted to keep up with him and almost succeeded, despite my rucksack doing its utmost to make life as difficult as possible. As we neared the peak of this first climb, I looked down and saw that our group was stretched out over a considerable distance. This meant we now had to stand still at the top and wait for the others to catch up. I was drenched with sweat and the cold attacked the vulnerable areas. Within seconds I was shaking like some drug addict doing cold turkey. I hated this loss of momentum and inwardly cursed those comrades who were holding us up. On the simplest 'civilian' level, you know how it is if you're nicely balanced with bags of heavy shopping in each hand – you can somehow swing along fine once you hit your rhythm and absolutely dread meeting a friend in the street who wants to stop for a chat?

After an interminable wait, we got going again. I wanted to impress so I stayed with Fennel at the front, although I knew this would mean standing around waiting for others to catch up again while I froze my knackers off once more. There didn't seem to be a halfway point where I could satisfy both Fennel and pace myself. I had to show I could keep up. If I was to be cold occasionally, then so be it; it was only for three days and surely I could cope with that? There was another problem with stopping; I would begin to stiffen up and it was quite difficult to get going again, particularly the first few metres, until I got the muscles working and warmed up.

We had climbed the foothills of the range non-tactically, walking as if we were on holiday instead of soldiers, just to get into the swing of things. From now on, the march would become completely tactical and we could expect to be ambushed at any time. We would have to cross the ground and negotiate any obstacles in the proper tactical manner, as we had been taught. Fennel took a lot of the pressure off us by doing all the map reading and navigation, thereby sparing us from getting lost and adding extra kilometres to the already long route. Even when we eventually arrived at our various regiments, only NCOs would do the map reading and navigation. This particular skill is only taught on the NCOs training cadre; and as we were not required to navigate at this early stage, there was no point in teaching us. I got to wondering what would happen if the *caporal* in charge was killed or wounded? I had learned, however, not to question their techniques, so the question remained unanswered.

Moving tactically is both time-consuming and tiring. Everything has to be checked out and then made safe and apparently undisturbed before you can move on. We came across smallholdings occupied by hill farmers and these had to be skirted as if an enemy was nearby. The occasional farmer we did see carried on with his work as if a section of Legionnaires pepper-potting while he was clearing his outbuildings and yard was the norm. Mind you, he'd probably seen this all so many times he could have told us if we were doing it correctly or not. Any damage to farm property, including animals, was handsomely compensated to the owner by the Legion. Indeed, it was suggested by one farmer that if we were to 'accidentally' damage an outbuilding in order for him to claim compensation, then he would supply us with fresh produce. This allegedly was common practice here in France and I know for sure it happens in the UK.

Pepper-potting is the art of moving forward whilst under threat of attack; your comrades cover you with a blanket of fire, hoping to keep the enemy's head down. One man moves forward, while his mates lay down fire. Once he is in position another man moves forward to a place of cover and so on. It may sound complicated, but it isn't, merely tiring. You are essentially being covered by your comrades when you move and you cover them when they move. It is very effective and ground can be covered quickly and safely when the technique is applied properly.

We occasionally stopped and immediately went into all-round defence mode so that Fennel could take a compass bearing and confirm our course. It was very tempting to drink from your *bidon*, water-bottle, during these unscheduled stops as despite the cold all the physical exertion caused considerable loss of body fluids. It would have been so easy to gulp water down and refill the bottle from one of the many mountain streams. Rule one, however, was to be self-disciplined and conserve water. If you really did need to drink, then small sips were of greater benefit than gulping it down. The principle applies as much in the desert as it does in mountain brush, and it's not just part of the generally sound principle of conserving supplies: a good gargle really can

GHT *Quartier Lapassat*, the 'Old
ort' at Castelnaudary, home to
e 4ème Regiment before their
ove to a new purpose built
artier on the outskirts of town.
was from here that we had our
rst *permission* and were allowed
» wear the kepi blanc in public
r the first time. (© *John Robert
oung/Military Picture Library*)

ABOVE '*The grandest assembly of real fighting men
that I have ever seen; marching with their heads held
up as if they owned the world. Lean, hard-looking
men, carrying their arms admirably and marching in
perfect precision. They are devils, not men.*' Field
Marshal Lord Alanbrooke. (© *Alain Nogues/
Corbis Sygma*)

LEFT Kit issued to a new Legionnaire. The kepi,
at front, is issued but may not be worn until the
Legionnaire comes back from the Farm. Note
the troops at rear carrying their kit in holdalls.
(© *John Robert Young/Military Picture Library*)

LEFT A Legionnaire on guard at
the main gate to Camp Raffali,
Corsica, home of the 2ème REP.
The *caporal* is *en garde*, his wing
worn on the right breast and th
regimental badge on the right
chest pocket. (*EPA/PA Photos*)
RIGHT Section attack man-
oeuvres in French Guyana. The
Legionnaire on the right, in
prone position, is firing the
FAMAS. The Legionnaire on
the left is firing the 7.5mm
light machine gun. (© *Robbie
Cooper/Corbis Sygma*)

LEFT The infamous and gruelling assault course in French Guyana. Legionnaires from the 3ème *Régiment Etranger d'Infantrie* have been crawling beneath a barbed-wire covered obstacle, up to their eyes in mud and slime. (© *Robbie Cooper/Corbis Sygma*)

ABOVE Patrolling the river Oyapock in *pirouges*, a quick and efficient way to move through the jungle. The locals use this mode of transport throughout Guyana. (*Yves Debay © Military Picture Library*)

BELOW Bayonet practice in Djibouti, north-eastern Africa. Using the bayonet proficiently and to its maximum effect depends on the amount of violence generated by its user – as displayed here. (© Jacques Langevin/Corbis Sygma)

RIGHT Fresh rations being issued at the base camp in Guyana. The bench is there to keep foul-smelling Legionnaires apart from the permanent staff. Note the sludgy mud on the ground, and the man-made shelter on the right. (© Robbie Cooper/Corbis Sygma)

LEFT Camerone Day festivities at the Legion 'home' at Sidi Bel-Abbes, Algeria. The memorial seen here was later transferred to Aubagne, the new administrative headquarters of the Legion in southern France. (Yves Debay © Military Picture Library)

ABOVE Songs will be sung before the Legionnaires are unleashed onto the beer laid out on the table. Rigid discipline ensures no man moves before the officer, seen here on the extreme right, allows them to. (© *Robbie Cooper/Corbis Sygma*)

RIGHT A young lad being introduced to the Legion on Camerone Day. He has borrowed a friendly Legionnaire's kepi. This is the day when some Legion *quartiers* allow civilians into the camp so they can see Legion life at firsthand. (© *John Robert Young/Military Picture Library*)

ABOVE Singing is a daily fact of life in the Legion. Here a colonel leads his men in a song of his choice, most probably a *chant de régiment*, the regimental song. (© *John Robert Young/Military Picture Library*)

RIGHT A 'dry' drop onto the DZ in Corsica – one of the many training drops undertaken by the REP. Note that there is no container, or *sac à dos*, dangling beneath the Legionnaires, as there would be in the 'real thing'. The close proximity of the parachutes means the Legionnaires probably exited their Transall aircraft at a rapid rate. (*Peter Russell; The Military Picture Library/Corbis*)

LEFT 'Just checking!' After a successful landing this Legionnaire is looking up to the rest of the drop to ensure that another parachute will not land on top of him. (*Peter Russell © Military Picture Library*)

LEFT In a rare solitary moment at Camp Raffali, Corsica, a Legionnaire catches up on his letter writing. Times like this are treasured – time to be alone with your thoughts and, for some, memories of home. (© *John Robert Young/Military Picture Library*)

RIGHT An ultra-modern Legionnaire. He has a telescopic sight on top of his FAMAS, wears high-tec night vision goggles and has a throat mike for his radio so that he can keep his hands free for firing. (*Defence Picture Library*)

LEFT Legionnaires preparing lying-up positio The Legionnair on the right is covering his comrade, who i sending secret data back to ba via his battlefie laptop and its message scrambling system. (*Defence Picture Library*)

slake thirst almost as effectively as a long drink. Brownie points were earned if at the next official water stop you had plenty left in your *bidon*. Furthermore, we were advised at the outset of *le Raid* not to drink water directly from the streams and rivers in France, even if treated with sterilization tablets. The water can make you very ill for a week or more – you may feel like your insides are going to pass through your arse. The point was emphasized a couple of hours later. We had followed the course of a mountain stream for a few hundred metres. As we came over the top of a rise we saw the decomposing carcass of a sheep lying in the flow of water of the stream. Point proven, and noted.

Food also plays a very important part in a soldier's life. Not just for replenishing and storing calories and energy but the undeniable fact that hot scoff immediately warms you up, raising not only your body temperature but morale as well. Strictly speaking there may be as many nutrients in a well-filled sandwich, or even in some dried foods, but nothing beats hot, cooked food and this can't be just psychological. On marches I used to fantasize about plates stacked high with steaming vegetables, as I had always loved fresh vegetables at home straight from the garden. A great image but I didn't do myself any favours; it was a form of torture. Our food on this tactical stage of the march was mainly in snack form, usually a *casse-croûte* – a hunk of crusty bread covered with pâté. It filled a hole but did little to replace spent energy and calories and consequently we became hungry again more quickly than we would have liked. However, as I kept reminding myself, and I'm sure the other lads did as well, *le Raid* was supposed to replicate action proper. If we'd really been in a field of conflict we'd have had no choice about our rations and could scarcely have sauntered into an agreeable little mountain auberge and ordered *le plat du jour*.

Because the march was tactical, we had to carry our rifles in the 'ready' position. This meant putting the butt of the rifle into your shoulder and keeping it there at all times, ready to fire off a couple of rounds quickly should we come under attack. Again, it may not sound terribly arduous, but after four or five hours scrambling and clambering the FAMAS felt very heavy. This method of patrolling fitted in perfectly with the Legion's aggressive style. Fire off a couple of quick rounds, just to get enemy heads down and then launch a counter-attack in their direction. Always forward, always aggressive, always putting the enemy on the back foot. We never worried about the enemy or their activities; let them worry about us. Definitely not School of Infantry tactics, but damned effective. The School, at Warminster, would always teach a commander to lead his troops away from the scene of an ambush, and then reorganize at a safe distance before launching a counter-attack. Not the Legion though; aggression is paramount, always startle and scatter your enemy.

All through the day, I noticed Fennel making discreet notes. He always seemed to be watching and listening to everything we did, nothing escaped him. Towards dusk we approached another collection of shabby outbuildings and about one hundred metres away from them we halted. The section was split into two and tasked with carrying out a reconnaissance patrol around the area, ensuring it was safe for the rest of the company to enter. We had been given tasks like this all day, with notes being taken on individual and section performances. Once we were in the hut, empty and barren, Fennel stood us down for the night and we went non-tactical. A large fire was lit, the *RCIRs* – the *Ration de Combat Individuelle Réchauffable* or food in bags that you heated in boiling water – came out and a relaxed atmosphere prevailed. At times like this I felt like a boy scout and not a Legionnaire. A guard still had to be mounted, however, and we drew lots for the rota. Steve and I managed to get the first watch. Fantastic, we would be on guard when everyone was still up and about. We should also be able to get a decent night's sleep.

A dazzling flash, the type that blinds you temporarily, and a bang so loud it deafened me for a minute, was our early morning wake-up call. I jumped out of my doss-bag in swift movement, trying to orientate myself. I must have been in a deep sleep for I didn't know where I was, as I stood in the middle of the hut, vainly attempting to discover exactly what had woken us so violently. Herchsfeld had thrown a thunderflash, a simulated grenade, into the hut and as we stumbled and blundered into each other in the darkness he shouted that we were under attack. He had simulated a grenade attack and he wanted to see how we reacted half asleep and disorganized. Grabbing our rucksacks and *brouillage*, our webbing – at any rate, some of us remembered to do so – the section staggered out of the hut, at least carrying rifles. We burst into the woods behind to reorganize.

Steve's experience took over and he immediately assumed command, organizing us into all-round defence and plotting a counter-attack. As our eyes became accustomed to the half-light, I think we were all pleased that Steve had assumed command. Fennel and Herchsfeld were observing closely to one side, saying nothing about the pandemonium they witnessed. My ears were still ringing, as if someone had smashed a tuning fork into them and the high-pitched wail was almost unbearable. My sight was also askew and all I could see for several minutes were two little white dots.

Before Steve could put his master plan into operation, Herchsfeld called a halt to things and motioned for everyone to group together. He was not a happy man. Behind him lay a mountain of equipment and uniform which had been abandoned when we burst, almost literally blindly, out of the hut. I was one of a minority that had left only their sleeping bag behind. There wasn't time to pack that in such a panic, although I know there are some who'd say you shouldn't leave any gear at all, for any reason. Some of the section had left webbing and rucksacks as well as sleeping bags. The instructor stressed that this kit was all vital for survival when out on operations. Once lost it may never be reclaimed. He emphasized how an entire operation could be jeopardized if crucial equipment was not in place for whatever reason. We'd rarely get a second chance.

Our small group had not performed too badly and were allowed back into the hut for a couple of hours' kip. The others, once they had recovered their kit, had to form all-round defence in the vicinity of the building and remain alert. God help them if they were to fall asleep. The exercise was to remind us to think all the time, rifle and kit, rifle and kit. Take care of those first, and yourself next. Rifle and kit.

It took a while to settle after the uproar of the simulated attack – the air was icy, I knew that dawn and a new day were only hours away and I found it impossible to sleep. The cold was again nipping into the very marrow of my bones. I dozed briefly, only to wake up startled, shaking and shivering violently. I curled into a foetal position, both hands clasped together as if in prayer. Even if I clamped them between my legs it was hard to keep them warm. To this day I often sleep like that under the weightless warmth of my duvet at home and still get flashbacks to that freezing cold night. My body remembers the icy misery of it.

Dawn could not come quickly enough. At least then we would be moving and therefore keeping warm. Breakfast was water and hard, crunchy biscuits, like dog treats – far from ideal when a long, hard march lies ahead. My feet had held up pretty well, considering the punishment they endured back at the Farm. Apart from a couple of small blisters and losing the odd toenail they were fine. We marched all that next day and I could feel the air getting gradually warmer. Although I didn't ever notice going down a steep or even gentle gradient, we were clearly descending. The snow had turned to a sleety slush and the wind had dropped considerably, losing its bite as it did so. At certain points during the day we would stop where a truck and tent had been set up. Here we would be tested on various skills from first aid to setting up a radio link. All very basic stuff, but we would need to be competent at these skills before we could go on to more serious training at our regiments.

The light faded quickly that afternoon and we once again came across a smuggler's safe haven, an even more tattered barn. I noticed straight away that the whole *2ème Compagnie* was here, including Lt. Colomb. The sections already there were sorting their kit out and making themselves comfortable. Fennel told us that we would be hunkering down up here tonight. It would be non-tactical again, although a guard would be posted. But the ordeal was as good as over. We had lost a couple of lads during this march, not from my section. They were taken back to Castel for treatment to the injuries they had sustained and then would be given the good news. They would be on the next available course – right from the beginning, what a bastard! Philippe told Steve and I that he had really struggled on the march and that he had made his mind up which regiment he wanted. The cavalry. We were both surprised at his choice but he answered our question before we even asked it. It was simple, he could sit down; the cavalry were mechanized, they drove everywhere and that suited him right down to the ground. Bloody hill climbing and running everywhere could be left to those 'mad *Anglais*'.

At the rear of the barn I saw several crates of beer and wine, together with piles of real food. Tonight we would drink, sing and celebrate the completion of our basic training. This is an old Legion tradition, but it is up to the company's commander as to whether the *engagés* were allowed this privilege. We must have got more things right than wrong because we were clearly to have a night on the drink. Tomorrow would see the last few kilometres and we'd march back into Castel as newly fledged Legionnaires, upright and proud, Colomb at our head as we strode through the gates of *Quartier Capitaine Danjou*, singing out loud. When we passed through the gates, the *Chef du Poste* would bring the guard to present arms and we would have arrived, in more ways than one.

THE DAY AFTER OUR TRIUMPHANT return to Castel was spent cleaning equipment and having medical check-ups ensuring that no lasting damage had been suffered on *le Raid*. All the equipment we used during training, in the block we lived in and the classroom was meticulously scrubbed, cleaned and polished. We were to leave for Aubagne in a couple of days for regiment allocation. I had become used to the life and routine here at Castel and knew I would miss the place very much. There is no formal pass-out parade as you would expect in the British forces – it's not as if we could invite families down here for the big day. But we did have a final presentation in front of Colomb, who told me I was a *très bon* Legionnaire and could go far. He wished me luck and shook my hand. It all felt quite surreal and rather an anti-climax for it to finish this way. I certainly didn't expect a big parade by any means, but I didn't think it would end quite so flatly.

The *Chef du Poste* spoke to us on the square at Castel for the last time before we returned to Aubagne as a company for regimental postings. Both Steve and I reaffirmed our determination to go to 2ème REP, while Philippe hoped for the *1er Régiment Étranger de Cavalerie*, based at Orange in France. I was very disappointed that he wouldn't be coming with us but though wiry, he didn't have the physique for strenuous demands. He'd done brilliantly to get this far. We would all have a good drink in Aubagne before we went our separate ways and I hoped, really hoped, that we would meet up again sometime, someplace. I knew I would miss him. We had become very close during the months of training and I will never forget how Philippe had helped me during those early days when I was physically and mentally unsure of just about everything. I am not saying that I wouldn't have succeeded without him, but he helped me enormously, especially when I was struggling to learn French. A good man indeed. I wish you peace, my friend, wherever you are.

My *bonhomie*, Henri, had also applied for the Cavalry and it was doubtful that I'd ever see him again. We were not so close but he had also helped me considerably and I owe him a debt of gratitude. I haven't gone into much detail about others in the company, basically because I didn't have a great deal to do with them and didn't know them well enough to form opinions. They were comrades only in the widest sense and not real friends. I didn't want to strike up too many friendships with people I would never see again and the other guys had no influence on me during training; they were simply there. But I wished them well, too.

The atmosphere at Aubagne was now much more relaxed than at Castel, for obvious reasons. A saving grace for us was the presence of another batch of several hundred prospective *engagés*. Only a few would actually make it to Castel and I knew they hadn't a clue as to what they had let themselves in for. They got assigned all the crap jobs around the *quartier*, the chores which we'd had before. It was great to be excused latrine duty and so forth. 'New kids' always get the shit jobs, no matter which army they serve in. It just happened that these new boys were thought even less of than we were, thank God, for we were far from strutting around with arrogance, even now.

While waiting for our postings to come through, I began to think of home again, of what I had left behind and how far I had come, both physically and mentally. I did regret, even more, hurting my parents about just vanishing but that was done now and maybe time would heal. Perhaps at some level I was faintly surprised that they had been bothered at all and that somehow made things worse. I was certainly a stronger and more confident person as a result of my Legion training. And I valued true friendship more than I could ever have understood before. Certain friends made here were more to me than traditional family had ever been – people I knew I could turn to in terrible times.

I felt a real sense of belonging in the Legion, a closeness difficult to explain. My parents would probably not agree, but I felt I was becoming a better person. I was experiencing different cultures, opinions and customs. My mind had been broadened in every possible way. Having said that, there were times when only a punch-up would clear the air, such as that time at the Farm. I was less prejudiced and more tolerant of others, for sure, but at the same time I was aware that I had become almost obsessive in my desire to fulfil my ambitions.

The night before our postings were announced, we gathered in the foyer to drink gallons of beer and recount tales of our basic training. I would imagine this sort of malarkey is replicated in armies throughout the world. It was harmless and quite humorous as we sat there reminiscing about all the laughs and also the bad times during training. Then Steve quietly staved off too much sentimental nonsense by saying: 'Let it lie there in peace, because if I cannot remember it, then it didn't happen.' However, celebrating the good times and coping with adversity in a droll manner really were the best ways to deal with training. As the evening wore on, the beer flowed and the tone of the conversation again became boisterous. For once there was no one around to tell us to keep the noise down. That would change, for me, Steve and the other lads going to the REP.

The great day arrived and we sat waiting for news of our fate. Philippe did get 1er REC, his name being read out first and as I leant over to shake his hand, I heard my name being called, immediately followed by 2ème REP, Calvi. I was overjoyed, doubly so when Steve's name was shortly added to the half dozen of us who would be heading towards Corsica within the next couple of days. We were handed joining instructions and dismissed. The three of us headed straight for the foyer and bought a crate of beer. We toasted each other until there was no more left.

As Philippe's posting was in France he was to leave the following morning. As we lurched back towards our accommodation, I couldn't have known that this would be the last time I would see Philippe alive. A tragic accident, almost a year later, claimed the life of one of the nicest blokes I have ever known. Philippe's death was not a valorous sacrifice, sustained during a bold and fearless Legion operation, but sheer bad luck. Wrong place at the wrong time. Whilst drunk in Orange one Saturday night, he walked into the path of a motorcycle, neither seeing nor hearing its approach. He died almost immediately from severe head injuries. An appalling waste of life. I didn't manage to attend his funeral, or meet his family so I couldn't tell them how proud they should have been of their son. I hope they would have known that already and didn't need an oaf like me intruding on their grief. I miss him terribly and – as I wrote earlier – hope he is at peace somewhere. That reunion we had spoken of will now have to take place in that great meeting hall in the sky.

WHAT LAY AHEAD NOW WAS CAMP RAFFALI, Calvi on Corsica. An island that basks in the Mediterranean, between France and Italy, north of the coast of Morocco. I had an extra bounce in my walk now and foolishly thought that I had made it. That swagger would soon be mercilessly knocked out of me during my first months in the REP.

CHAPTER EIGHT

LEGION LEGENDS

MY CONVERSATIONS WITH THE *ANCIENS* got me thinking again about the Legion's history and how its ethos has changed over the decades. The old men had surprised me by saying that modern Legionnaires were more bolshie and questioning than they had dared to be, less disciplined somehow. This was at odds with the idea that old campaigners were all on short fuses and forever risking the slammer.

I didn't entirely buy into what they said about this because any old soldier, anywhere in the world, will say that standards have slipped since their day. I had mixed feelings: if what they said was true I half deplored it and half agreed with the implication that a Legionnaire should operate on a 'need to know' basis, because too much information – particularly if facts have shifted somewhat down the line of Chinese whispers – can be disruptive. But I couldn't approve of mindless obedience either.

It all began to connect with what a man's expectations and aspirations were when he joined the Legion and the points at which the fictions faced the facts, or intersected with them. The novel *Beau Geste*, by Percival Christopher (P C) Wren was published in 1924, when the author was thirty-nine. Wren had spent time in the Legion after a quiet early life in

Devon and his tale of honour, savagery and a missing gem smacked of authenticity. It became an immediate international bestseller. As recently as 2003, Barry Humphreys (aka Dame Edna Everage) affectionately remembered how as a boy in Melbourne, Australia, *Beau Geste* and its sequel, *Beau Sabreur* (1926), embodied his favourite escapist fantasies. In Britain during the 1950s and 1960s the seminal boys' comic *Eagle* featured illustrated strips of Dan Dare on the front cover and Luck of the Legion on the back (Captain Pugwash was somewhere in the middle), neatly expressing both the space-age and nostalgia.

There was never anything amusing about Luck's adventures, but in *The Goon Show*, the classic BBC radio comedy of the 1950s, there was often a Legion sketch punctuated by Peter Sellers' strangulated cries of 'Mon Capitaine'. There was something for everyone in *Beau Geste* – little boys, jolly egg-heads, armchair adventurers of any age and women, who found the stories romantic. Perhaps even Prince Charles, who claims the Goons as an influence, was affected. Few stories exert an enduring grip on worldwide public imagination unless they are grounded in some timeless emotional truth and satisfy a basic need to see justice prevail. That it also satisfied the blood lust of some readers indubitably added to the appeal.

Hollywood was not slow to recognize this and the first *Beau Geste* film, a silent, was made in 1926. It starred the British heart-throb Ronald Coleman and cashed in nicely on the vogue for raunchy and romantic desert action created by Rudolph Valentino in *The Sheik*. Countless films have followed, including the classic talkie starring Gary Cooper in 1936, to Mel Brooks' 1976 pastiche *Silent Movie*, and some very macho recent films starring Jean-Claude van Damm. In greatly differing ways all address themes of rejection, isolation and rugged individualism, brutality, heroism, moral courage, redemption, justice and romance. Many of the ideas embodied in the Beau Geste myth overlap with those in other manly legends, from the Odyssey to Robin Hood, from the Arthurian legends to Indiana Jones in *Raiders of the Lost Ark* – wherein the desert made a comeback, big time. These being some of the principal fictional inspirations for the Legion's hold on the imagination of men all over the world – and some women, too, particularly as they have recently been allowed to enlist – what of the other factors?

In my case there was certainly an element of running away from intolerable pressures at home and something more: hopelessness. You might almost say it was a way of staving off thoughts of suicide. Anyway, there was certainly a tinge of that petulant little-boy sulk of 'they'll be sorry' as the child plans to run away from home. I can't say that *I* was much influenced by books or films, but I'd been in the armed forces and knew that what little self-respect I retained stemmed from my years as a soldier. Others may have just longed for a military life that was not on offer at home. Many European countries, particularly the neutral Scandinavian ones, just can't provide a minded lad with service training.

Those on the run, and no-questions-asked? Well, I've explained how the Legion cooperates with Interpol and similar agencies, rooting out dangerous reprobates at Fort du Nogent and other recruiting centres or at basic training camps like Aubagne – which is not to say that a fair few do hope that a contract with the Legion and a new identity will allow them to lie low for a few years and emerge 'laundered' like stolen banknotes ready for recirculation. Few pull this off.

Bullies? Lads with a real appetite for a kick-in, and some pathetic need to frighten others? Well, yes, there will always be a few of these and maybe the Legion is the best place for them. Like every other rookie they will be observed and monitored, punished fiercely if they transgress, dismissed if they transgress once too often. But maybe, just maybe, some shred of the good character that resides somewhere within even the scummiest bastard will eventually emerge. Maybe.

Loners, losers and the broken-hearted? Sometimes a man can be all three. The Legion is, by and large, a good place for loners although sooner or later the solitary man will need to become a team player. Besides, there's very little privacy, so solitude must remain an internalized state. It's quite good for 'losers', too, as often an apparently aimless and disappointed life can be snapped into focus by both the discipline and the comradeship that the Legion brings. Self-respect is built in a way that may have seemed, possibly unfairly, unattainable in civilian life. Perhaps I'm thinking of my comrade Philippe here. As for the broken-hearted – I guess there must be a few, though retiring from the 'real world' for five years is a pretty extreme way of getting over a love affair that's gone wrong. I can't really say much else as in my experience such matters were so seldom discussed.

Finally, wanting to hang out with the boys may have been more of a motivation many years ago before all that became legal. They say that one man in ten is homosexual, which means that once someone on each side gets the red card, two men left on any football pitch will be gay and a third will be wavering – and that's not counting the referee. Good luck to them. I can only say that despite the absence of female company most of the time and the 24/7 proximity to other men, no one ever made a pass at me and I was seldom aware of any gay friendships.

Some may enlist, even today, with images of a little fort in a desert oasis, the flag limp above the ramparts except when a storm draws wind and rustles the branches of the nearby palm tree. Men with immaculate tunics and white breeches may patrol and salute in this infantile fantasy. Today the fort will be a gleaming modern complex and the uniforms as likely to be combats or tracksuits, except on ceremonial days. Yet do not quite dismiss this picture of the toy-soldier fort or the men who served in such places in the nineteenth century, from the Crimea, to the desert, to Mexico.

Laws in every country of the world were different in those times and certain reforms remain long overdue in some places, even today. At first the Legion *was* a hiding place, if not exactly a haven, for some ruffians and criminals. Even so, Legion practice made men of them, men with big hearts and the courage that was exemplified as early as April 1863 at Camerone in Mexico. It was an early template for everything that the Legion has always stood for – fight till the last man can stand no more, never surrender and tend to your wounded brothers. Since its creation in 1831, the Legion has been dogged by the perception of it being a colonial tool of oppressive bullying, manned by mercenaries and n'er-do-wells. The Legion has fought in all of France's political skirmishes through-out the world; I list some of their notable campaigns here, in alphabetical order so as not to confuse the reader as to their importance or outcome: Algeria, in the sixties, which was a pivotal time for them; the Crimea; France in World War One; Italy during World War Two; Mexico; Morocco; and Syria. Let us not forget Indo-China in the fifties, where the strength of the Legion grew to 35,000 troops.

Recent deployments to various African nations have sealed the Legion's place in military history: Chad, Central Africa, Rwanda and Zaire. Modern day conflicts, in Lebanon in 1982 with the United Nation peacekeeping force, and again under the UN mandate to Bosnia in 1993, confirm the ease with which the Legion can adapt its role, under the most strenuous and arduous of conditions. During the Gulf war in 1991, France was asked to send forces to assist General Schwarzkopf and the Allied forces in the removal of Saddam Hussein's forces from Kuwait. Three regiments from the Legion, 1eme REC, 2ème REP and 6eme REG were dispatched and played a major part in Operation Desert Storm. Observing strict Muslim law was, however, difficult for some Legionnaires. Legend has it that one officer complained bitterly about the lack of red wine at meal times: there are times when it is just impossible to adapt totally.

YOU WILL READ IN OTHER CHAPTERS of some of the action – rearguard and otherwise – in which the Legion has distinguished itself over the past 140-odd years. I suspect, however, that the crucial role it played within the relatively recent French conflict in Algiers is what a good many people think of when they picture the Legion entering fields of modern warfare and its dirty realities, rather than that noble old myth. Once again the cinema has played its part, for millions read *The Day of the Jackal* or saw the film, made from Frederick Forsyth's novel, concerning an assassination attempt on Charles de Gaulle. It's true that the modern Legion was born out of the war in Algiers. After that a new kind of Legionnaire emerged. In retrospect Algiers represents a bridge in the Legion's history, a time on the cusp of change when the FFL of old was pitched into the modern world.

My chosen Regiment, the 2ème REP, had been formed in 1955 as a result of the reorganization of the French airborne forces, already heavily involved in the Algerian mess and already over-stretched in Indo-China. All the old empires seemed to totter, falter and fall after World War Two. The war for Algerian independence, which began in 1954, was a patriotic struggle, a classic David and Goliath face-off or a shabby and tiresome little revolt, depending on your politics. The 2ème BEP, (*Bataillon Étranger de Parachutistes*) was fully occupied in Indo-China, another famous Legion battlefield at the time, so a new para force had to be mustered. Algeria was a French colony and the Algerian FLN (National Liberation Front) was conducting reasonably successful guerrilla strikes, aiming to rid their country of the French. The colonial master's naval base was, of course, at Toulon, not far along the coast from Marseilles, and just a stretch of seawater away from the coast of North Africa.

Armed groups of FLN would attack isolated French-owned farms and any passing French Army patrols, effectively taking control of whole regions. The Legion had suffered horrific casualties during the conflict in Indo-China but those who returned to lead the men of the 2ème REP were consequently experienced in counter-revolutionary warfare and in anti-guerrilla tactics. These battle-hardened soldiers were determined to best the FLN. Algeria, and specifically a town called Sidi-bel-Abbes, the Legion's base depot, was officially a part of France and this time, unlike in Indo-China, there would be no question of ceding home territory to nationalist guerrillas.

The arrival of the 2ème BEP, later to become the 2ème REP, in Algeria was fraught with uncertainty. It was a Major Masselot, an experienced BEP officer with extensive contacts within the regular French Army, who convinced the commander of the French Airborne forces to disband the BEP and create two parachute regiments. On 1 December 1955, the 2ème REP was born and they linked up with the 1ème REP, their comrades in arms from Indo-China, to fight in an Algerian conflict which was threatening to spiral out of control. It would take more than some latter-day Wild Geese – that Irish private army of legendary loose cannons – to help regular army forces prevent this potential tinder box from igniting into an even worse conflagration.

The situation was unique in that it ignored the traditional rules of war, introducing completely new procedures. Legion patrols were subjected to typical guerrilla warfare tactics such as hit and run ambushes and terrorist attacks employing booby-traps. Counter-tactics introduced by the Legion included the perusal of the enemy, encircling and trapping them, and calling in reserve forces to imprison the enemy, leaving the troops on the ground to continue in their relentless hunting down of the terrorist. Helicopters were invaluable during these operations and were used to transport troops to various locations in the continuous search for the enemy or to med-evac any casualties. The burning heat of the desert and the ankle-breaking ground of rocks were as much of an enemy as the wiles and forces of the local *Fellagha* guerrillas. The entire protracted episode was a confusing combination of colonial collapse and nationalism which led to resentment on both sides and to revenge. As the tensions escalated, both heroism and brutality from each side reached new heights and depths. I do not wish to offer a full-blooded history lesson on this conflict. Simon Murray has already given us a brilliant first-hand account of many battles and patrols of the war, but perhaps it is worth explaining again something about the relatively short sequence of events which led to the birth of such a proud Legion regiment.

French politicians had told their countrymen that Algeria would remain a department of France – a department equating to an area with some local political autonomy, like a county in Britain. The army, they said, was coming in to protect them. The French settlers, actual numbers are unknown, wanted the army to build solidly-fixed defensive positions, in order to protect them, their property and investments. The REP and the other heli-borne operations instead pursued the FLN during mobile patrols, thereby leaving the settlers feeling abandoned, isolated and vulnerable to terrorist attack. This caused civilian–military tension which lasted throughout the war and led to the formation of the OAS (*Organisation de l'Armée Secrète*), French civilians hell-bent on preventing Algerian independence.

This was a classic guerrilla war. Sudden terrorist strikes, ambushes and hit and run operations were followed by governmental forces – namely the Legion – sweeping the desert in search of rebel groups. Arguments raged between traditional officers who wanted to play it by the book and the REP officers who wanted to employ new methods, more mobile operations and the airborne means to implement them. Indeed, officers from the 2ème REP wrote a study of helicopter operations, tactics and the rapid deployment of troops to cut off retreating groups of rebel fighters which has proved to anticipate tactics used today. The internal conflict was resolved because of the stunning success of the paras' operations. The evidence was clear for all to see and could not possibly be refuted.

The 2ème REP were involved in several major engagements in Algeria, in one alone killing nearly 200 FLN activists. This was a brutal war and savagery was not confined to the rebels as the forces of 'order' fought fire with fire. Many captured rebels were beaten and tortured by the French forces. The Algerian war had a profound effect on the Legion – the 2ème REP in particular – and it is important to remember certain events and their consequences.

General de Gaulle had returned to power in 1958 and over the following year had made a series of both secret and public approaches to the FLN. His reputation remains that of the aggressive patriot, but here he attempted to end the conflict by offering them some sort of self-determination. The army were dismayed and felt betrayed, almost as if their past sacrifices had been ignored. The army commander at the time said he would not execute the orders of the Head of State and was immediately reassigned another posting. He had many sympathizers, however, and militant anti-government protesters took to the streets in Algiers. Shots were fired at the *National Gendarmerie*, there to uphold law and order. The seeds of rebellion had been sown. An ominous sign of things to come was that soldiers of the 1er REP had stood idly by during these riots, for many supported the French Algerian cause. Such subordination was punished and was to prove pivotal in subsequent Legion reorganization.

The army rebellion gathered speed and in 1961, four French generals and the Inspector General of the Legion attempted what became known as 'The Generals' Putsch', the 1er REP supporting the generals. Their purpose was to defy de Gaulle's government, indeed topple it, and keep Algeria French. Meanwhile, the 2ème REP had returned from operations, astonishingly, despite radio contact and codes, completely unaware of recent developments and were greeted by rumour and confusion. By the time they had been properly briefed by their officers the situation had been defused and the revolt quelled. They were astounded to learn how the 1er REP had taken over Algiers city, the government buildings there and its radio station. Anti-government protest, leading to a parachute drop on Paris in support of a *coup d'état*, was being widely rumoured. On the night of the 'putsch', 22 April 1961, the 2ème REP's commanding officer led them into Algiers city. They secured the airport and drove away defending French marines, using weapons which included sharpened sticks, as they did not want to be seen to take arms on fellow French servicemen.

De Gaulle, in a piece of superb political manoeuvring, spoke to the nation, rallied most Frenchmen back to his side and snuffed out the revolt as if the mutineers were petulant children. By 26 April, the Generals had fled and the 1er REP's days were numbered. The regiment was struck from the rolls of the French Army forever. The 2ème REP, although exonerated from any blame and back on operations, was unsure of its future.

In July 1962 Algiers become independent. Many within the French government called for the 'mercenaries', the Legion, to be disbanded once and for all. The 2ème REP continued with operations throughout the delicate time of the hand over of Algiers and through loyalty and professionalism even managed to silence those who had called for their dissolution.

In 1967, a Lt. Colonel Cailaub took charge of the 2ème REP. A man of vision, he wanted the REP to become ready for any mission, anywhere, no matter how dangerous or unusual. He wanted to dispatch outdated notions of an exclusively focused parachute force and look to the future. Cailaub used his considerable contacts within the French high command, cajoling and harassing them for equipment and broader training facilities. The regiment was to be an elite force and each of its proposed four companies would have specialized skills and tasks. It would evolve into a fully flexible air-commando unit.

Cailaub frightened the traditionalists, but they listened to him and his persuasiveness eventually won them over. By June 1967, the 2ème REP was encamped at Camp Raffali, named in honour of Major Raffali who was killed in action in September 1952 during the fighting in Indo-China, as he lead an attack by the 2ème BEP. It had become part of the French Rapid Reaction Force, whose motto is 'Fast, Strong and Far'. Thanks to Lt. Colonel Cailaub's vision, the Legion threw off the shackles that had for so long kept it apart, even estranged from the regular army and fostered so many of the old misconceptions. It learned to change and move with modern thinking and innovations and has thoroughly earned its place amongst the world's elite forces.

QUITE HOW MANY OF THE *ANCIENS* had played some doubtful role during World War Two, before they joined the Legion, I didn't know and I really didn't want to know. If they were involved in any atrocities during the war I hope the Legion gave them some redemption. Maybe they were just taking orders. Not even a *képi blanc* can sweep some slates clean and I admit to an unease here, but perhaps one of the great unsung glories of the French Foreign Legion is that it has so often been prepared to give a man a second chance. There is no greater humanity – and no man should ask for more.

CHAPTER NINE

CORSICA AND 2ème REP

AT THE START OF THIS BOOK I WROTE that I always wanted a bit more. Perhaps that's why I had always aspired to be a para despite my worst personal fear – of heights. I wasn't afraid of discipline and rigour. I wasn't afraid of physical pain and danger. I wanted and almost relished all those things. But I was afraid of letting myself and my comrades down because of that truly dreadful phobia.

However, in the 'wanting more' department I certainly got my wish now because, if anything, the bullshit and being fucked about was worse here than at Castel. The *2ème Régiment Étranger de Parachutistes* (REP), prides itself on being the most professional and exclusive of all the Legion regiments. There is *appel* and inspection three times daily; first thing in the morning, after lunch and at 2100 hours. As new arrivals, we weren't going to be allowed off camp for some time, so it never really bothered me; the rules were just a bit tiresome. In fact, we would not be allowed off camp until we were badged – awarded our parachute brevet – and operations aside, regimental tradition dictated that we would not be allowed off the island fort for about twelve months. I thought it just another way of the Legion letting us know that they controlled us, on or off duty.

Camp Raffali is set on the outskirts of Calvi, birthplace of Napoleon Bonaparte. Whitewashed buildings with red roof tiles majestically face the sparkling blue Mediterranean and rugged mountains tower behind them. A beach lies 500 metres from the main gate, but it is guarded at all times and is thus, sadly, not a place to relax after a swim. Raffali's resemblance to a quiet Corsican village – if slightly sprucer and grander than the real thing tends to be – is reinforced by its 'streets', which subtly divide the barracks into smaller, even more enclosed work areas. Buildings are surrounded by flower beds, pines and palms line the immaculately kept thoroughfares. A monument to Legion paratroopers killed in action stands, like any village war memorial, just inside the entrance to the camp and behind this is the headquarters building, with *Legio Patria Nostra* emblazoned on the white walls in huge black letters. The monument had been brought to Corsica when the 2ème REP moved from Algeria at the end of the war there in the early sixties. A *voie sacrée* (sacred path) leads to this memorial, which is inscribed in Latin, *More Majorum* – in the footsteps of our predecessors.

It is a wonderful place on a remarkable island and over the years my comrades and I were to enjoy many of the pleasures which have made it a holiday destination – the climate, the landscape, the good local wine and a cuisine which is poised between French, Italian and North African. Nor was there ever any shortage of Legion groupies, a particularly sexually rapacious breed of camp follower, who were sometimes local girls but more often than not sophisticated independent women from all over the world who flew to the island in the hopes of landing a Legionnaire. Ladies from the Scandinavian countries and from Italy were particularly taken by the glamour of the *képi blanc*.

Once, after the punishing cross-island march that the REP endures occasionally, I went into Calvi with Steve, Roger, a Legionnaire from Sweden, and a German lad named Horst. The prodigious quantities of beer we consumed soon replaced body fluids lost during the march and meant that we became inebriated pretty fast. We were a bit noisy and laughing at anything and everything. I think we were just normal young men enjoying a night out. We could have been anywhere.

In a bar called *Au Son des Guitares*, a renowned Legion haunt, Horst and Steve were playing pool when they were challenged to a game by two very attractive young women. A great cheer rose from the gathered Legionnaires as they forecast some embarrassment for my two pals. The girls were on holiday from Italy. Roger acted as a self-appointed interpreter, claiming he could speak Italian. It later transpired that he had learned any Italian he knew from the film *The Godfather* and he knew no more Italian than the rest of us. Still, it was a great icebreaker and soon we were all getting on fine, communicating reasonably well in English. The beer flowed, the music thumped out and games of pool were interspersed with hoots of raucous laughter. I was really enjoying the company of women once again after being in a male-dominated environment for so long, but I certainly wasn't looking for anything else. Raw wounds were still open and hurting deeply. It had been less than a year, after all...

At one point I disappeared to the gents for a leak and was followed a short time later by Steve.

'You jammy bastard!' he said. 'That little 'un, Maria, for some bizarre reason, fancies you, my old mucker.'

Horst had by this time paired off with the other girl, Lucia, and presently it became obvious that we were now a foursome. Steve and Roger went off to another bar to try their luck there.

The four of us strolled away to a quieter part of town, away from the noisier bars and the prying gaze of other Legionnaires. We feared they would either cramp our style or take the piss mercilessly. It was fantastic to be experiencing a sense of normality again. We just walked and talked and it all felt so natural. The musky aroma of perfume, the sound of a soft giggle evoked a completely different world. Our money didn't go far on this very expensive island – we hadn't yet completed the jumps course which would entitle us to parachute pay. The girls, however, stood their rounds and bought us several beers.

Later the four of us walked hand in hand through the now quiet streets of Calvi. Earlier we had drawn knowing glances from the Corsicans we passed: they had no doubt seen all this before. We took the girls back to their hotel. I knew there was no chance of being invited in, but I hadn't really wanted that. It had been enough, on this magical evening, to act in a normal way, do what young men and young women do. Anyway, we had to be back at Raffali and ready for work at 0600. It was by now gone four, so it was a goodnight kiss, no promise of another date and the night was over.

Horst and I wandered slowly back to camp, up the hill and past the deserted holiday village that the REP used for exercises. The dark Mediterranean glistened in the moonlight.

'Do you think we will see them again?' he asked. 'No,' I answered. 'We're on guard tomorrow; then it will be someone else's turn.'

It had been nice while it lasted, but I had sensed from the outset that it was to be for that night only. She had been lovely and who knows what might have been? Another time, another place? The world is full of people asking that same question. A sweet novelty for the girls, perhaps, something to tell their friends back home; certainly something different. For me though, it had been a wonderfully romantic escape, no matter how short. It would keep me going for weeks.

ANY NOTION THAT I MIGHT ALMOST be here on a sybaritic holiday had evaporated the morning after our arrival at Raffali. The half-dozen of us newcomers completed the *promo*, a short class held before jump school actually began. It was designed to monitor our levels of fitness and morale. The instructors had to ensure that we were physically capable of enduring the course and that we were mentally prepared as well. The regiment was going to invest a lot of time and money in training us and they needed to be sure that not a single franc was going to be wasted. That completed we joined about fifteen other trainee paras that made up our group. The course proper would begin the following day.

Wearing T-shirts, shorts and trainers, we set off on a brisk run at 0600 on a bright morning, the damp and demoralizing weather of the Pyrenees fast fading to memory. The only sound in the camp was the soft thud of our trainers as they hit the tarmac in perfect time. Although not yet warm, the sun was dazzling and we breathed the early morning fragrance of pine and fresh flowers. For a moment this did feel like a holiday jog and one could almost imagine panting back an hour or so later for a shower, coffee, croissants and jam ... We trotted past the guard and onto the streets of Calvi. The pace increased and I could feel my thighs beginning to strain and tighten. I learned that this fifteen kilometre daily run was only a warm-up to get the lungs open and deal with any residual Kronenbourg damage from the night before. I also realized that the REP's idea of fitness and Castel's were worlds apart. Although my general condition had drastically improved since I enlisted, I knew after this run, this gentle introduction, that I would still have a fearsome amount of work to do to come anywhere near the standard expected here and reckoned I'd be spending some time in the gym.

Anyone who has been to Corsica will remember how the mountains rear up almost immediately from the coast, the steep inclines, narrow hairpin bends and fearsome, rocky drops. Magnificent views, for sure, but the most excruciating terrain for any runner, let alone one with a 23kg (50lb) kit on his back. Day after day we ran or doubled (quick-time walking) everywhere and any back-sliding was summarily punished by press-ups or heaves to a bar or both, the number of them dependent on the instructor's mood.

The physical work was broken up by further weapon instruction. We learned how to assemble and disassemble our issued weapon, the

FAMAS, until we could do it blindfold in seconds. Other instruction including the use of the MINIMI, a 5.5mm magazine-fed light machine gun, and the BAB 9mm pistol quickly followed. We also had spells in the parachute preparation hangar, where we learned everything connected with the canopies we would be using. A 'sprog' para must learn all about the parachute he will depend upon to allow him to drift safely down to earth, just as he would need to be familiar with the weapons he uses on terra firma. Knowledge dispels fear – that was the theory. The classroom was in a huge building with tall windows and containing long tables where the vital work of repairing and packing chutes was carried out. No more than six chutes were prepared and packed by any operative in any one day. It is wisely believed that concentration levels lapse after this and potentially fatal mistakes can occur. The geometric precision required of us when we folded our bedding or shirts had sometimes seemed mindless; here it was clearly crucial.

The unit was led by an NCO from the regular French Army, attached to the Legion for a fixed tour of duty. A packed and prepared chute, made these days from strong but incredibly light synthetic silk, would have passed through four quality control inspections, each recorded and signed before being stacked in the 'ready' pile. The system works well and the safety record of the REP is second to none.

We also had lectures on the origins and history of the REP. I was enthralled by these lessons, which included visits to the regimental museum on the camp outside of which there is a marble slab inscribed with 'The sun never sets on earth soaked with the blood of Legionnaires'. The museum encompasses everything that is associated with the REP. As with the archive in Aubagne, this is a quiet, almost reverent, place where the visitor is reminded of the Legion's past glories and honours, leaving him with no doubts about its demands. Room by room, battle after battle, the citations and honours awarded to the REP are proudly on display. The bravery of members of this regiment in the past was what we had to live up to. We would learn even more from other Legionnaires about famous battles and extraordinary courage shown by soldiers of the REP.

Runs were followed by circuit training in the gym, followed by weapon training, after which came instruction in the parachute repair hangar and then more running. The food here wasn't bad, but meal-times were not lingered over, partly because there never seemed to be quite enough to eat. We all had various non-military tasks, like tending the gardens, camp maintenance and cookhouse duties. This last was a popular chore because work in the kitchens at least ensured you got at the food first. We were all issued with a daily ration of cigarettes and as I've never smoked, and the cigarettes were something of a camp currency, I was once again often able to barter for work in the kitchens with my freebies and thus avoid latrine duties or some other unpopular job.

The daily schedule was testing, to say the least. I barely had time to think of home, but one Sunday, a free day as usual, I decided to write a letter to my folks. Since we rookies were not yet allowed to spend our free time savouring the delights of the town off-camp, and hanging around in the foyer could pall after a while, it was as good a use of the day as any. I found a quiet place: at least the dormitory which I shared with nine others was likely to be undisturbed. The room was quite impersonal, with no outward signs of who lived there. There were no photographs or posters adorning the walls and it was a bolt-hole from the general clamour. I was roomed with Steve, the German lad Horst, Roger the Swede and some others. The four of us stuck fairly close together often enjoying a few beers in the foyer, or later on in down-town Calvi. You had to take people as you found them here: it still wasn't the done thing to delve into anybody's past or background. Unless infor-mation was volunteered, any secrets remained within that man's own head. I considered myself very fortunate to have come across three fine blokes with whom I could get along. We could talk if we wanted to or just as important, be left alone with no questions asked.

It suited me just fine. I had a difficult letter to write and needed a clear mind. I tried, in vain, to explain myself to my parents. I should have written of my inability to talk to them, and told them how I really felt, instead of telling them what I thought they wanted to hear. I was exceptionally proud of what I had achieved so far but I didn't tell them that. I thought it would be rubbing salt into a wound I had caused by leaving in the first place. That letter went through many clumsy drafts and was never replied to.

These early days consisted mainly of physical tests, their results all carefully recorded. We may have completed basic training but here at Calvi we were treated worse than new *engagés volontaires*. We were here under sufferance, caught in the middle. Among the elite, we were nothing. Last to be fed, first for the shit duties, cleaning or guard. Ignored by all, with the exception of our instructors. I suspected that this would last until we were awarded our wings, the brevet, and had the lanyard, the *fourragère*, the regimental identification, pinned onto our left shoulder. We had to prove ourselves all over again. Only our *moniteurs*, the instructors, spoke to us and I often thought that if they could use sign language to communicate then they would. None of us admitted to it but I think we all felt lower than the lowest mangy cur. We sat by ourselves in the cookhouse and the foyer. I wished these six weeks would end. Maybe that's why I chose a sad Sunday to write that letter home.

Feeling ostracized did bring the section closer together. We felt like a unit within a unit. Steve was obviously my best mate: we had bonded together right from the start, way back in Paris. He was a big, confident sort of bloke, very much like the big brother most boys would wish for. He always seemed to have an answer to problems that arose, a solution for everything. He was a natural leader and he spoke a lot of sense. He would stand his ground and fight if the situation called for it; but he would also know when to walk away, to leave things alone and to fight another day. I felt slightly jealous at times because nothing seemed to bother or trouble him. It wasn't that he had no conscience and didn't consider his actions but that he could deal with most of life's annoyances with a *'C'est la vie'* attitude. Apart from knowing he'd been on the run, I still had no idea what had driven him to the Legion. I knew some of the others from the *2ème Compagnie* at Aubagne, too, so I didn't always feel totally alone but I occasionally wondered if I had done the right thing by coming here. We had gone from walking with a swagger at Aubagne to having all our confidence crushed out of us, barely able to speak. In retrospect I see that, in a subtle way, endurance of this was part of our training too.

Our section consisted of men from many different nationalities and cultures, but here we were really one – the Legion. We were being pushed to the limit of our physical and mental endurance; we learnt immediate, unquestioning obedience to any instruction or order. We were bound together by collective misery, united by the marching and almost defiant singing, all of us hoping that soon we would be accepted Legionnaires of the 2ème REP and then it would have been worth it.

Everyone knows that all soldiering is ninety per cent boredom and ten per cent action, if that, and that the colourful tales old campaigners repeat usually concern heroic defeat rather than glorious victory – think of Dunkirk and the Legion's own Camerone. But I doubt if any of us was prepared for the apparently cruel and tedious graft we were put through or the sense that it might only end in some pointless, forgotten debacle in a place that interested no one.

Over beers in the foyer we would recount our differing experiences, attempting to out-do each other on the suffering scale; we would sing some more and many of us became proud of being able to say 'fuck off' in five languages. Although segregated from the troops of the REP, as each day passed we felt a little closer to joining this elite family within a family. We were becoming comrades. Naturally there was a tendency for the Germans to huddle together, the Brits too and the Spanish, Italians or whoever. The Swiss or Belgians, who were often actually French (France does not officially permit her nationals to join the Legion), also kept their own company much of the time. These last were the only ones who usually spoke French at the camp – none of the rest of us would do so unless speaking to an officer. It is a matter of slight regret that in all my years with the Legion I never acquired any real fluency in the language. When we all gathered together we'd generally converse in English. Most Europeans can speak some English and we found it easier to correct their mispronunciations than bother to learn their language properly. Some of the French lads would try to help us speak as a native, a sort of 'street French' using slang, and attempt to teach us idiom and accent, which is very important when conversing in French. After many futile efforts, a combination of rough, deep voices and the fact that all were laughing at us, we decided it would be a lot less effort to speak in English. A Frenchman, Paul, had tried to help me and I genuinely did my best to learn more of his language. Paul even told me that using a decent accent and at least trying to talk correctly would generate respect. Respect is a big word in the Legion.

One morning, after our usual beasting – running along being shouted at, cursed at and generally abused – around the calf-killing hills of Calvi, the section sat outside the parachute repair building devouring crusty bread with jam. Our *moniteur* approached so we stood and snapped to attention, uneaten bread flying in all directions, a feast for the gulls wheeling over the camp. We were told that a section was going to jump later that morning and that we were to board the aircraft to observe an operational jump. An excited babble emanated from the group and we were left to finish what was left of our food.

Camp Raffali is unique in that it has its own airstrip and drop zone, DZ, nearby. It is reasonably flat, considering the mountainous local terrain and it is also fairly free of the ankle-breaking scrub bushes so often found in Mediterranean areas. A huge observation tower equipped with wind-measuring devices and radio antennae dominates the DZ and there are always ambulances on stand-by when a jump is taking place. The notion that a Legionnaire could break a leg and then be forced to march back to barracks is best left to the novelists. Nothing is left to chance and safety is paramount. Perversely, I really looked forward to this little jaunt, perhaps because I knew that I wouldn't have to jump this time so it would be like watching a film in an engaged and yet detached sort of way.

At home I have a minor panic if I have to stand on a chair to change a light bulb. Getting up a ladder to clear the guttering is out of the question. I can face snakes and spiders, the dentist and other rats. I've faced the eyes of men who've meant to kill me. I can even face opening the brown envelopes that come in the post. But I can't face heights. Quite why someone with this classic phobia actually chose to join a parachute regiment may be something for the shrinks to ponder. Even an amateur psychologist could deduce that it has something to do with challenge and the wish to conquer one's deepest fear, to almost masochistically confront the greatest personal test. I didn't understand it then and I still don't. All I knew was that I wanted to be a para however paradoxical my motives and reasons were. I just had to do it – whatever that proves.

The Transall C-160 is the workhorse of the French Air Force, some-what similar to the RAF Hercules. The insides are minimal: canvas seats and straps, emergency instructions painted on the shiny metal bulkhead and gleaming metal wires tangling overhead where the jumpers 'hook-up' prior to exiting this faithful old dear. When the interior light above the exit door glows red, the entire 'stick', which is the group of men to jump, stands up and secures a line to a metal hawser above them. This line is attached to the main parachute and on departure from the aircraft will automatically deploy the chute; the man only has to concern himself with getting set for the landing. Above a door on the port side of the bulkhead, our gateway to the abyss below, were two lights, one red and one green. Our time in the aircraft, whether short or long, would be dictated by whichever of the lights shone in the semi-darkness. The stench of hydraulics and aviation fuel is foul, causing many first-timers to be overcome by dizziness and nausea. Then again there are the combined human smells of sweat, vomit and shit. And that of panic.

We stood in rigid squad formation and watched the section board using the rear-loading ramp to walk onto the aircraft, each man straining to manage the extraordinary amount of kit tethered to his body – it could be as much as 38kg (84lb). Sometimes it wasn't so much a walk as a waddle: for complex aerodynamic reasons, the smaller and lighter the man, the heavier his kit had to be to ensure a safely balanced landing of man and gear at the same time as the rest of the stick. A long-forgotten science lesson about ants carrying their own body weight sprang to mind.

Imagine any man, tall or slight, jumping – particularly at night – into unknown and hostile terrain with that kind of weight strapped to his back, even if he had no fear of the jump itself. Adrenalin is a fine and useful thing and enables us all to rise (or in this case drop) to the occasion but I believe few paras leave their aircraft without a moment of fear – hence some of those human smells. It is a testament to the skills of pilots and navigators, as well as to the courage of parachutists, that despite turbulence, slipstream and darkness thirty soldiers can usually land safely within half a square mile of each other.

The main parachute is harnessed across the back and a smaller one is slung over the lower abdomen, which constantly bashes against the thighs. This has a rip cord and is in case the main automatic chute fails to open. It is not a dignified way for an elite soldier to enter the fray, however perfectly he lands and however many elegant, rolling landfalls you may have seen in the cinema. In the plane, on the day of our observation, the guys checked each other's kit, harnesses, straps and fastenings, pulling and tugging at everything until they were satisfied that the equipment was secure. A slap on the helmet signalled that everything was OK. The jumping section sat on the port side of the aircraft and we faced them. These young, hard-faced Legionnaires did not give us so much as a glance, concentrating and absorbed in thoughts of the minutes ahead. Once strapped in safely, the loadmaster spoke into his intercom and with a lurch the huge engines engaged and the aircraft taxied away. The engines roared again and we surged forward as if released by a catapult. Heavy thumps rebounded off the tarmac as speed gathered and then, after what seemed to be a ridiculously short run, we lifted off and while still climbing, went into a sweeping turn over the bay. The aircraft climbed steeply and banked once more. After only a few minutes in the air, the jumpmaster, a French Air Force NCO, ordered the stick to stand and hook up. The side door opened, the red light above the door flickered and the loadmaster shouted more instructions. It was almost impossible to hear him as cold air rushed into the hold, creating a tunnel of noise and replacing the malodorous stale air within. The stick moved closer together on automatic obedience; every man knew exactly what was required of him. Then, a shout of 'Allez!' and in a matter of seconds the entire stick was gone. As if connected by an invisible umbilical cord, they all went through the door like a giant caterpillar.

The Transall climbed steeply once more as the jumpmaster pulled in the trailing static lines, the only evidence that anyone else had been aboard. The noise inside the aircraft precluded any attempt at conversation. I didn't need to talk though. I looked at Steve and he at me. I think we both tacitly felt profound admiration for those lads. It had been one of the most awesome things I had ever seen. I wondered how I would react given the same circumstances. I didn't want to disgrace myself and I really wanted to behave in the same way as the Legionnaires I had just witnessed. I looked about the aircraft and wondered if anyone else was thinking the same as me? If they were, then they kept it well hidden.

I don't know whether to be saddened that the role of the para in modern warfare – God forbid – is probably over. It is unlikely that there will ever be another Arnhem or Normandy invasion, when hundreds or even thousands of paras descend to join a ground force. Future conflicts will be handled differently. We live in a world where the threat of conflict is still very real but I think that long drawn-out wars, involving troops on the ground, where the outcome is doubtful to say the least, are gone. A modern war involves air superiority and bombing the enemy into submission. This is followed up by a barrage of artillery, and then ground troops moving in to mop up any resistance. It is the era of 'push-button' war. Battles are fought via computer from long distances. There is still the need, however, for a fast, rapid reaction force ready to carry out the wishes of its political masters, and that is the reason the French will always rely on the Legion, no matter the dark mutterings from those who will insist even now on calling them mercenaries.

There was still an immense amount of work to do, however, before we could even think of jumping out of a Transall ourselves. The work would be eighty per cent physical and twenty per cent theory of parachuting. Few people realize how tough a para has to be. Here I was being worked even harder and pushed even further than I thought possible. I wasn't bothered about being confined to camp, nor that we had so little free time. Once we had finished for the day, eaten our evening meal and sorted out our kit for the following day, I was ready for bed. I've never been much of a one for silence and solitude but every man likes some privacy at times. Now our days were so full, so exhausting, that I didn't even miss a few minutes reflection before sleep. I couldn't even tell you what time lights-out was because most nights I was already snoring like a baby before I could think much about what would happen next.

During my time the regiment was made up mainly of British and

German lads with a smattering of Frenchmen, Spaniards and some Italians – which surprised me as I'd bought into their reputation for not really being up for this type of work. All formal orders on the parade ground, or when presenting yourself to a higher rank, were in French so the fact that English was generally spoken in the foyer and cookhouse made the regiment seem almost a home from home. We were still largely ignored by most of the seasoned troops but were becoming quite matey with our *moniteurs*, the NCOs who ran the pre-parachute training course. They were widely known and respected and would discuss the new batch of trainees with Legionnaires in other companies. We knew that whatever the *moniteurs* said about you in these early days might haunt or help you throughout your career, so it made sense to make a good early impression. Work hard, do your best and then a little bit more, keep your ears open and mouth shut. Keeping to these principles would always make life a little easier.

After a deep, if brief, sleep it was time to return to the duties and practicalities of the day, from learning how to steer the parachute, to slowing down the rate of your descent – also quite important – as well as what to do if your main chute failed to open. While we listened to these lessons carefully each of us knew that the theory, essential as it was, would have to be physically tested one day soon. We were also well aware that since a single training jump was an expensive enterprise – well over £1,000 per man if you costed in fuel, chutes, instruction, kit and all the rest – any idle moment in class was a waste of money as well as time. It is a strange irony that governments as well as the Legion expend vast sums of money on training men to achieve what most people concerned hope will never be necessary. In the business world I suppose it is called insurance or damage limitation.

We learned how to exit the aircraft correctly, how to fall properly and how to roll once landed – in daylight, in darkness, with maximum kit or a lighter load. Nothing was left to chance. We were taught how to put the chute on and how to harness up without causing a nasty personal injury: there were two straps on our parachutes that came through the legs from behind and attached to a d-ring by the abdomen. The trick was to place your testicles on either side of the straps. If you didn't do so, when the chute opened up and all the straps and rigging went rigid, your knackers were crushed by your pelvic bone.

ALL TOO SOON THE DAY OF OUR FIRST jump approached, weather permitting. My sense of dread mounted until it felt like I had been punched in the chest. I'd always found it difficult to admit to, let alone explain, my phobia and I wasn't going to start doing so now, amidst a bunch of guys who prided themselves on being fearless. I'd never had to confront it before, not like this. As a boy, playing with friends and with trees to climb, I would just stop: *not doing that, fuck off!* I knew I had to conquer it and that this was the place to do so. Refusals to jump in the Legion are extremely rare. Legion paras are often described as 'two time volunteers'. They volunteer once for the Legion, and then again for the REP. It is assumed they know exactly what the score is and what is expected of them. They do not let anyone down. Upon landing and return to camp any refusnik's locker is emptied and he and his kit are summarily removed to another regiment. It is instant and non-negotiable. A refusnik's bottling-out is thought to endanger the confidence of his comrades, to be almost contagious.

'Are you fucking mad?', Steve blurted out, spitting pieces of semi-digested food over the table during our evening meal. 'I've heard the shagging lot now. You're scared of heights and you've volunteered for this lot. Fucking class!'

I muttered something about him lowering his voice in case anyone else should hear him. Too late. Some obnoxious German in our section had overheard Foghorn Burns and burst into contemptuous guffaws. The news then spread quicker than a dose of dysentery in an African village. Other Legionnaires were smirking and pointing at me as our *moniteur* approached the table. 'Hey, *Anglais*, you are scared of height, no? OK, tomorrow you can go Number One. You have the honour to jump first.'

By now Foghorn's face was purple as he struggled to keep both his laughter and his food down. Bastard! I suppose I should have expected it and I would have done the same given half a chance.

I lay awake most of the night, half praying for rain and thunder for the next day and half praying that it was actually the day after, all this crap was done with and I hadn't made a prat of myself. Those prayers were ignored, but maybe my more reasonable request of 'Please God, give me the courage to do this' would be heard. Don't mess with God: don't ask for more than you deserve. That night seemed interminable and when dawn broke the weather was absolutely bloody perfect. Bright, clear and still. The others' excited chatter made it feel like being in an aviary again. I was very subdued and felt quite sick. I did notice, however, that as time passed some of the others didn't seem to be as confident as they had been during my ordeal in the cookhouse the previous evening. Steve had tried to allay my fears, now realizing I was deadly serious, but he failed.

There was no way I could stomach anything at breakfast, not even a bowl of coffee. The reality of what was happening had by now hit the others and I ceased to be the butt of their inane jokes. They too were wrapped up in their own thoughts. The *moniteurs* were not, and they had an ace up their sleeve, especially for me – the ace of all practical jokes.

During our training in the theory of parachuting we spent a lot of time in the repair facility and learned how to pack a chute correctly. There were stringent checks made on all parachutes and it was highly improbable that you would be allowed to actually use a chute you'd packed yourself. Despite the old reputation of the Legion, safety is paramount and all equipment used is, where possible, thoroughly checked by suitably qualified people. Until that day. The day before we had stood behind the long trestles in the facility and, under instruction from the NCO, we had each meticulously packed a parachute and then labelled it with our name, rank and number. The chute was then stacked separately upon the many racks of shelving within the facility's vast interior. When the chutes were checked for the last time and ready for use you could see four distinctive ticks and signatures on the attached tags, stating it had passed all quality control checks.

The instructions were, of course, all in French and barked out fast. My French had improved, but not by that much. I was struggling to keep up and I couldn't expect the instructor to slow down just for me. I didn't want to appear to be the class idiot, so instead of asking the instructor to clarify things, I had the idea of watching one of my fellow students, whom I knew could understand exactly what was being said, and copying him. Brilliant. Whatever he did, I would follow. Every fold or tuck he made, I would replicate. There, foolproof, nothing could go wrong. We were not yet proficient in the art of parachute packing so there was no way, I managed to convince myself, that the Legion would allow unqualified Legionnaires to use a chute that was not one hundred per cent safe.

Armed with this desperate confidence, I began to relax and followed exactly what my fellow student, Jean, was doing. I reminded myself that there was not the remotest danger of my badly packed chute making it past one quality check, never mind four. After the lesson we wrote our names and number on a tag and attached them to the chute before placing them on the relevant racks. During the mid-morning *casse-croûte* I approached Jean along with Steve. Making a joke of it, I told him what I had done during the lesson. He immediately stopped eating and gave me a worried look.

'I think I have missed some of the instruction,' he faltered. 'I did not hear it all. I hope I have not led you into the same mistake.'

'Don't worry, *mon ami*, they get checked. If it's wrong, it won't pass inspection.' And that was that. I'd become bloody good at bravado.

Anyway, it was now D-day and after breakfast we had a quick parade and then it was time to get equipped for our debut jump. We were only jumping in light order today, that is to say without any *sac à dos*, the issued rucksack in which we usually carried all our kit, or rifles. The only gear we would need was our helmet and, of course, the two parachutes. We went to draw them from the stores and when I laid eyes on mine I very nearly passed out. For there on the shelf was a packed and ready main chute with a tag on it, bearing my fucking name in clear block capital letters. No other marks or signatures. This babe had obviously not passed through *any* checks, never mind the four it was supposed to have cleared. I cannot adequately describe the horror and dread I felt just then. I tried to explain to the storeman but he just pushed them towards me and hustled me out into the sunshine. I was not beside myself, I was *past* myself. I grabbed Steve and in gibberish told him what had happened. Before he could do or say anything, one of the *moniteurs* came over and bawled at me to get ready. I can't remember how I managed to fasten any of the buckles and clasps on my gear, I was shaking so much, I felt as if I had lost all control.

I was tortured by it all and felt as if my life was ebbing away, so desperate, in fact, that I didn't notice the *moniteurs* disappear back into the stores. Steve came over to me so that I could check his chute and webbing.

'I can't fucking do this mate,' I gasped. 'It's not gonna open, man, it's not fucking safe. I am dead, I just know it.'

'For fuck's sake, shut up and stop snivelling,' he retorted, without a glimmer of sympathy. No one on earth could have described my abject terror right then. If you're scared shitless, then you're scared to death and there is nothing you can do about it, except face it.

Suddenly I heard laughter. Raucous, almost lewd laughter. The mirth that indicates that a seriously good joke has been played upon someone. Coming from behind me, the sound of guffawing slowly penetrated my panic. I turned slowly in an attempt to join in, hoping laughter would lessen my morbid fears. Then I saw that it was directed at me and the whole nightmare began to dissipate. Standing in a line like the Three Stooges were the storeman and the two *moniteurs*. Looking very smug they held aloft a beautiful and perfectly packed main parachute, along with an equally fine reserve chute. The rotten, filthy, dirty bastards had wound me up good and fucking proper. For about ten minutes, though, it had felt like ten days. They had let me think I was going to jump with a parachute which we all knew was utterly useless.

They stood there, laughing like drains at their perfectly executed prank. The rest of the stick, including that traitorous shite Burns, were falling all over the place unable to control themselves under the weight of their kit. Jean, who I had looked to for help, stood there appearing oddly forlorn. I suppose I'd done them all a favour as the nerves that they too must have had were dissipated with this outburst at my expense. I could only stand there and take it. Most had tears of mirth streaming down their faces. The whole tale became common knowledge, spread on the wings of laughter. It certainly took everyone's mind off what was going to happen fairly soon. But the incident, funny as it may have been, did nothing to allay my fear.

Once everyone had been thoroughly checked by the *moniteurs*, we boarded a truck for the short ride to the aircraft from which we would eventually jump. The general levity had all but disappeared and an air of hushed anticipation enveloped the truck. When it arrived at the aircraft pan, the holding area for the plane, I noticed how cautiously the lads disembarked from the truck and I found this amusing, bearing in mind that within the next thirty minutes we were going to jump out of a perfectly serviceable aircraft at about 800 feet. It was now my turn to attempt an inward snigger.

We lined up to the rear of the aircraft; its huge tail door open like some ravening maw waiting for its next meal, a dark chasm from which there was to be only one way out. The fear returned and intensified as we stepped towards the loading ramp. It seemed to reach up from my stomach, slowly strangling my airway. We were checked yet again and as each passed the *moniteur* going into the bowels of the Transall, I remember thinking, 'You can check and check all you want. Just make sure that I am safe.' The odour, which was to become so familiar, assaulted my nostrils and stuck in the back of my throat. At last we were all in and sat in the canvas seats, the tailgate closed and we went from dazzling sunlight into a shadowless gloom. A roar from the turbo-prop engines and the Transall lurched forward to begin its taxi run along the tarmac. It was impossible to talk, if anyone could have been bothered to try anyway, such was the intensity of noise inside the hold. A burst of acceleration and within seconds we were airborne. Communication was by eye contact and hand signals only. I felt as if my eyes were bursting from their sockets. My face must have been terror personified. The expression 'shit-scared' comes to mind. But everything was OK so far. I had avoided tripping over anything and hadn't been sick.

Without warning, the side door opened and simultaneously the red light above flashed. It changed to a ghostly green as I hooked up onto the gleaming metal cable over my head

'*Allez! Debout!*' yelled the loadmaster, urging me forward. I only remained standing, I am sure, because of the huge surge of adrenalin that shot through my body. Despite blazing sunshine outside, the air that poured into the aircraft was icy. Amidst the grip of panic I was aware of the mounting urgency. Somehow I shuffled forward, then I was standing in the doorway and this was my moment of truth. I called upon any shred of bravery or courage at my command. There was a hefty slap on the back and a cry of '*Bon voyage!*' Then nothing.

Silence. I seemed to explode from the door rather than step out in the orderly way we had been practising for weeks. I launched myself as hard and as far as I could, eyes and mouth firmly clamped shut. There was a sharp crack as the canopy filled with air and the supporting straps went tight. The static line attached to the hook on the anchor line inside the aircraft had pulled back the cover from my main chute. At the same time another cord, this one fitted to the apex of the chute, pulled the canopy out of the pack and instantly snapped.

A rush of air had filled the canopy and I began to drift, rather than tumble, down to earth. It was an amazing sensation, being suspended in such silence and serenity. I felt as if I was floating. I thanked the God to whom I had earlier prayed that the chute had opened correctly and that I didn't have to begin emergency procedures. I felt a surge of relief as I saw that blessed material open above me. In those few seconds any sense of being crowded and constantly under observation, the lack of privacy and frustrated need for solitude that I might occasionally have felt, evaporated: this was intense, sublime, magnificent, personal peace and space. Then, just as suddenly, 'Bastard!' and I'd forgotten everything that I had been taught about landing. The ground was rushing up to greet me; I could hear a lot of people shouting, instructors I think. I didn't even get time to shit myself. I braced myself with only milliseconds to spare and, *crash*, hit the ground hard in an undignified heap of bone and flesh which happily seemed to have stayed in one piece. I lay in a crumpled mess, the chute now refilling with air and threatening to drag me all over the airstrip. The drop zone is away from the main runway and is a hard, unforgiving desert-type wilderness. Small but thick and very prickly gorse bushes which can rip a man's skin to shreds are interspersed with rocks. It is sometimes not enough to land safely; you have to be watchful of where you land. Now the training did kick in. I scrambled to my feet, albeit unsteadily and began to pull the straps in tightly. The parachute collapsed and I thought, 'It can't be over already, surely?' I had spent so long worrying about it, there had to be more to it than that.

I've heard others say that your first jump is the best, the one you remember above all others, as everything seems to take an age to happen. Well, from my point of view, that is bollocks. The whole escapade took only seconds and I wished it had lasted a lot longer. I was so relieved that I had not let myself down; I had performed exactly as I had been trained and felt elated at that. But I was still bloody terrified of having to do it all over again even though I'd 'broken my duck'.

Once on terra firma, chutes collected and dumped for the servicing guys to check and repack, we headed for the foyer and gallons of Kronenbourg, singing and generally releasing the tension that had driven us all for the past few days. Everyone had their own story to tell and everyone was determined to be heard above the pandemonium. It was a great day, brought to an abrupt end by one of the *moniteurs* who broke up our party. When we had separated the swearing from what he actually meant, we were left in no doubt that we hadn't completed the course yet and were still under instruction. There would be time for celebration when the work was complete. He eventually calmed down and said severely, 'First you must walk, then you can run, *d'accord?*' Of course, he was right and we headed back to the block, chastened. Lying in the strangely quiet room that night, exultancy having mellowed to a quieter satisfaction, I called out to Steve, 'It was still great though.' He could only agree.

The good, comfortable feeling didn't last long, however. About half an hour later, the lights were switched on in the room and I heard an English voice call out, 'I am looking for Burns and Parker.' Legionnaires are almost always referred to by their surname. The tone of the voice did not make it seem like a request.

'Here,' I answered, bemused as to what was going to happen next. A *caporal* I recognized from walking around the camp sat at the end of my bed.

'Just a word of warning boys. Some of the troops', he meant

seasoned Legionnaires, 'are getting the impression that you lot are a bit cocky, gobbing off. Pack it in and play the white man. Mouth shut, do the course and go to your companies. Don't go pissing it up in the foyer. You're not there yet, OK? It's only advice, you can take it or leave it.' Then he was gone. I knew from his accent that he was a Scouse, but I never spoke to him again and never knew his name. Had I the chance, I would have thanked him because it was shrewd advice. We were only part of the way there, we hadn't made it by a long stretch and yet there we were acting like old sweats. Time to screw the nut and keep these slightly swollen heads down. I forgave myself the brief over-exuberance but knew it wouldn't happen again.

The second jump, the following day, seemed even worse than the first one, strangely. I suppose that because I knew what to expect I was even more apprehensive than I had been the day before. Yes, I'd done it once and hadn't ended up as a heap of crushed bones, all had gone well and – I reminded myself – there had been those moments of exhilaration between being carried by the slipstream and hitting the ground. But any hopes of deluding myself that the fear of heights could be dispatched as an imaginary demon were now forever scotched. There was nothing imaginary about it and some level of apprehension would always remain because try as I might, the terror always remained real, even if it didn't consume me as it had before my first jump and it largely became confined to the time in the aircraft beforehand.

The second jump passed without incident and without wishing to lay a curse upon myself, I even began to enjoy the sensation of exiting the aircraft and the twenty-five or so seconds that I had within my own small, silent world in the air. Because the weather was so idyllic over the next few days and our aircraft was available we completed the five daylight jumps quickly and without anyone sustaining serious injury. The setting really was perfect and I thought of the lads in the British airborne who must depend upon the weather to complete their jumps and seldom have the luxury of the 'let's get this over and done with' approach to a dreaded task.

The final qualifying jump was to be made at night and carrying full kit, i.e. *sac à dos*, rifles and webbing, the whole lot weighing about 55kg (120lb). After feeling that I had moved on in conquering my fear of heights, the thought of this particular jump frightened the shit out of me again. Jumping at night is very different from daytime jumping and it was the fear of the unknown that again frightened me. I certainly wasn't going to make the same mistake again and announce my fear and concern to all and sundry. Would I ever be free of this phobia?

The conditions were as usual perfect for us as we boarded the faithful Transall, this time with the knowledge that once this jump was over we would be in and could celebrate properly, flaunting our newly awarded wings and lanyards. Although I had only five jumps to my name, when the red light cast an eerie ambience in the darkened hold, it now seemed second nature to stand, hooking up as I did so, without being told. The red changed to green and, like racing cars speeding from their grid, we were gone, hurling ourselves into an abyss. As darkness amplifies any sound, an even louder crack echoed in the night air when my canopy opened and I floated downwards; the roar of the Transall engines faded as it headed home and I saw on the horizon the flickering lights of Calvi contrasting with the indistinct and hostile mountains ranging up behind. The town seemed to be on the edge of the world. The few seconds of that startling sight will remain with me forever. Then I experienced for the first time the sensation of 'ground rush'. As you approach land there is a noise like a tube train roaring into a station on the underground. Because of the dark it is difficult to judge distance and know how far away from the ground you actually are. The DZ was in total darkness yet I was aware of this blackness surging up towards me.

Think, think. Knees tight together, keep those ankles close; then *thump*. I hit the ground with such force that the wind was knocked out of me. I had misjudged everything and I crash-landed or 'piled in'. The training and my survival instincts took over, saving me from serious injury and only my pride had been hurt this time. I rolled over onto my stomach and began to gather in the fast-collapsing chute, my *sac à dos* acting as an anchor. One of the ground staff on the DZ party ran to where I had clattered down, asking if I was OK. It must have looked worse than it was, for I was on my feet in no time. One thing I did know for sure, there was no way I would let them know if I *had* been hurt. That might have buggered my passing out. It was over and I had passed, thank God, Allah and the rest. We didn't need to be told how good we had been on the course, nor how clever anyone thought we may be any time we did something right – which is only what should be expected. A good soldier just quietly gets on with it.

Back at Raffali, late as it was, we attacked a great feast accompanied by an immoderate quantity of Kronenbourg. This was the recognition I wanted, to be accepted by the men of the 2ème REP, this was all I needed. There was a great atmosphere and I felt as if I had earned my part in it. Now we had all completed jump training – no refusniks, no bottling out, no ignominious departure, no threat to group morale. A lone, deep voice began to sing 'Le Boudin'. After a short respectful silence, we all joined in, NCOs, *moniteurs* and officers alike. My feelings of triumph, pride and camaraderie were beyond words. The sense of the invisible ropes that now bound us even more firmly together added to the absolute joy I experienced that evening. At the morning parade we would be presented with our brevets and lanyards. A day to look forward to, of course, but that night was for celebrating.

Horst felt particularly proud as he too was afraid of heights and had been unsure of how he would react when the light turned green. Steve, as usual, took the whole thing in his stride but I think he was just as bucked as the rest of us. Maybe he was just good at disguising his true feelings. It had been a fantastic course and great experience.

Next morning I stood rigidly to attention, my arms stiffly by my side, hands flat against my thighs and fingers stretched following the seams of my trousers. Lt. Colonel Hogard, back at Raffali after yet another tour of duty in Chad, pinned the silver wings to my right breast. That was followed by the placement of the lanyard upon my left shoulder. He took one pace back, saluted and offered me his right hand which I shook firmly.

'Parker,' he said, *'Tu est un très bon Légionnaire'*. My chest swelled and I grew six inches taller. This man was a Legion legend and he was paying me the highest compliment I could imagine. At the end of the parade, we were told to which company of the regiment we had been allocated. I was going to the *1ère Compagnie*, and so, thank God, was Steve and as our names were read, a *caporal-chef* appeared as if from nowhere, indicating that we should follow him. I am unsure whether it was just good fortune that Steve and I were sent to the same company, or whether the Legion had kept together two good friends. Personal thoughts and feelings seldom come into it with the Legion.

The four of us going to the *1ère Compagnie* were led into the administrative block to await an interview by the company commander and to be officially welcomed to the regiment. We would then be separated and each sent to different platoons. As we were dismissed, the company commander instructed me to remain behind. He went on to say that I had received a very good report from Castel and had also achieved an above average performance during jump training. He smiled, I think in reference to the joke played upon me. I had 'shown a remarkable attitude when faced with adversity.' He had recommended that I be placed on that *fut-fut* fast-track training which lead to promotion to *caporal*.

'I am very honoured, *mon capitaine*, but I do not feel I can command other Legionnaires.' I wasn't trying to be a smart arse; Christ, I had only been in five minutes. How would it look to other, more experienced Legionnaires?

He smiled again. 'Do not worry. Here at the REP you will gain experience of many things, very quickly.' This swiftly proved to be all too true.

I went along a corridor hung with photos and memorabilia from differing campaigns to the office of the company adjutant, equivalent to a warrant officer in the British Army. He told me that I was going on the Jungle Commando course in two weeks, in French Guyana, South America. I was caught in a tornado with no possible means of escape, although none was desired. At *la soupe* that evening, I couldn't wait to tell Steve about it. When I had finished I was nearly breathless and Steve appeared to be genuinely pleased. He couldn't help adding archly, 'Of course, I always knew that you would do it. Easily, in fact'.

Steve had been concerned about my fear of heights and had wondered if I would actually refuse. He said that if he could see how much courage it had taken for me to leap from that aircraft, then so could the Legion. Courage is a prerequisite of all soldiers. Leaders who display courage will command the respect of their men. Those men will follow that leader into any situation and under any circumstances. He was being sarcastic and knew it had taken effort to jump. It hadn't been 'easy' at all, and he knew that.

There was, meanwhile, another Legion tradition looming, one which I was really looking forward to: Camerone Day, one of the biggest days in the Legion calendar.

CHAPTER TEN

JUNGLE HELL

ON 30 APRIL 1863 AT CAMERONE HACIENDA, Mexico, Capitaine Danjou and sixty Legionnaires fought nearly 2,000 Mexican Army regular soldiers. The battle raged all day under a blistering sun. Eventually only five fighting Legionnaires remained, their Capitaine killed. They had no water, no food and no ammunition. Dead and mortally wounded comrades lay all around but even with the Mexican bayonets at their chests and throats, the Legion *caporal* still standing refused to surrender unless the Mexicans treated the wounded and allowed any surviving Legionnaires permission to retain their arms. Thus, the legend of Camerone was born. At every Legion base, anywhere in the world, Camerone Day is marked with respect and enthusiasm by all ranks. Individual regiments may have slightly differing ways of celebrating the day, depending on the *Chef du Corps*, but the main theme remains basically the same.

Roles are reversed throughout the *quartier*. The most junior Legionnaire, the newest to the section, is granted the honour of being *caporal de jour*. It is he who then decides on the allocation of the various duties to be performed that day, and it is he who leads the section onto La Place Darne, the parade square. I had thought that this would be a great opportunity for some payback. All those petty little punishments and beastings could be revenged on this day. But then you remember that this is only one day of the year; for the remaining 364, your life could be abject misery. Maybe it would be wise to play the white man and enjoy the day for what it was. Bloody tempting though! All cleaning duties normally performed by Legionnaires, even cleaning the showers and toilets, would be executed by the NCOs and officers. It is all completed with great humour and good grace.

Permanent barracks open their doors to outsiders for the day, which happens only rarely. Some members of the public, mostly tourists, do enter the *quartier* and gaze at this secret world into which they have been invited, but with all the recent security scares, I wonder if this practice has now ceased. The Irish Republican Army always wanted to carry out a spectacular attack against the British Army's Parachute Regiment, their arch enemy. How many similar groups would love to put one over on the Legion? If the practice has stopped now it's a shame but quite understandable.

Only the hardest-looking and best-dressed Legionnaires are called upon to perform the guard on the day; even more care than usual being taken in preparing their *tenue de garde*, so that they and the Legion look their immaculate best.

Arrangements for Camerone Day would probably have been underway for months, but because of our intense training programme, we missed most of these. Important as Christmas is to the Legion, this day supersedes it. The preparations included the construction of display stands, side-shows such as games of skill and chance, and the erection of huge marquees around the camp. Everyone was dressed in spotless, best uniform; snowy white kepis covered our shaven heads and men appeared to grow in stature as they swaggered around the camp.

The day began when the sous officers brought us lowly Legionnaires breakfast in our rooms. Coffee, croissants and pastries were taken at leisure instead of coarse bread being gulped or rammed down our throats so as not to be late for parade. After breakfast, the sous officers had to start *corvée*, as directed by the *caporal de jour*. It was all taken in good heart and is a tradition warmly welcomed by both Legionnaires and NCOs. On this occasion, the *caporal de jour* was a German lad known as Helmut. He paced slowly behind the line of non-coms as they vainly attempted *corvée* around our accommodation block, the rest of us hanging out of windows, shouting both abuse and encouragement. Helmut had previously collected several discarded cigarette butts from the foyer and placed them in his trouser pockets. Every so often he would drop one of them on the ground behind the advancing line of NCOs. At this point, we began to jeer and taunt them at their piss poor performance. Helmut called them back, gave them a proper Legion bollocking on how they had let us all down and then gave them ten press-ups for not doing the job properly. Sure, they all laughed, but I wondered if someone logged all this in his mind, ready to recall it the minute Helmut returned to the parade square.

Although the day was one of festivity and jubilant spirits, we were still soldiers and some things had to be done, come what may. Physical fitness was as much of a tool of our trade as deft confidence with any weapon we had to handle. Thus we had a quick ten kilometre run before we got down to enjoying ourselves.

The sun, beating down from cloudless blue skies, accentuated the glorious scenes at Raffali. *Anciens* and their families had been invited to the camp to join in the festivities, still part of the brotherhood and not forgotten, especially on this sacred day. The whole scene was reminiscent of a hospital fund raiser, not home to a fearsome fighting unit. The tricolour fluttered in the cooling breeze coming off the Mediterranean. Alongside the flag was the Legion ensign, its green and red colour dazzling in the sunshine. In the centre of this flag was the Legion emblem, the exploding grenade. After the run there was a parade and we were inspected by high-ranking officers. I was a little surprised to notice that they were from the regular French Army; it is considered an honour for a serving officer to be invited by their Legion counterparts to inspect Legionnaires. Some come on attachment and it is thought to be a good career move for ambitious men, for if they can command Legionnaires, they can command anyone. Perhaps they were merely curious and maybe some of them just wanted to see how this day was celebrated.

On Camerone Day we will lived and ate like kings, with no scrimping or restrictions. The lunch menu read thus:

Onion tart
Roast pork in wine sauce
Fresh vegetables, Croquet potatoes
Salads and Cheese
Coffee

Copious amounts of food, wine and Kronenbourg were consumed by all in a wonderfully relaxed and friendly environment. It has been known for Legionnaires in jail on Camerone Day to be freed, dependent on the nature of their crime, and to have their transgression struck from the record. This is a form of amnesty if you like, in remembrance of our comrades who gave their lives at Camerone all those years ago.

The *anciens* regaled us with tales of battles past and various heroic rucks they were involved in. They told us how much the Legion had changed over the years. In some ways, they said, for the better, in others for the worst. And as is the way of old men – especially old soldiers – all over the world, they told us how much easier it was for us these days. The older sweats always think they've had it harder: mind you in this case, I think they were probably right. Then the singing started and we tried to out-sing each other deep into the night, crates of Kronenbourg to hand for lubrication.

The next morning, heavily hung-over, I was told to report to the Adjutant's office, where I was instructed to make ready for my departure to French Guyana and the Jungle Commando Warfare School. It was not a course I had applied for nor had any intention of applying for.

I had been ordered to go there so off I would go, despite not looking forward to it. I was to fly in three days time. This was surely not enough time to be properly inoculated, I immediately thought, but was reassured that I would be vaccinated at Raffali and then have nearly two weeks to acclimatize before the training course began. I spent the next couple of days drawing all the necessary kit: special canvas boots – a mighty relief from the Ranger boots – plastic sheeting for building shelter, insect repellent and rations (RCIRs), and prepared to hear all types of horror stories about the jungle.

Steve was happy to stay on at Raffali as he'd settled into regimental life very easily. He was especially chipper because Michelle, the girl who'd written to him around Christmas, was planning to visit Corsica soon especially to see him. By then, we should be allowed off camp and into town when off duty and I aimed to accompany him, playing gooseberry, if I came back from Guyana unharmed. Who knows, I might even meet some nice young lady myself.

THE FIRST THING THAT HITS YOU about Guyana when you step off the aircraft at Regina is the heat – a hot, heavy, airless punch that makes you gasp as you leave the comfort of an air-conditioned plane. It was hazy but the temperature felt near to ninety. Attempting strenuously to draw in air which just wasn't there made my whole body break out in sweats. The atmosphere was suffocating and I feared that this was going to be a very unpleasant experience. Normally before I go anywhere I like to discover as much as I can about my destination. Due to the suddenness of this deployment I hadn't had the chance to assimilate any information about Guyana so I was going in blind, so to speak.

After the euphoria of passing jump training and joining the regiment properly, the build-up to and celebration of Camerone, this was a complete shitter. I felt very low, knowing that I – born and bred in crisp northern climes, even if the air around Tyneside was sometimes polluted – was going to suffer badly in tropical conditions. Added to that,

I didn't know anyone here at all. I did, however, know that I would have to get my head sorted out and double quick. This course wouldn't last too long but I knew that if I went into it, and into the jungle, with low morale, it would seem interminable. I had to get enthusiastic about things and look at this as the stepping stone to getting those stripes.

There is a permanent Legion regiment based in French Guyana, the 3eme REI, which has been there since 1973. Their main tasks were to defend the French space centre at Kourou and to maintain surveillance of the borders with Brazil and a lesser known country, Surinam, where a tattered civil war had raged for some years. The war had been escalating for years and, as usual, it concerned borders and disputes about which country owned what land. To my knowledge the dispute is to this day unresolved. The Jungle Commando School is in the heart of the tropical forest and can be reached only by motorized *pirogue,* the main form of transport used by both the Legion and natives in this Jurassic Park-like landscape. This boat is essentially a hollowed-out tree trunk and as these primitive canoes meander slowly along the River Approuage they occasionally disturb bloated floating bodies, a result of the many mercenary operations carried out in the civil war in Surinam. Such sights do not turn the heads of jungle hardened Legionnaires. Nor, indeed, do the smells.

We – this small course of ten students, some of us *1ère Classe* and others *caporals* – had lectures on safety in the jungle before we left the confines of Regina and all its relative comforts. The accommodation was spartan but comfortable enough, in fact palatial compared to where we were going. However, I soon found it tough to adjust to the humidity. Some days it was ninety per cent, and because of my fair skin the sun also bothered me as I tend to burn easily. I had heard that a man who is sunburnt in the jungle can stay that way for many, many months, so deep does the sun penetrate the skin. Daily runs, short distances in terms of length, felt like running a marathon, so draining were they of strength and fluids. I was drinking gallons of water every day but still felt thirsty. The attitude of the instructors was laid back, almost horizontal compared to Castel and Calvi. I wouldn't go as far as to say that I was respected here, but I was treated as an adult and soldier, unlike the previous training when they treated you like an imbecile.

If nothing else came out of these early lectures, they taught us to respect the jungle at all times, to anticipate that it could destroy a man both physically and mentally. The briefing officer was from the 2ème REP, here on attachment. I do not recall his name but I remember straining to absorb everything this lean, tanned and authoritative man said. My French had improved enough to make these vital classes interesting.

The atmosphere at Regina was fairly relaxed, bearing in mind that it was a place of instruction. The permanent staff were more concerned with making sure we were ready to go into the jungle than with giving us the aggressive bullshit which is common on most courses of instruction. Instead of trying to scare the shit out of us with horror stories, they reiterated the need to treat this place with the utmost respect. Learning to work in the jungle was going to be hard enough without unnecessary obstacles being put in the way. We were given all the right jabs, some of which made me feel ill and even hallucinate. I've even been told that these medicines may have influenced my current state of health, but life's too short to consider this very much. Anyway, it was all relatively comfortable there and all too soon, the acclimatization period was over and we made ready to move into the jungle proper and begin the real work. I had paid special attention to the lesson on a tremendous piece of kit, the Global Positioning System, which can pinpoint your position to less than ten metres even in the dense jungle.

The course was to be a gradual build-up to a special three-day exercise deep in the heart of the rainforest. On this exercise we would have limited equipment, no food and be expected to survive for the duration. I couldn't see how I could be completely happy, having being selected for what was, after all, a prestigious course, but living in the vast and mighty animated compost heap before us. The thought of the exercise was both exhilarating and frightening. I felt physically ready for the challenge but was I strong enough mentally?

We moved out from Regina and into the jungle, where we built a small camp and from where we'd be taught more 'on site' skills: building shelters, starting fires and learning how to move without leaving any evidence of having been there. Then there would be the move into the interior of concentrated mass vegetation for the final exercise. Throughout the course we would be watched extremely closely, all the time being examined – every day was a test in itself. This course is recognized as one of the toughest and most demanding of its type in the world. Indeed, both the SAS and American Special Forces have been known to use the school and its facilities, such are the difficult and arduous conditions, particularly the oppressive heat, though I saw no sign of either bunch during my stay. Perhaps their camouflage was too good – entirely possible. Expert jungle fighters can be camouflaged and lie within inches of their pursuers and yet remain completely unnoticed.

All the time one message above all was hammered home: respect. Respect the jungle – it can be your friend or your worst enemy. French Guyana, as far as jungle training goes, is as good as it gets. The country was claimed by the French as far back as 1642 and was seen as a way for France to grab a piece of the South American colonial action that attracted most of Europe's seafaring nations at that time. The French government was keen to gain a foothold there and thus dispatched many of its prisoners to accomplish the hard labour. They built an infrastructure, both in the jungle and on the now legendary Devil's Island. This rocky outcrop had been a brutal penal colony for many decades and France had sent many fearsome criminals into exile there. It was reported that escape was impossible and even if you managed to escape the island, the sea would willingly add you to its collection of victims. Any soul that beat the impossible odds and actually reached land would surely die in the merciless jungle that was their first landfall. Early settlements succumbed to starvation and disease and even the penal colony could not endure the extremely harsh conditions and eventually floundered. Today maladies such as malaria and dysentery are still rife. In the 1950s, amid much international condemnation, the penal colony was closed and the area, almost modern against the jungle background, was handed over to the European Space Agency.

This is a country of French culture, though, and it fiercely resists being enveloped by the rest of South America. In Cayenne, a modern town, croissant shops and Citroën dealerships nudge against more ethnic concerns. The currency (in my time there) was the French franc; the airport has a French name, Rochambeau. No tourist, however, should let the gleaming airport and the smart hotels lull them into a false sense of cleansed security, as just a few kilometres away from Cayenne the jungle sits and waits, untamed.

The Space Centre is very important: almost half the world's commercial satellites are launched from there, including our friend the Astra, responsible for broadcasting Sky TV programmes. When the ultra-modern Ariane rockets streak over this equatorial rainforest, they pass over the hidden, ancient villages of the Arawak and Wayana tribes. Time will tell which culture and civilization proves to last the longer.

Using our *pirogues*, we paddled for about thirty kilometres down river, our bergens tightly packed in the front of the boat, and headed for the training camp, a remote bivouacked shanty village beside the River Approuage and close to the Brazilian border. After just a few strokes of a wooden paddle, I was drenched in sweat and I remained damp at best for the duration of the course. I was perpetually soaked to the skin by sweating in the humidity. One minute I could be almost suffocated by intense heat and the next virtually drowned by one of the torrential downpours of rain that break up the day. Not only was I awash, but my kit was wet as well. Everything, including my sleeping bag, was wet. The whole fucking, stinking jungle was fucking wet.

And the noise. Noise in the jungle can drive a man insane. It is a cacophony of screeching birds, chirping insects and monkeys, I presumed, squealing and screaming. It is incessant, day and night. Some reckon you get used to it but I could never see that day coming for me, even after only a couple of hours of paddling to the camp.

Day two was our first introduction to the perils of the jungle. It was a lesson steeped in legend and even those who have not endured the course, but know of the legend of confronting the 'Beast of Guyana', may be awed by what we had to do next. A German officer, named Walter, I think, showed us what to do when confronted by a boa constrictor snake measuring easily three metres (or did it just seem that long?). We followed Walter into a mosquito-infested swamp and were immediately up to our ankles in foul-smelling mud. I saw this evil serpent for the first time as it reclined semi-submerged in the mud. This creature, which squeezes its prey to death and squashes the bones before eating it, lay in the quagmire of rotting leaves and undergrowth awaiting its next meal. There have been stories of human victims. We stood in a quadrant, none of us wishing to be at the front and all jostling for the furthest position away. Walter pointed to one unfortunate, the rest of us heaved a collective sigh of relief and the victim – sorry, the soldier – stepped forward. As he did so the constrictor stirred, its jaws snapping at the air, hissing and spitting his protest at being wakened. At last it rested back, but was coiled now and ready to launch another attack. Nervous laughter sporadically broke out amongst our group but was silenced when Walter snarled, '*Avec amour!*', 'With love!'

He approached the snake, slowly waving his beret like a hypnotist's pendulum in front of the reptile, approaching quietly and never taking his eyes off it, not for a second. A second Legionnaire, from the instructor's group, snuck up behind the boa and began to tickle its head. Incredible. If I hadn't seen it, there's no way I would have believed it. The huge boa was motionless, immobilized and unrecognizable from the hissing, spitting beast we had witnessed moments earlier. The initial fear now dispelled, we were all quite keen to hold and stroke this monster.

This was an introduction that has been carried out – one might even say staged – for decades and may still be performed to this day, although probably not with the same snake, who could have earned a fortune in appearance fees by now. Everyone who attends the course sees this remarkable demonstration. But there is a serious point to the show and that is a sense that quiet, steady calm in the jungle will more times than not win over brutal toughness. To survive, one must use finesse, not force.

To call the base a camp is a misrepresentation. The word 'camp' gives a false impression, maybe even recalling the order of Raffali. Here it was, in fact, a bamboo hut with a roof made of palm leaves, and raised some four feet off the ground in the middle of a small clearing. That was it. No cookhouse, no latrines. When we went into the jungle proper on exercise we would defecate into plastic bags, place them into our bergens and carry the waste with us. The idea behind this apparently disgusting action is that you leave no trace whatsoever of your presence in the bush. An expert tracker will notice that the earth has been moved and will discover the excrement, thereby giving clues as to who has been there and how long ago. It could lead to your death so, as ever, nothing is left to chance. For the duration of the course we would live in a self-constructed A-frame shelter, using a poncho and any lengths of wood that came to hand. The whole thing was put together using rope and bungees, ensuring that it was at least two feet off the ground, thereby keeping away the scorpions, ants and other crawling beasts who liked nothing better than to feast on sleeping Legionnaires during the night. We were given a couple of hours to sort our shelters out and stow away any kit before the instructors explained our routine and how we would be spending the days there.

By the time I had been in the jungle for two days I smelt like a decomposing corpse. It is thought that a soldier's morale will drop fast after the first forty-eight hours in the jungle and, unless caught in time, the soldier will go downhill very quickly, to the point of losing his mind. A place to sleep and clean, dry kit are vital in keeping soldiers' morale high.

I had already lost a good part of the battle because my kit was damp. But I made sure my A-frame was solid and above the ground and that it wouldn't collapse the minute I laid my weary body upon it.

'The most important equipment you will carry are your FAMAS, your machete and the *brouillage* [webbing belt]. Never go anywhere, even for a shit, without these things. The machete will be your friend. You will build with it, kill for food with it and it gets you out of the shit in the jungle. Never leave it, not for one second.' This was the opening lecture we received and was one the instructors reminded us of constantly. 'You will be severely punished for not obeying this command. And never leave the camp [we sniggered at this description] on your own. Always take another person with you, even for a shit. You can become lost and disorientated in a short time here in the jungle. Everything, every tree, looks the same. Now, pay attention, so I can tell you what you can and what you can't eat from the jungle.'

As attentive and interested as I was, it was impossible to concentrate fully on all this. I and my fellow students were under airborne attack from mosquitoes and countless other flying disease carriers. A constant tattoo of slapping noises, as we swatted these infernal creatures, made us sound more like an appreciative audience than a class of soldiers learning how to survive in a hostile environment. The insect repellent we had been issued with must have been the icing on the cake for the insects which hummed and buzzed around us constantly: far from deterring them they seemed to love the taste and couldn't get enough of it. The back of my neck must have been particularly delicious as I was attacked there mercilessly, and any uncovered area of skin was now a lumpy mass of open bites, each weeping and ripe for infection. Sweat dripped into the open sores, the salt stinging as it entered the wound. It dripped into my eyes, causing them to sting as well.

I was severely pissed off, very uncomfortable and I could feel myself sinking. I was in that period where my morale could spiral helplessly downwards and I knew I would have to make a massive effort to retain interest in the course, thereby keeping me alert and alive. I didn't want to give in and anyway, pulling out of the course just wasn't an option. Completing it would look good on my service record but I knew deep down that this would be the last time I would have anything to do with the jungle. Legionnaires volunteer to serve here and there are always more volunteers than vacancies, if only for the enhanced pay. They deserve every franc; I would have to be dragged kicking and screaming back here. I reminded myself that no one had said it would be easy.

The jungle, we were informed, was full of food; all good nourishing stuff and chock-a-block with proteins. From the humble beetle to the bark of a tree, it was all there, just waiting to be discovered and utilized. There is a simple test to perform to see if anything you find is suitable to eat. You just rub the item onto your skin and look to see if there is any allergic reaction: a rash or spots breaking out. If not, rub it onto your lips, wait a while and then taste it with the tip of your tongue. If you experience no problems, then eat a little, if no reaction, take a chance and wolf the whole thing down. This may sound fussy but it could be the difference between eating something healthy or being poisoned. You choose. I can't actually remember tasting anything nice or nasty. Whatever it was, I tried to swallow it whole and wash it down with a mouthful of water. We were told to forget eating lizards or snakes. For one thing, the energy expended in catching them was far more than the energy received from the prey and thus a pointless exercise. Also, they are more inclined to give the recipient belly ache and/or the shits and the jungle is no place to go down with either of those. But everything we could possibly need to live on was here in the jungle: bamboo and trees for shelter, wood to burn for fire, fruit and vegetables to eat and fluids to drink, if you knew where to look and how to utilize them.

Inside the canopy of the jungle, beneath the thick tree tops, was another world of darkness and claustrophobia. Huge trees that seemed to climb ever upwards blocked out the sun's rays completely, save for the occasional break where glimmering shafts would stream through and cause the dampness on the foliage to evaporate. The wispy steam that rose towards the sky added to the prehistoric atmosphere. The humidity was stifling inside the canopy and sapped the energy from your body. Even the slightest movement caused breathlessness. So far we had learned only to look after ourselves. The next lesson would be even tougher – learning how to patrol and fight in the jungle, how to ascertain your position should you become separated or lost and how to make it back to camp.

As rookie *caporals* it would be unusual for us to do any operational navigating in the jungle. That would be left to the more experienced *caporal-chefs* or sergeants who used the Global Positioning System for navigation. This thing can tell you your position, accurate to a few metres, anywhere in the world. We had to prepare for any eventuality though, so we had lessons in its use. We might just have to lead the section if all the NCOs and officers were killed. During this stage of training we were to combine patrolling with navigation, while using live ammunition on a close-quarter battle range. Now this was certainly more to my liking.

The canopy hid the morning sun from us but you could tell it had risen as the early muggy and damp heat intensified. One day we were practising recce patrols in teams of six with one of our instructors to make up the numbers. Before we set off the staff reminded us of safety procedures – pretty much standard operational routines. Should a man become lost or separated he must try to get back to the last rendezvous (RV). If that failed or he still had no idea of where he was, he should stay still, set up a defensive area and protect it. It is much easier to find and rescue someone who is standing still, rather than a man blundering around the bush.

We set off, very slowly and deliberately. Moving through the jungle is not like being Indiana Jones, lashing out with a machete and wiping out acre after acre of vegetation. The ideal way is to be so careful as to make it appear that the ground has been untouched by human hand or foot.

Stealthily moving through the jungle so as not to let the enemy know of your presence is tiring, both physically and mentally. It is never advisable to use the high ground. Although clearer of the vegetation you will encounter at the bottom of a ravine, the high ground is where most ambushes would be laid, and all but the cleverest enemy who has second-guessed you will use tracks or clearings in the jungle as their killing zones.

After only a few minutes we were ordered to halt in a small clearing. We sat and listened. Above the usual jungle commotion the only discernible sound was that of us Legionnaires and our heavy breathing, even though we had only just begun the patrol. Suddenly a tremendous noise, like a farmer's shotgun being discharged, shook the small clearing. Birds, their wings flapping in double time, flew upwards away from impending danger, while other creatures unable to flee so quickly screeched and squawked their alarm calls as they scurried along the ground. A twenty-second flurry of intense activity died down and we were left to ponder just what the fuck had happened. A grinning instructor appeared from behind a tree carrying two pieces of dead bamboo. He had snapped the bamboo as we had sat in the clearing. The point of the demonstration was to reiterate how noise is carried in the jungle and that any unusual noise will send hundreds of animals scattering. This would alert any potential enemy to your presence. If any one of us had inadvertently stood on that bamboo while on patrol, noise like gunfire would have been heard for miles.

Stealth is the key word when moving along the jungle floor. A potential booby trap can be anywhere, compromising the patrol or even worse, killing a patrol member. Walking through the thick vegetation is hard enough on its own. We had to go through the stuff and leave it as if nobody had been there. Any enemy following you will be on the look-out for any signs of disturbance. Broken branches, leaves turned over and even disturbed spiders' webs give away the fact that someone has passed through recently. To cover even the shortest distance could take hours of energy-sapping effort. We were reminded that even one dead and rotting leaf is classed as an obstruction, and not to crash through the wood and trees. The golden rule when patrolling the jungle is to move an obstruction out of the way, pass through it and then replace it.

We had to regularly stop and check our position. It was not enough to rely on compass bearings and there were few ground features that you could orientate your map to. I was pleased that I had learned map reading back in the UK: it is a difficult skill to acquire anyway, never mind out here in the jungle where everything looks the same. I am sure that the fact that I could read a map and navigate, which had come out during my interviews with the *Deuxième Bureau* all those months ago, had a great bearing on my selection for this course.

'Why can't we use the Global Positioning System?' someone cried as fatigue overcame him. Our instructor replied with a glare that could have stopped a charging rhino. The student went very quiet, hoping no doubt that the jungle would open up and swallow him whole. Having equipment like the GPS was great, but we had to be able to work out locations manually in case the equipment was lost or damaged. So much to learn.

That night, when we returned to base camp, I was absolutely shattered. Even though we were not covering any great distance on the patrols, it seemed to be much harder work even than basic training. You were on constant alert, careful so as not to damage any vegetation, looking for any enemy or signs of enemy. Carefully placed targets behind trees or in the undergrowth could spring up at any time, at the press of a switch the instructors carried. We had to be watchful for the ever-present threat of killer snakes and even keeping a bead on the instructors was tiring. We could cook on open fires for now and all around the camp plumes of smoke spiralled upwards. The normal dank and musty smell of decaying greenery was replaced by the far more pleasant aromas of ration packs being boiled up. The stewed meat and potatoes were bloody delicious and I didn't care what kind of meat it was. It was a time to get hot scoff down you, drink plenty of fluids and sort out any medical problems. I had a few mozzie bites that had gone septic and horrible sores on the inside of my thighs where the constant abrasive rubbing of my damp trousers had worn away the skin. I didn't want these to get out of hand, so I tended to them with a good clean and applied some cream that I had managed to cadge from one of the medics back at Raffali. It is really quite astonishing how much your morale is lifted by a bellyful of hot food, some clean (even if not completely dry) socks and underwear. Actual cost, pennies. Benefit, immeasurable.

Even after just a couple of days we were very dirty, our faces ingrained with camouflage cream and unshaven. We must have stunk although when a whole team is equally rank no one notices. They say that people on the ground practically pass out from the fumes when astronauts exit their capsule but none of the space cadets ever notice a stench while they're up in space. Anyway, glorious soldiering this was not. I often asked myself how people could live and exist in such terrible conditions, but again, if this is all you are used to, it isn't really a problem. I knew this type of combat wasn't for me though. I felt as if I was under observation 24/7, if not from instructors then from God knows what types of creature that were lurking in the dense thickness of vegetation all around me.

We practised with a considerable number of patrols and their differing drills. We learned how to get out of an ambush, firstly by locating the enemy and laying down as much fire as you can in his direction. Once his head is down, and it will be unless he is already dead, you move and fire, covering each other's advance until you have overrun the enemy's position. Then you regroup, check casualties and reorganize. It depends on the number and type of casualties whether the patrol continues, or helicopters are called into predesignated landing sites for evacuation of the wounded. It would have to be a pretty serious contact, sustaining many casualties, for a mission to be abandoned. Observation posts were set up almost within touching distance of our targets, sometimes as close as twenty metres away, and we learned how to patrol in teams of two, four and six.

Transporting injured comrades away from the danger area and how to tend to them without being killed oneself, became second nature. At Castel we had been taught basic first aid and how to treat battlefield injuries. Stabilizing the casualty is your first priority, making sure he is breathing and doing your best to stem any blood loss. Reassuring your stricken comrade and getting him to a place of safety, while avoiding becoming a target yourself, is no easy task, but it is something you do without thinking of the danger. All that you have time for in a firefight is to put a dressing over the wound and hope that stops the bleeding. We had been taught mouth to mouth resuscitation and how to give morphine injections, not forgetting to mark the casualty's forehead with a large letter M. This is to let the medics at the hospital know that he has had a dose of the good stuff. This letter is usually written with the only fluid available: the casualty's own blood. There isn't a great deal else you can do when under fire except make your comrade as comfortable as possible, bearing in mind that your own life is in danger and the mission has still to be accomplished. I could see the reasoning behind the attachment of Legionnaire medics at the hospital at Castel, but remember my Canadian friend? The best way to learn anything is to do it for yourself.

The pressure was intense and ceaseless. Instructors attacked us verbally during meal times and sometimes we would be forced to crash out of the camp at one o'clock in the morning when the instructors launched a surprise attack. There simply wasn't the time or opportunity for the occasional laugh we'd enjoyed at Calvi. We didn't even have the time to really get to know one another on this course. Everyone treated the others there as professional soldiers, each knowing what their job was and what was expected of them. We each knew what was required of us and that it slotted into the overall team picture, leaving no room for loners or people wanting to do their own thing.

There was no respite at night and thus very little sleep. This wasn't always the instructors' fault but that of those bastard mosquitoes. As we were near a river there were swarms of them. Thinking about it, maybe the instructors were to blame after all because they chose the locality of the camp in the first place, the devious buggers. Darkness would envelop the camp early, coming without warning, like someone extinguishing a light; it could be as quick as that. You could quite clearly see the advance party of mosquitoes hovering close to the hurricane lamp near the instructors' side of the camp. Those mozzies were doing my head in. The main squadron of flying parasites, thousands of them, advanced to our position and nothing could stop them. You would swat at them, but still they came. Whining (and indeed dining) and buzzing and stinging, they excelled at making vicious nuisances of themselves and depriving us of sleep. Each wound inflicted by these tiny terrorists of the night was a potential septic puncture waiting to flare up and cause untold misery. Every morning, as the sun struggled to break through the dense tree cover, one of those imponderable questions came to mind: last night there were tens of thousands of mosquitoes, creating a cloud above us, a cloud that would not disperse, no matter what you threw at it. Now they had vanished so where did all the little bastards go?

We faced other dangers while out on patrol. There were weeds and vines that attached themselves to other vegetation. They were bramble-like with thorns and had small but nasty spikes which could become attached to the skin and clothing as you brushed past. They dug into the flesh and because of the angle of insertion, the more you pulled and struggled with them, the deeper they got embedded. It was important to resist the overwhelming and natural temptation to simply rip them away as such impatience could easily lead to skin torn to shreds. Then there would be open wounds on the body which in turn could very quickly become infected.

Although I never saw it on this course, another potential problem is a psychological one, for men can go crazy whilst in the jungle. Living in shit, some people try to fight it and become clean. This is impossible, as well as being tactically naive. The shit in the jungle will always come back and envelope you. Don't fight the dirt, use it and live with it. A scruffy soldier in the jungle will always survive. No washing, except to clean wounds. Accept that you must smell like the jungle, not like a make-up counter in a department store. You can always degunge after the operation – this disgusting personal lapse isn't for ever. The perpetual darkness and half-light gets to people as well. They feel enclosed all the time. Although, according to your body clock, it is daytime, it is never quite light as the jungle canopy is so opaque. Occasionally, a single beam of light will shine through, as if a Holy Grail has been found, but you never actually see the sky or clouds or the sun. That deprivation becomes a torture for some people, just as a slowly dripping tap can wear away at nerves.

Eventually the instructors decided that we were ready for the final exercise – that three-day survival test. We were given only basic equipment: a fishing line, FAMAS with ten rounds of live ammunition, a hook, the invaluable machete and three matches, one for each day. A thorough body search was carried out before we were set loose to ensure no cheating. We would eat whatever we managed to catch or scavenge and drink whatever we could collect. This was to be a real test of physical and mental endurance. And we would be observed...

As we set off into the wilderness, one by one we were tapped on the shoulder by an instructor as the signal to drop away from the rest of the section and begin the exercise. I was the fourth to drop away and although we seemed to be in an area of only fifty square metres, once you were on your own, that was it. No last minute advice, no wishes of good luck. You simply melted into the bush. The sounds of the section moving away quickly disappeared and were replaced by the incessant chatter of jungle wildlife. We were in their territory and I don't think they liked that one little bit.

The first and most important task was to construct a shelter. I chose somewhere that I thought had good drainage, on a slope so the rain ran away from me. Then I set about collecting the wood to make somewhere to rest. I made the shelter with two long pieces of bamboo slung between two trees, using vines as rope, with long, very leathery leaves that were incredibly strong, fixed as a base. This may sound a bit Robinson Crusoe, but it was very effective. I didn't bother with a cover as I knew it would inevitably rain and as I was already wet through it wouldn't make any difference. No point in using energy when there's no need to. Also, I found the downpour of rain very refreshing in this stifling heat. As darkness fell, I thought about making a fire. The whole course was in a fairly small area but we had been told to work individually. I wasn't going to take any chances, knowing how good the instructor's concealment skills were; they could be anywhere, watching and noting how we performed.

My stomach had shrunk. We hadn't eaten a wholesome meal for what seemed like weeks so it didn't take very much to make me feel quite stuffed. With some fruit I had managed to retrieve from the ground and some nice, healthy grubs I had dislodged from a fungal growth under a fallen tree, added to the earthworms I had stashed away earlier, I had quite a little buffet meal for myself. I took several deep breaths and built up the courage to eat these creatures of the earth. Even before the first had passed my lips, I began to gag and wretch. But I was very hungry and I had to have something, anything and in a flash, I threw a few bugs into my open mouth and swallowed. It wasn't as bad as I had feared; they had no taste – well, I had just swallowed them whole and never gave it a chance. The first hurdle had been crossed and I had done it: eaten worms like I was a six-year-old trying to frighten my sister. When a man is hungry he will eat anything, just to survive.

This was purely a survival exercise so it didn't matter about the fires or the noise we made as we stumbled around. But the instructors were trying to see what we were made of, and I figured that lighting a fire could be seen as a sign of weakness. As much as I disliked the course and the jungle, I didn't want to fail the course or receive a dodgy report to take back to Calvi. The Legion didn't expect us to be expert jungle fighters after this brief course, but it was designed to give us an insight as to what we could expect to come across in similar circumstances. We could now also pass on vital lessons to comrades who had not experienced such hostile conditions.

As darkness fell I lay on my 'bed' and tried to catch up on the lack of sleep I had suffered recently. I kept my boots on, nervous of the stories I had heard about beasties climbing into them during the night and the consequences that followed the next morning. I didn't fancy a foot-long centipede curled up in the warm confines of my toe caps waiting to bite into and then hold onto my foot the next day. Scorpions also love the musty, warm atmosphere of a discarded boot as it lies by someone's bed. No, once I'd inspected my feet, my boots remained firmly laced on. I was also pleased that I had raised my bed off the jungle floor; there were so many indescribable creatures just waiting to bite or sting you. If your bed wasn't raised, you spent the night worrying exactly what the horrible beasts were going to do, and then couldn't sleep anyway. Even with my bed raised, I still bloody worried about what might crawl into any orifice I hadn't covered. I cuddled, yes cuddled, my FAMAS and with an accompanying lullaby of chirping, squeaking and clicking noises, I fell asleep.

Shouting and swearing woke me early on Day Two. I rubbed my eyes. One of them felt especially gritty and sure enough something had found a bed for the night in my eyebrow and I found I had rubbed it and all its poison into my eyeball. That morning reflex of eye-rubbing was a big mistake. Some unknown beast had kipped in my eyebrow and I had squashed the shagging thing all over my eyes. But there were no nasty effects, so it couldn't have been that dangerous. It transpired that a comrade on the far side of the encampment had woken to discover his FAMAS had been taken during the night, obviously by one of the instructors. The kid, a Spanish lad, was beside himself with worry and panic. There was little we could do but begin a search of the immediate area in a hopeless attempt to find it. We had all guessed what had really happened and I felt that we were only trying to make ourselves look better by mounting this futile search. The instructors had it, they were watching us and, I have no doubt, were sadistically enjoying themselves.

After about an hour of floundering, unsuccessfully looking for the missing weapon, an instructor broke his cover and showed himself. The FAMAS was returned to its owner and he left without saying a word. As far as our Spanish friend was concerned, he had gotten away with it and could continue the exercise. He was clearly overjoyed but I and a few others knew that he wouldn't get good news when we returned to Regina at the conclusion of the exercise. It was an obvious fail.

We muddled through the next days, more by luck than skill, and before we knew it, the exercise was called to a halt. I had lost track of time and didn't know what day it was. In the semi-darkness of the jungle, time had no meaning. I had spent entire days looking for food, just to survive from one meal to the next. I ate when I could and what I could. I was completely exhausted. I had been conscious of every single movement or sound I heard. Was it a beast? Or was it an instructor watching my every move? I had become a little paranoid, I feared.

We were by no means as robust as when we started the course, all of us even leaner, having burnt off any excess fat and not having eaten a substantial meal for weeks. Our pasty, white bodies hadn't seen the sun for days because we had been permanently under the forest canopy. Skin that was visible was obscenely scarred from bites and stings. Dirt was ingrained under our now suppurating scabs. Everyone had deep-sunken eyes, cheek and jawbones were prominent. This was after only two weeks; I don't think I could have stood it for any longer. I was elated to be on the way out and back to civilization. If ever, in all my Legion years, I'd been tempted to request a transfer it would have been from here. But honour prevented me from even thinking of bottling out.

No matter how many times I washed and shaved I couldn't rid myself of all the dirt on my hands, face and neck. I thought I would be left with a permanent reminder of my days in the jungle. The kit I had used was only fit for burning, the boots so rotten they almost fell apart in my hands. It took a couple of days to clean and return all the kit. We sat in a lecture room two weeks later and were told that we had all passed, even the Spanish lad. He was beaming until he was told that he would have to complete the survival exercise again. He thought it a big joke and began laughing. It suddenly dawned on him that he was the only one laughing, the instructor being completely serious. He would have to go through it all over again, so I don't really understand why they told him he'd passed. I am sure that I saw tears in that kid's eyes.

After this we all went outside and intended to feast upon a barbecue and loads of beer. I had one piece of chicken, three bottles of beer and then threw up on the ground. It would take some time, I feared, for my stomach to become accustomed to receiving proper food again.

Although I knew I had passed the course, I wasn't naive enough to imagine I had done particularly well. I must have only just passed, simply not giving the instructors enough reason to fail me. It had probably been noted that I had detested the jungle, every second of it. I hated the feeling of being perpetually wet, the dirt, the filth and the incessant noise. For me it had no redeeming graces whatsoever. I'd felt like an animal, dehumanized and basic.

CHAPTER ELEVEN

RESCUE IN RWANDA

WAVE AFTER WAVE OF RELIEF POURED over me as the aircraft touched down onto the airstrip at Calvi. I was so pleased to be 'home' and away from my jungle nightmare. I was looking forward to seeing Steve and the other lads and catching up with all the latest news, particularly about Steve's love life. And I was really looking forward to renewing my association with some Kronenbourg. There was some administration to be completed in the Adjutant's office on my first day back. It included receiving mail that had arrived for me whilst I had been in Guyana. There was a letter from my parents; although they could not and would not accept what I had done, they didn't want to break off all contact with me, which was a great relief. I would write regularly from now on, I swore to myself.

But this felt like my home now, so much had I taken Camp Raffali to heart. It was late September, still pleasantly warm and the sun shone brilliantly. A wind, nicknamed 'Traumantin', blew in from the northern Po Valley in Italy, taking the edge off a potentially extreme heat. We got used to the various winds that affected Corsica. Nice in summer but in winter, the same wind can cut through you like a swordsman's blade.

'Spider!' The nickname had been given to me because of the coincidence between my Legion-bestowed name and a certain cartoon super-hero. Hard to believe it was a year since Parris went to Paris and became Parker...

'You fat bastard,' yelled Steve from across the parade square, 'too many cake shops in the jungle, I see.' I hadn't realized just how thin I had become. I must have lost between two and three stones.

'Aye, good to see you too. Hope you get some sexually transmitted disease before Michelle arrives,' was the only reply I could think of, unfunny as it undoubtedly was.

'What was it like then?'

'Fucking horrible. Wet, dark and fucking wet. I hated every fucking minute of it.'

'Yeah, well if you can't take a joke, you shouldn't have joined.'

Odd, how men sometimes express friendship. There wasn't much more to be said. He went off to weapon training and I headed somewhere else. I never told him, but it was really great to see him again. I felt normality was returning at long last.

That same evening, I sat with Steve and some of the other troops, drinking and singing. I found it quite peculiar to be among ordinary people again; although none of the men that sat with me could be described as ordinary. We were all clean-shaven, wore neatly pressed uniform and smelt fresh. If some of the boys had slightly overdone it on the aftershave I wasn't complaining after the stenches of Guyana. I wasn't soaked with sweat, nor swatting away at indescribable flying insects, real or imaginary. When my eyes flitted upwards, I could see the sky and the stars and it was beautiful. Steve was ecstatic that night. His potential girlfriend, Michelle, was arriving the following week for a holiday. Our intake had now been granted permission to leave the camp and go into town. Tomorrow we would head off for the first time, in uniform and with a pocketful of dosh after going to the cashier's office to draw wages. I couldn't wait.

It was a wonderfully balmy night as we strolled down the narrow cobbled street that leads from the Citadel towards town. As we passed cafés, we attracted little or no attention, so used were the people of Calvi to the Legion. I was nonetheless slightly disappointed. I had wanted someone to at least acknowledge that I was there. All that bloody training and suffering, and nobody gave a toss. Great. I fought off this self-pity and concentrated on the pleasures of the evening to come.

Calvi, in some respects, is no different from other garrison towns the world over. The Corsicans had their bars where they drank and played cards, while the Legion had their own particular watering holes. Nothing sinister in it, just the way it is. I felt rather like a tourist, wandering past the bars and cafés, stopping occasionally to watch the locals as arguments suddenly erupted over a game. Loud shouts soon gave way to quieter mumbling and Gallic shrugs of the shoulders.

We walked down the Boulevard Wilson and headed for the Café Select, a popular Legion bar. Thumping music could be heard some distance from the bar and our step involuntarily quickened. A record by the Communards, 'Don't leave me this way', was belting out and I remembered it was one of the last records I had heard before I left England. A bunch of us from the regiment had been in a local town and when this particular song came on the lads jumped up on to the bar tables and began dancing on them. We were asked to leave by the landlord, once he had turned the music off, and it was with this thought that I approached the bar tonight. It struck me at that point that I couldn't remember the last time I had heard a news broadcast or seen an English newspaper. I felt like I had been ostracized from society. I had no idea what was happening outside of the world I was now in. It was if nothing else mattered except this haven called the Legion. I vowed that I would buy myself a radio soonest, so I could at least listen to the BBC. Those thoughts didn't bother me too much, it was just a bit strange for a short while. Anyway, there was beer to be drunk, so I pushed the images of England to the back of my mind.

Entering the dark room, we were greeted by blasting music, flashing lights and the buzz of loud conversation. The huge room was packed with Legionnaires and a surprisingly large number of women. What looked like a fairly serious game of pool was taking place in the far corner; there were piles of banknotes on the side of the table and the players' faces were contorted in concentration. Nobody appeared to take any notice of us as we forced our way through the crowd to the bar. I had had this ghastly apparition of everything coming to a halt as we entered the bar, like in a Clint Eastwood film. Music stops, conversations are halted mid stream and everybody turns and stares. Thank God no one noticed us.

As we sipped beer from the bottle I could see through the smoky haze that the women were young, pretty and well dressed. You could tell that they knew their way around a Legion bar, such was their aura of confidence. They were so confident in fact, that they were slightly intimidating and anyway, I wasn't particularly interested. I hadn't ever been very good at approaching women and the last thing I wanted to do was make a fool of myself in front of all these Legionnaires, or worse, face rejection again as I had been rejected in England. I had to stop myself thinking too much or else I could have slipped into depression, because I did have a lump in my throat and a heavy heart right then. So I did what soldiers do best, I ordered some more beer. The two of us stood back and drank both the beer and the atmosphere. It was boisterous to say the least and I suppose to any civilian walking in the atmosphere could be intimidating, almost frightening. That is why they had their bars and we had ours.

A few beers later Steve suggested we try another bar, Au Son des Guitares, which advertised itself as *La Maison de Légionnaire*, and so off we staggered. Again the place was packed with Legionnaires and women. We were talking, above the din of loud music, to an experienced NCO, who warned us off some of the all-too-willing ladies who confronted us. They were, for the most part, predatory Legionnaire hunters, mainly Italian and Scandinavian, but from other European countries too, ladies who leave their husbands and head for Corsica and a fortnight of rampant sex. Some, he told us, his words slurred from beer and cognac, have their fun and go home. Others, well, they couldn't for one reason or another, and simply hated to leave the fun behind, which could lead to difficult situations. They, when they returned for their Legionnaire, may find he was now someone else's. Whether he was taking the piss, I didn't know. But, looking out from this bar, situated on a hillside overlooking the calm Bay of Calvi on a warm night with a full moon, well, anything could happen, couldn't it? I wondered how this atmosphere would affect Steve and his impending date with destiny. Alas, poor Steve was not to discover the answer to these romantic notions, not this time anyway.

We paraded next morning to a distinctly different atmosphere at Camp Raffali. The camp was a hive of activity, with people rushing about with a definite sense of urgency. You could feel it in the air, something was up. Something big was definitely kicking off.

We were put on twenty-four hour alert to go to Rwanda. Where the fuck was Rwanda? I had never heard of the place. Pretty soon I knew it was in central Africa. After a brief parade and no inspection, which was very unusual, everyone was dismissed. We all dashed back to the block to check kit and go to the stores to draw any specialist kit we might need. Excitement and anticipation quivered through the air. At this stage, however, I didn't know exactly where we were going or why. All sorts of theories flew around. The boys were really up for it, whatever it was.

After lunch our company, plus quite a few others from other companies, remained in the *réfectoire*, a huge cinema screen filling one complete end of the hall. The Commanding Officer walked in with slow purpose. We all snapped immediately to attention and a hush descended. It was like sitting in church. The lights went out and simultaneously the screen lit up. Two words filled the screen. *Operation Noroit* (Operation

North-west Wind). The CO spoke first in French and the *Adjudant* repeated in English moments later. Now I knew this was going to be huge, dealing with a rescue mission in Rwanda. The Commanding Officer reiterated the importance of getting the French nationals out of this place which had ignited into a dangerous hot spot and he stressed that we, as a regiment, must act correctly and properly at every stage. He wanted us all to come back to Calvi safely, with reputation and honour enhanced.

A series of brutal and bloody clashes between the Hutu and Tutsi tribes in Rwanda had become so severe that white foreigners in the country feared for their lives. Large-scale ethnic massacres were forecast and it appeared that the whole country was about to slide into complete anarchy and that a civil war was ready to erupt. Intelligence reported that after being exiled for nigh on thirty years, the Tutsis were now rearmed, allegedly by Idi Amin's regime in neighbouring Uganda, and were moving on to the capital city, Kigali. Anything or anyone that wasn't Tutsi was being destroyed or killed as the rebels made their way to claim what they thought was rightfully theirs. There were some 700 French nationals in the country and we were going to get them out.

The up-to-date intelligence read out did not make for pleasant listening. The Tutsis, although single-minded in their aim, were totally disorganized and were operating in groups of twenty to thirty strong. There was no cohesion between the groups and the only common tactic they appeared to have was to slaughter anything or anyone in their way. There did not appear to be a tribe leader and these small but brutal groups were behaving exactly as they pleased, killing, raping and looting as they went. It was emphatically forced upon us that we were not there to police the country but simply to get the French nationals out to safety as quickly as possible. Our rules of engagement, when we could legally open fire, would be given later but it was emphasized that if we or a national were not under actual threat or fear of death, then we did not open fire. This was going to be a very difficult and potentially hazardous operation. The Legion's quick reaction capability made it a natural choice for missions of this type. The fact that it can sustain casualties with no political fallout is another consideration. Only his comrades weep for a fallen Legionnaire. There are never grieving relatives banging on politicians' doors demanding to know why their kin died in some forsaken far-off country. The Legion will go in hard and fast, achieve the objective and return, hopefully without fatalities, to barracks where it waits until summoned again.

Once the CO had given his brief outline we went off into individual platoons and sections for a more detailed brief about exactly what our role in this operation was to be. Going with us would be the Legion's Special Forces, the *Commandos de Recherche et d'Action en le Profondeur.* No proud and feared combat unit should have to go to war with the acronym CRAP, surely? There have been, allegedly, many heads scratched and hours wasted attempting to rewrite the name, all to no avail. One would imagine that these things would be thought out – but I never heard of anyone going to the unit and saying, 'By the way, do you know you're crap?'

The operation was going to be in two stages. First, we would be flown to a town called Bouar in the Central African Republic where we would have time to rehearse and practise the second stage, the actual rescue mission. My platoon was to secure the airport including the control tower, while other units would rush straight to the French Embassy and the French school in Kigali, the capital. Once the operation began, speed was of the essence. We had been warned that the Tutsis were not well organized and had little discipline. This could make them more dangerous because they were not answerable to anyone and could virtually do what they liked. Reports were coming in of rogue elements butchering opposition soldiers in the streets and in front of women and children. Sometimes even those women and children would feel the sharpened edge of a machete. They were left in the road lying in pools of their own blood. The killers had no conscience and no sense of right and wrong. There was no concept of law and order and normal rules of civilization had no meaning.

Seasoned Legion veterans were horrified by the tales of barbarity that were coming from this place. I too was horrified by what I could expect to witness and also feared that I would be worse than useless when it came to ignoring whatever barbarous acts I saw and having to walk on by. We would be there only to rescue French nationals. Anyone else would have to fend for themselves.

Personal kit was checked and rechecked as the build-up progressed rapidly. Each platoon, each section, gathered in lecture rooms to be given up-to-the-minute situation reports and details of our duties once we hit the ground. We'd rather hoped that we could parachute into Kigali, thereby emulating our comrades from the late 1970s who dropped into Kolwezi, Zaire, and executed one of the most famous rescue missions of our time.

May 1978 has gone down in the annals of Legion history and folklore. Operation Bonite was commanded by a Colonel Erulin, a veteran of the Algerian conflict. The mission was straightforward: to rescue almost 2,500 Europeans and Zaire nationals threatened with massacre by the 'Tigers', *Front de Libération Nationale Congolais* (FLNC), and put an end to the threat to the town and surrounding areas imposed by these so-called rebels. Assistance in transporting equipment was provided by the American Air Force under an agreement with the US Government. A Belgian commando unit was also being prepared but political argument delayed their arrival. French civilian lives were at risk and a personal plea for help from the President, Mobuto Sese Banga, hardened the French resolve and they decided to act on their own.

Africa was in turmoil during the late 1970s. The Cold War was supposed to be long over, but in reality the superpowers were attempting to gain influence wherever they could in this vast continent. Agents under various disguises, military advisers from the Eastern bloc, supplied the 'Katangais' with all types of weapons and equipment, actively encouraging them to attack the mineral-rich region of the Shaba Province. Its strategic position and wealth of minerals such as zinc, uranium, diamonds and copper made it the ultimate prize. The French, aided by the Belgians and Americans, rallied to the aid of President Mobuto. Zaire's huge francophone population and position within an unstable Africa was seen as an important cornerstone in keeping the continent non-communist. Who could the French High Command rely on to respond quickly and effectively to such a dangerous situation? The Legion's 2ème REP was tasked immediately. One of its sub-units was already in Africa, assisting Chad to halt the many incursions into its territory by neighbouring Libya. Although practised and exercised many times, when the alert was raised, mid morning on 17 May 1978, everybody knew this was to be the real thing.

A siren had blasted from the camp on Corsica, and Calvi burst into action as duty PM (*Police Militaire*) patrols in town passed on the vital messages. Within a matter of hours, the regiment was mobilized. A small fleet of commercial aircraft had been commandeered and early the following morning the advance party left Corsica for a long flight into a combat mission 4,000 miles from their base. This on its own was a remarkable logistical feat.

As the Legionnaires parachuted into Kolwezi only the rescue of the nationals was on their minds, but they soon became embroiled in bitter house-to-house fighting and inevitably took casualties. The enemy were not ancient tribesmen who believed that bangles, body paint and spears would defeat their foes. These were well-trained, well-motivated and extremely well-armed soldiers. Although on the back foot from the sudden appearance and aggressive tactics of the REP, they soon reorganized and launched vicious counter-attacks. The following day, a second drop of Legionnaires arrived and ground taken was consolidated. Over the next forty-eight hours, other units, including a Belgian Army unit, arrived in Kolwezi. They continued the evacuation, while the 2ème REP maintained their task of clearing up the remaining groups of Tiger rebels. Occasional and isolated fighting continued until the end of May and by the 27th, the regiment had regrouped at Lubumbashi, mission completed. The surviving Europeans – some 190 had been killed by the Tigers and a further forty who had been held hostage were later discovered to have been murdered – were transported away from Zaire by US aircraft and it was aboard US Airforce Starlifter aircraft that the 2ème REP were repatriated to Calvi. It had been a very impressive victory. Reports indicated that the rebel forces had fled over the border into Marxist Angola and an African multi-force was on its way to relieve the Legionnaires

The success of the mission was due to many factors, not least of which was the superb physical condition of those involved. A long flight, then waiting in baking heat in a holding area with the inevitable tension and stress of what was effectively a combat jump into completely unknown territory, all contributed to enduring fatigue. Along with the success came a number of problems, some logistical and others caused by thoroughly bad communications, delays and orders immediately followed by counter-orders. A detailed analysis of the whole operation provided a checklist for improvements to be instigated when the regiment was next called into action.

This is not an exact examination of that mission: I do not have the expertise or knowledge to cast any opinion on its political consequences. I merely wished to write something here about 2ème REP's glorious record in being able to respond to, evaluate and execute missions of this nature at short notice, under any circumstances and in any theatre of operation. The experiences of some of those officers still at Raffali meant that when we received our orders to go to Rwanda we were going with troops whose calm savvy and basic knowledge would prove invaluable to the rest of us – a bit like the Legion's trust that my jungle training could prove to be valuable with rookies during a tropical assignment at some point, I guess.

Training intensified over the next couple of days. We practised live firing until I thought the barrel would melt on my rifle, we studied patrolling techniques in built-up areas, anti-ambush drills and first aid, i.e. how to stop bleeding, keeping the wound free from infection and how to treat a casualty who is in shock. Most fatalities are caused not by the actual bullet wound but by the body going into shock and effectively closing down. The casualty has to be kept warm, reassured (even if his condition is hopeless) and conscious. Resuscitation skills, mouth to mouth, and the treatment of broken and shattered limbs were practised.

There was a derelict, unfinished holiday village on the road from Calvi to Raffali. Scant regard for local planning regulations had been observed by the owner and halfway through the project he was told to stop. The Legion took the site over and we now had the perfect training area for fighting in built-up areas. Somehow we could tell that soon, very soon, our time would come. All this training would be for a reason. I could see boxes and stacks of stores and ammunition being ferried to the airstrip. Then, just after we'd paraded in platoon strength one day we were told that we were off to Africa the next day. As from then we were confined to camp. A taste of real combat to come was tantalizing. My only worry now was how I would react when the bullets started flying and people began to die. I would soon find out because Operation Noroit was on.

A strange atmosphere steeped the block that night, the eve of our rescue mission. The bolshie, super-confident troops of only twelve hours ago tended now to be thoughtful young men, each silently running through the possible sequence of forthcoming events. It was during this time of reflection that Steve burst into my room.

'You gotta help me mate. This is fucking serious.

I didn't know what he was banging on about. But he did look pretty wound up and so I tried to cope. 'Just tell me what the hell you're going on about. Calm down and start at the bloody start.'

'Michelle's due here and I am heading for fucking Africa. What the hell do I tell her? I can't get off camp to phone and tomorrow we are heading off for God knows where.'

We eventually came up with a plan. One of the guys from another company that was remaining behind would go into town tomorrow and send Michelle a telegram telling her to postpone the trip for a month. He would sign it in Steve's name and tell her he would phone soon and to watch the news over the next few days. He was setting himself up as a war hero. The guy sending the message was also setting himself up. If this little scam got back, there would be hell to pay. What things we do for friends and comrades. It was the best we could think of at such short notice. We had to concoct something. Dramatic, but bloody effective.

The reality that the Legion suffers fatal casualties of one in ten made us all reflect on what might happen soon. Would we come back and if we did, what injuries would we have? Would I be able to walk? Would I be able to run, or jump out of planes again? These were real possibilities we each had to fight privately in our heads. I felt confident that once we boarded the aircraft, all these doubts would disappear. I wrote home, not exactly telling them what was going on but the letter was written in such a way that if anything did happen and I wasn't to return, my family would know of my love and respect and the genuine remorse I felt if I had ever hurt them.

I bumped into Steve later and said one of those stupid things that have been uttered many times before any conflict in history. I made him promise that if he saw me really hurt or about to be captured he would shoot me. He just stared, said nothing and nodded. He didn't ask the same of me. Later I felt quite stupid: it had been an outrageous thing to ask and it was never mentioned again. What I was really afraid of was not death or capture but of letting my comrades down once we were under fire.

This was to be a joint operation between the French and Belgian governments, but it was us, the 2ème REP, who would arrive first at Bouar. This, initially, was to be a holding base where we could rehearse various plans before actually heading off into Rwanda. We would rehearse actions on ambush, casualty evacuation and what to do if we came across French nationals in what would become the battlefield. Every man had to know exactly what was expected from him and what he was to do in certain circumstances. We practised entering buildings and securing safe areas, where any casualties could be treated.

The situation in Rwanda had deteriorated to such an extent that in only twenty-four hours we took off for Kigali. Speed and surprise were imperative and the main reasons we would fly into Kigali and not parachute in as had been hoped. For a parachute drop to work perfectly, you are dependent upon too many outside and uncontrollable elements. The weather and suitable drop zones close to the target are just a couple. A freak gust of wind that had not been forecast and half your troops plus their equipment are spread over a considerable area. Command and control suffers and it can take some time to get everyone together again and by then both surprise and speed are lost. We only had one shot at this. It had to be right first time otherwise innocent civilians could be seriously hurt. At least this way, climbing from a plane, although less dramatic, all our men and equipment would reach the ground at the same time and, importantly, in the same place and intact. Many of us had hoped to emulate our comrades of Kolwezi fame and place ourselves in the annals of Legion history, but it was not to be. Not this time anyway.

It was early evening when we landed at Kigali and disembarked. The aircraft had taxied to a pan on the far side of the airfield, away from the main buildings and control tower. Everyone fell into their respective platoons and sections, only the raised voices of sergeants ordering people into place could be heard over the incessant clicking and buzzing of insects from the surrounding bush. For a horrible moment I had flash back to the jungle and I shuddered. I hoped nobody noticed and got the wrong idea. A huge, orange sun was fast disappearing over the horizon and with that came the welcome relief of cooler evening air. A group of about thirty soldiers was kept apart, hidden from us by the fuselage of the parked aircraft. This was the CRAP team and they were going to head straight off for the Embassy, which had been given priority. Officers and NCOs were brought up to speed with the latest situation via updates from the advance party which had been *in situ* for the past twelve hours. The reports made for grim listening.

Apparently, the Tutsi gunmen (we refused to honour them by calling them soldiers) had degenerated into a lawless rabble. Shooting, killing, looting and raping at will. Anyone and everyone outside their small groups were seen as potential victims. So far they had given the Europeans here a wide berth but the feeling was that once they had run out of local prey the Europeans would be next. Our orders had changed considerably and we were told that the evacuation of every European, not just the French, was of paramount importance, hence the quick move to Kigali and no time for rehearsals in Bouar. There simply was not the time now in a situation fast becoming desperate.

The rebels had obviously heard of our arrival and about forty-five minutes later mortar shells began landing at various locations around the airfield, kicking up the red African soil. The firing had no direction and there was little skill or marksmanship involved. However, many good soldiers have died as a result of poor shooting. Luck is all that matters once the round has been fired. In fact, this haphazard method of laying down fire is exceptionally dangerous because you cannot judge where the next round will fall. It could be literally anywhere and although we knew it was amateur fire it still had to be taken very seriously. The decision to move was taken quickly and we got off the airfield in double quick time.

My section had been given the task of clearing the area surrounding the airport, a type of sterile zone. We needed some extra men as the task was going to be massive, involving the clearing of many buildings, in case of hidden snipers and what passed for farms in the locale. Not farms as you'd expect to see in England, with an orderly, if sprawling, house, a barn or two, maybe a hayloft surrounding a cobbled yard and stables facing out onto green fields where healthy animals were baying for their feed. No, these 'farms' consisted of run down shacks and sick, emaciated beasts who must have hoped that that death would arrive before the next dawn. Of course the people who had scratched a living from these smallholdings cannot be blamed for such atrocious conditions. I was delighted to see the large frame of Steve ambling towards us, together with a German called Wolfgang. For some reason, I always felt better and safer when he was around. Steve had an air of confidence and calmness about him. If I stayed with him and watched him, then maybe I could get out of this without a scratch. A sergeant called us to order and prepared to explain exactly how this operation was going to be executed. We listened intently, as in the distance the unmistakable sound of small arms fire could be heard, interspersed with the dull crump of mortar rounds landing.

'OK, listen in here,' began the huge sergeant. 'Do exactly as I tell you and you will be OK.' His heavy German accent had authority. 'We must patrol the perimeter of the airfield and clear all the buildings close to it. Once that is complete, we do it again in case any enemy sneak in behind us. We will keep the airport safe until everyone is gone. Then maybe we can go. Do not be afraid to open fire. Things have changed now, we fight to our rules. If you see a man with a weapon, shoot him. Do not ask questions. Just shoot. I want to take you all home [to Calvi] alive. *D'accord?*'

He then showed us a map, outlined the route we would take and where the friendly forces would be. My stomach was in knots and I struggled to breathe. I felt my heart banging against my ribcage and I imagined that everyone else could hear it too. I looked around at the others. No one showed any signs of nerves or fear and that made me feel worse, stupid, because I was shitting myself.

As the darkness closed in we began our first patrol. Noise seems to be amplified at night and travels further, as I had noticed during that first Calvi night jump and in the rainforest. Our boots crunched against the hardened soil and the dry vegetation that lay dead across the ground. Communication between the patrol was whispered hoarsely. I could hear the unmistakable sound of drunken men on a rampage some distance away, their slurred shouts and the shrill screams of women who were clearly begging for mercy. I heard the less sickening sounds of breaking glass and shattering wood as a door or window gave in. And there was laughter and the futile bellowing of a single man trying to regain some sort of order. A *caporal* walked by me: 'Forget these sounds *mon ami*. You are not here for them.' What I had heard was going to be a damn sight easier to forget than what I was about to see.

We had patrolled only a couple of hundred metres when we were officially welcomed to Kigali. A burst of about ten rounds kicked the earth into the air ten metres behind the last man of the patrol. We hit the ground and quickly located the enemy. As soon as the man fired, he stood up, possibly in misguided exultation. Brilliantly silhouetted by the late evening sun he was hit by the collective fire of at least ten FAMAS rifles. I saw him somersault backwards over a small wall. We were the last thing he saw. This little incident suddenly changed the attitude of the patrol. These bastards were trying to kill us so we would kill them first. All our alert discipline swung into bloody-minded aggression. If force was the only thing they understood we were just the blokes to give it to them. The words from our sergeant rang in our ears. Just shoot. We would do that alright. The radio man took quite a while to radio in contact to HQ. All the platoons had come under some sort of fire within minutes of being on the streets and there was a lot of radio traffic.

The commander had decided that as we approached and then cleared a building, any building, it was to be destroyed as we left the area. It mattered not how this was achieved: explosives, burning or by calling in vehicles to flatten it. The poor construction of some of these shacks invariably meant that a few bursts of sustained fire, followed by either grenade or rocket attack, flattened them anyway. The order did, however, make for a very long first night. Suddenly we came under more accurate and sustained fire from thick bush only 200 metres to our front. My section sprayed the area of bush but we couldn't locate the exact position of the gunmen or man.

'Can you see him?' I yelled above the noise and confusion to Steve. He shook his head. The gunman could see us, however, and his fire was getting better and closer to us, the rounds smacking into the red earth all around us. We lay there helpless and frightened to move, not wanting to present a bigger target. After just a couple of minutes Steve jumped up and zigzagged at full speed towards a large tree off to his right. Bullets zapped and cracked past, giving the gunman's position away. Flash from his muzzle told us where he was and countless rounds then hammered into his position. Surely no one could withstand this vicious onslaught. Silence fell, the smoke from this ferocious, brief engagement spiralled slowly upwards in the now curiously still air. The smell of cordite was thick and nauseating. Steve stood in his position. The gunman was dead: Steve had been incredibly brave in calling fire like that. Our patrol began moving, slowly and stealthily again. Another contact, another kill.

'You're fucking mad, mate,' I said. He simply grinned and continued to scan his arc of fire for more enemy.

My nervousness accentuated my senses. Behind every bush, every wall was a sniper. Each tuft of grass hid a mine; I avoided twigs and branches on the ground, lest they be booby-trapped. The ground ahead had not been cleared so we were particularly on the look-out for signs that mines may have been laid: mounds of earth in unusual locations or freshly dug. In the background was the steady chattering of semi-automatic fire as other Legion patrols came into contact with rebel gunmen. The patrol was long and arduous. Each building we came across had to be dealt with in the same way. It was a long night.

Steve and I were tasked with destroying one particular outbuilding. Our sergeant got us together and dished out a quick set of orders. A sub-section would go up to the house and clear it as per operational orders. Then we were to place explosives around the foundations and blow it up. We were slightly behind the main assault group as they launched their part of the plan. As planned they hurled in a few grenades and then blew the insides of the house through the windows and into the gardens, following through by raking the place with automatic fire. Nothing could possibly have survived that type of heavy and merciless attack. If any poor soul had been inside, then they wouldn't have suffered such was the fierceness of the assault. All that was left for me and Steve to do was to demolish what was left. The section, meantime, had moved on to its next objective. Steve then whispered something.

'Was it 4 kilos or 4 grams per charge?' The stupid bastard had forgotten how much explosive to put into each charge. Neither of us had much training in demolition, so this was mostly guess work, and neither of us wanted to make pricks of ourselves by giving the explosives back. This was not the time to ask for some extra instruction; all hell was breaking loose.

'I don't fucking know.'

'Tell you what. Just to be safe I shall put 4 kilos in. That should do it. Fuck me, 4 grams wouldn't blow off my beret.'

Looking at the building, I thought that a good shove from a lorry would have been enough to collapse the shack, but Steve was hell bent and 4 kilos it was. I will say that 4 grams doesn't really look very much at all, about the size of a boiled egg, so I had to agree with him. He placed the charges at opposite corners of the building and put the detonators on a twenty-second delay. Then, we ran as hard and as fast as we could, remembering there was hardly any cover around here. With only milliseconds remaining, he screamed, 'Down, for fuck's sake, down!'

The roar that reverberated might have woken the entire African continent, completely out of proportion to the small job we had just done. For what seemed like hours pieces of terracotta tiling and small bits of white plasterboard fell upon us and we were covered in a thick white dust. The explosions had deafened me; but conversely that loud ringing in my ears let me know I had survived. Through the swirling clouds of dust and smoke around us I could just make out the silhouette of one very pissed-off sergeant. He stood, hands on hips and menacingly tall, as we dared to raise our heads to look at the devastation that we had caused. He did not say a word, merely waved us forward. Steve attempted to justify his mistake by telling anyone who would listen that he was actually sending a message to the Tutsis. Don't mess with us, or we will destroy everything you own. So much for the Legion Code of Honour and respecting the enemy and his property!

The clearing patrol was taking a long time because of the constant sniper fire we came under. At this point, the firing didn't put us in much danger because it was so ineffective, but it did delay us and make the patrol extremely hard work. By 0200, we were only halfway through; we should have finished over an hour ago. We were exhausted, hungry and thirsty but there would be no rest or relief until the job was done.

About 0430, we came to the eastern edge of the airport, which bordered the outskirts of the town. The only traffic for the airport was the occasional military transport aeroplanes that screamed in. Then we would have to go to ground, keeping our eyes peeled for any attempt by the rebels to fire at the incoming planes. This delayed our real work, although those dawn patrols were unforgettable as one saw the sun rise, apparently in flames against the grey dawn skies. What the sun also did was to illuminate just what a terrible state this part of town was in. Burnt out motor vehicles lay abandoned and often overturned, enforcing a sense of defeat and helplessness. Local shops and businesses had clearly been looted and ransacked. Bodies, some horribly butchered, lay in pools of their own blood and there was no one to prevent the birds and insects from feasting on them. As the heat of the day intensified, so would the stench of death and decay.

We passed a horse, the wretched creature unable to move because of a shattered leg. Huge, brown eyes gazed up, seeming to plead that someone put it out of its misery. One shot from a Legionnaire to the animal's head ended the creature's pain. Man's brutality to fellow man is bad enough; to see innocent animals suffer through his actions makes it even more tragic.

A quick recce by our sergeant, and it was decided that there were too many buildings here for our relatively small patrol to destroy. We would patrol through, try to draw any enemy fire and then counter-attack. We were not under fire as we made our way back to the airport but we could see groups of men, gathered and armed with rifles and clubs. The crowd increased to about 150. We numbered only twelve; bravado was the most effective weapon we possessed, showing no fear whatsoever. They were chanting and waving their weapons in the air. They looked very threatening and followed us back to the main building, albeit at distance. No shots were fired but it was still a terrifying moment.

Back at the main event, which by now resembled a building site rather than an international airport, we were told to clean our weapons and get resupplied with ammunition and fresh water. Once that had been accomplished we had to grab some food while the patrol commander went off to give his report and receive further orders. We heard the other sections and platoons talking and from the sound of it we had got away pretty lightly last night. There had been some heavy fighting in the town and the regiment had taken casualties. It wasn't yet known if any of those casualties were fatal. Apparently some Rwandan army officers, allegedly on our side, had become so confused and frightened during the initial stages of the operation that they opened fire on one of our patrols. They were soon put right, although they did take fatal casualties during the brief firefight. They were simply terrified and had opened fire on anything that was moving or causing them worry. Confusion in battle is common and sometimes friendly forces will fire on each other. It is a fact of combat. The tales that came back were truly horrific and I felt that we were going to have to get our people out sooner rather than later. The other sections had advanced well, securing lots of ground, and it wouldn't be long until the hostages were under our control. Till then this was still mayhem.

Patrolling in daylight was both risky and frightening. It also let me see the utter devastation caused by these lawless ragamuffins who masqueraded as soldiers. They were simply well-armed bullies picking on innocent women, children and those who could not defend themselves. It was important to remind ourselves that we were professional soldiers and we couldn't let personal feelings get in the way of the operation. Once you let it become personal, discipline can be difficult to maintain, with people going off on differing tangents, each with their own agenda. We were making our way to the French school to assist another section in the evacuation of people, about ninety held there, effectively hostages. They included nuns who had been teachers at the school and had run an aid station near by. The situation had deteriorated during the night, with sporadic firefights erupting all over the place, once the rebels had cottoned on to what we were there for. It was now a matter of urgency to get these helpless people who had harmed no one out of this place. I sincerely hoped that their God would protect them and help us.

It became heartbreaking as we moved through the town. The mid-morning sun had broken through the cloud and it was getting hot. We needed to move quickly but also had to be alert to the possibility of ambush or sniper fire. As we patrolled, eyes wide open, turning, check-ing, looking out for each other, native women approached us. Their eyes were hollow and lifeless, begging us to help them. We walked on; patrolling is most effective when carried out on foot, and you see more and can react to any contact with the enemy quicker. They stood in front of us, barring our way, offering us their children. Couldn't we at least take the children? Please help the children. The wailing, the crying, the complete and utter hopelessness of these wretched people began to get to me. I couldn't look them in the eye or speak to them. They were getting in the way now. I wasn't concentrating on the job. I was close to becoming a liability and putting my comrades in danger. The more expe-rienced Legionnaires saw what was happening to us new boys and reacted quickly and brutally. Breaking formation, they grabbed hold of these miserable creatures, sometimes by the hair, and threw them to the ground. No explanation, no words, but the message to us was clear, get rid of them or you may be killed. When a big, tough *caporal* from one of the Eastern European countries saw how affected I had become he slapped me hard across the face and stared into my eyes.

'*Allez! Vite!*' was all he said. Come on! Quick! We weren't here to give assistance or aid. Whatever we saw, no matter how callous or wanton the brutality was, would have to be ignored. Leave them. I walked past the crumpled heap of a woman, two small children kneeling by her side. They were crying and begging her to wake up, 'Mama, mama'. From the dark crimson flow that puddled the earth around her head I deduced that she would never wake. Not in this world anyway. '*Allez*, leave them.'

A large crowd greeted us as we rounded the corner, covering each other's back and looking out for gunmen. They were chanting, shouting, waving bottles and farm implements in the air. It was pretty clear they wanted not merely to kill us but probably to butcher us and parade our carcasses as trophies – out of loyalty to leaders who cared nothing about them. A bottle was thrown. It arced into the air to land and shatter close to us. They were egging each other on, but only inching forward, seemingly unsure of how far to push us.

A shout went up, and we ran towards them, taking the initiative. This sudden rush took them by surprise; we were sprinting and each of us launched himself at the nearest target. I raised the butt of my rifle and brought it down, smashing it into a man's face. The juddering impact almost stopped *me* dead. I saw the rough skin split under his eye and his blood flowed freely. He fell backwards onto his arse and into a sitting position, a look of bewilderment on his face. His head then snapped back violently as my Ranger boot connected perfectly with his jaw. The crack, as his mouth shattered, sounded like a rifle shot. He laid, spread-eagled, unconscious, out of it. I stood over him, my breathing shallow and fast. Adrenalin was pumping through my body, making me feel invincible. It was my first blood for the Legion. Blood that flowed because of my actions. I looked around for my next victim.

We all behaved in much the same way during that confrontation and the sheer brutal efficiency and speed with which it was executed scared the shit out of the rebels. They immediately dispersed, shouting insults as they retreated, but leaving their injured behind, which summed them up perfectly to us. You never leave your dead or injured comrades at the scene of battle. You always, always, carry them away with you.

A similar scene greeted us at the school, but by now word had reached the rabble that we would take no shit and certainly no prisoners. It was weird, but as we approached the gates to the school, the crowd gathered there parted and let us through unhindered by anything more than sullen stares. Our comrades on the gate were obviously pleased to see us and welcomed us like brothers. The whole situation was, however, reaching a critical stage. We were told to man the perimeter fence while our NCOs went off for yet another briefing. The atmosphere was tense and we could feel the hatred these people had for us. We were spoiling their fun and they, being typical bullies, didn't like it, not one little bit. Next, my section was pulled off the fence and into a classroom for new orders. The school was a shambles. Everything that could be destroyed had been. Property that couldn't be destroyed had been defecated on and in, and the smell was vile and stomach turning. Why vandalize a school, of all places?

Our orders were brief and to the point. We had to escort all French nationals away to safety, nothing else mattered. Nothing else was to distract us from this mission, no matter what our personal thoughts or feelings. I had to clear my mind of the pitiful sights of women and children terrified and clinging onto each other for protection.

About a kilometre from the school was a small farm where a group of armed rebels were holed up. They had been giving other units a lot of hassle with small arms fire and were generally being a nuisance. It was thought that once this group had been eliminated the mission could proceed much more quickly and safely. No prisoners would be taken, we were just to get rid of them. And it had to be done that night, as French Air Force helicopters were on standby to evacuate the civilians.

There was an atmosphere of chaos on the streets. We could hear the shouts and screams of men, enemies of the Tutsis, being tortured and then killed. I saw a body being thrown onto the street from a house. It was followed by half a dozen lightly armed men; once again I refuse to describe them as soldiers. The chief torturer was a big man, playing at being an even bigger one. He looked like a gangster in a low budget film. He wore sun-glasses and a bright yellow Hawaiian-type shirt, unbuttoned to the waist. He held a machine pistol in front of him and kept it trained on us as we walked past. Our sergeant and the man held eye contact as we walked past. Each and every one of us wanted to do him in there and then. We silently prayed that he would give us an excuse to slot him. He was too clever though. He knew we wouldn't go out of our way to do anything, so he tried to taunt us. But we had a mission of far greater importance than decking some tin-pot heavy and nothing would stand in the way of us completing it.

We formed about 500 metres from the smallholding, each knowing what he had to do. My Legion training gave me a nerveless confidence that overcame any inner quaking; everything felt like second nature. I had been superbly trained and knew that as long as I remembered all I had been taught I'd be all right and probably get through this.

I knelt on one knee, a 66mm rocket launcher perched on my shoulder. At a given signal, I fired. *Whoosh!* The rocket zipped its deadly path towards the main farmhouse. *Bang!* Fucking brilliant. Right on target. A huge yellow-orange ball of flame and destruction exploded down-stairs, blowing out what remained of the windows. Glass and splinters of wood showered the earth. I threw the launcher away, remembering to stand on the tube to crush it useless – sometimes enemy troops attempt to use a spent tube as an improvised mortar launcher – and joined in the assault. My breathing was rapid and short again. I was keenly aware of everything around me and especially the incoming rounds that were kicking up the soil near my feet.

Once the assault had started my earlier lapse towards pity and doubt was forgotten. There was an air of inevitability about the whole thing and there was nothing I could change about it. In the heat of battle, I became calloused to the sight of death, the smells, the absolute destruc-tion we were inflicting, even the danger. The actual sight of a dead enemy gave me a feeling of righteousness, almost triumphant in the thought, 'Thank fuck it's him, not me.' We had a job to do and thinking about what was happening could wait until later.

Suddenly I realized that I was stranded out in the open. I saw a

Legionnaire crouched behind a small wall and ran like a man possessed to join him. Clearly we had badly underestimated the number of gunmen in the farm and this was going to be a right battle. The enemy had seen my run and now concentrated their fire at the wall. My comrade later thanked me for being so considerate! I instinctively ran from the wall and hit the deck, hard; I rolled over and crawled forward. All the time I was expecting the enemy to find their range and obliterate me. I wasn't going to risk drawing fire by lifting my head so I waited for the inevitable. Suddenly, I didn't feel so invincible.

'Fucking hell, Spider, get up, get up!' yelled Steve as he ran past. The attack was once again going forward. He got into a kneeling position and prepared to launch his 66 from the shoulder, the launcher perfectly balanced, and I lay down a blanket of fire to protect him. He shouted 'Ready'. Steve was not a man to forget little details, even in the full throes of battle. The 66 has a triangular back blast area of around fifteen metres, anyone within that area when the weapon is fired is likely to be burnt to death. The noise of the firefight completely drowned out his warning, but he fired anyway. The rocket powered away from us and entered the farmhouse by the front door.

'It didn't even knock,' said Steve, mockingly. The inside of the house exploded and enemy poured out of the gaping window frames into a hail of deadly accurate precision fire.

The firing of the rocket had drawn unwanted attention to us. We came under sustained fire but couldn't see where it was coming from. To my left, one of the boys was screaming in agony. He had taken rounds in his stomach; another Legionnaire was trying to bandage him. Blood and entrails covered his hands but he continued his task, oblivious to his own safety. Steve and I raced off to the right and found cover beside another small wall. Again, this movement drew fire and I thought the wall would collapse under the pressure of this renewed assault, thereby exposing us to the enemy. All around the farmyard lay dead and dying men, mostly theirs, thank God. Their screams and moans of agony were driving me mental. Why couldn't they just die?

The attack was again intensifying so we had to move. It is vitally important to keep up the momentum of an attack. Put the enemy on the back foot. Get them retreating under the speed and aggression of your force, and keep them running. Don't give them a second to reorganize. I made a huge mistake amid all the confusion around this small farm and I launched myself into a shed, not too far away from the wall that had, until now, been my saviour. As soon as I entered, I drew fire from a heavy machine gun. I was by now totally shattered. I was covered in brick dust and other debris, the sweat was pouring from every pore on my skin and I could hardly breathe. Worse still, I was on my own and African gunmen were attempting to demolish my little shack. I tried to gather my thoughts and come up with a plan. The screams and wailing from the wounded were really getting to me and again I feared for my sanity. The rounds pounded the area around the shed. The gunman wasn't a good shot but he would only have to be lucky once. I had to be lucky all the time.

Crash! The door of the shed exploded and in the doorway stood Steve. Thank fuck for that. Oh! You glorious, ugly bastard! I am so pleased to see you. And then we made our break for it and made it to that ditch…

We soon realized that the rounds going over our heads were coming from our own troops. The rebels in the farmhouse were either dead, wounded or had decided they'd had enough and done a runner. Whatever, the fighting was over and I had made it, along with Steve, unscathed.

We surveyed the farmyard when it was over. There really wasn't a farmyard anymore. Dead bodies lay all around, the smell of cordite hung heavily in the air, the destruction was hard to comprehend. Men had done this to each other. The moans of the wounded and calls from distressed animals brought me back to reality. We left their wounded as we entered the house to check that it really was empty, or that those inside were indeed dead. Our own traumatised comrades were treated and immediately evacuated to the airport.

'You OK?' enquired a voice behind me.

'Yeah, Steve, yeah. Course I am, why shouldn't I be?' I replied unconvincingly. It had been truly awful. I didn't want even him to see how I had been affected by the fighting. The respect and esteem that your comrades have for you is priceless. Maybe it's a stupid boy thing but it was a point of honour, even amongst comrades, not to show any sign of weakness.

The fire was now raging in the house, the moans of the wounded receded and diminished as they gave up their fight for life. The stench of the cordite in the air stuck in my throat; the smoke curling upwards to the heavens, taking with it, I hoped, the souls of those who had perished, whichever side they were on. We had lost three Legionnaires and two were wounded, evacuated to a safe area beside the airport buildings. A quietness, in stark contrast to the pandemonium that had recently prevailed, descended upon the once farm. When the death-toll had been confirmed the section reported back to HQ and we returned to the school.

As we approached the gates, not far from the scene of a fearsome battle, the dull thumping clatter of helicopter rotor blades caught our attention. They certainly weren't hanging about. In a short while, the civilians that we had come to rescue would be on their way to safety. They had little in the way of personal effects with them. The uprising had caught everyone by surprise and I think that they were happy to be escaping with their lives intact. They wouldn't stop to thank us, for they had no need to. We didn't really do it for them. Yes, they were the reason we were here, but they could have been anyone. We did it for ourselves, our comrades, our Legion. We simply had a job to do. People who tried to stop us for whatever reasons were dispatched. The job was done, with the Legion's honour and fidelity intact.

I saw the nationals as they passed us, terror etched upon their faces. I am not sure that they had expected the Legion to be their rescuers, and you could tell they were unsure of us. For their liberators, their saviours, were a band of thugs and mercenaries, or so legend would have them believe. I could see the weariness in the way they walked. Young men walked with a stoop, young men turned old beyond their years in a matter of days. After witnessing the cruel events they had, could the children I saw leaving ever be children again? Surely any innocence they had was now gone forever. The women were still sobbing, and not just from relief. Their children had lost, vacant faces looking as if they had just witnessed the end of the world. I watched them leave wondering how they would regale the tale of their rescue. Would we now be heroes or still the terrifying criminals of legend?

Only after the firing and the danger had passed was there any time to reflect. To think of comrades either wounded or killed. The times I had been so close to death without realizing it. A sense of calm returned and now that the callousness with which I had armed myself along with my hardware was gone, some human doubt and nervousness once again nagged.

A couple of days later, order now presiding in Kigali once more, French and Belgian troops arrived to take over from us. The Tutsi fighters had withdrawn over the border to lick their wounds before, no doubt, launching another attack on the people of Rwanda. We left by road for Bangui and then flew back to Calvi.

CHAPTER TWELVE

INTO THE DESERT

WE WERE GIVEN ONE WEEK'S LEAVE upon our return to Raffali. There was no flag waving or parade. The mission had simply been a job well done – no more than was expected of us.

We didn't own any civilian clothes – we weren't allowed to own any yet, that would come later – so we had to make do with mooching around the camp in Legion issue tracksuits. It is tradition within the REP that you do not leave the island on *permission* until you have completed at least eighteen months service with them, and even then it is at your *caporal chef*'s discretion, so we didn't really have much choice. Drinking in Calvi was twice as expensive as in the foyer and was generally reserved for special occasions only. So yes, maybe I soon became a little bored with this form of leisure.

The leave though, was very welcome. I caught up with a very browned-off Steve the following day. Amongst mail that had accumulated whilst we had been in Rwanda had been a letter from his Michelle. Only she wasn't his anymore. That telegram from Steve had indeed been posted when we left for Rwanda but Michelle had taken the news rather badly. She could not, as she explained in her letter, cope with being let down like that. It wasn't just this time, but the next time and the time after that. So far as she could see, the relationship had no future as long as he was in the Legion. There was no way she would sit at home, thousands of miles away, not knowing to what part of the world he would be sent next, whether he was dead or alive, or horribly injured. Steve was as upset as I had ever seen him but he eventually resigned himself to the facts. He was here, she was back in England, she had her family and he had his – the comrades – and neither could leave them. The choice in the end was easy. We did go into Calvi that night and got well and truly pissed. The town was quiet as much of it closes down for the winter months but we still did some damage to local supplies of Kronenbourg.

I soon settled back into the routine of day to day life on camp. Parachute drops followed by weapon training filled the days. It is important to keep troops as occupied as possible as boredom amongst combat-ready troops can easily lead to trouble. A wrong word or misjudged gesture can trigger a pointless brawl. Occasionally these are needed to clear the air and keep the pecking order intact but they should mostly be avoided. We lived in a world where threats of conflict and the risk of combat were real, daily possibilities. We had to be ready to mobilize quickly, sometimes within six hours, depending on the urgency of the situation. The move could be to the blistering heat of the desert in Chad, the green hell of some jungle or to the frozen plains of Eastern Europe. The key to this remarkable ability is preparation. Training and exercising for any eventuality is the Legion's strength. Each Legionnaire has appropriate clothing and equipment, separately packed and labelled with his name and number and ready to go, wherever the location.

The world is a big place for the young Legionnaire. Conflicts abound in many of its furthest pockets. Religious conflict, ethnic cleansing and the daily threat of organized terrorism. Various African states seem eternally divided by tribal conflicts, nurtured by corrupt military dictatorships. The Middle East countries also have smouldering long-standing grievances fuelled in the name of religion and stoked with alarming military power. Eastern Europe is another powder keg of unfinished business dating back centuries. All these potential theatres of operation present their own problems and if trouble flares in any of them the Legion is likely to be among the first troops sent there in an attempt to bring peace and harmony.

It was during one of these flare-ups, in Chad, that I was to undertake another operational tour with the 2ème REP. We were given a relatively luxurious twelve hours notice and, due to brilliant preparation, we departed Calvi exactly on time. As the desert is almost the Legion's spiritual home it seemed kind of right to be seeing active service there. Anyway, such tours of duty also added vital new tactics to the Legion's range of operational skills. The Legion had dusted off the principle of what they called 'nomadization', wherein fast-moving, long-reaching combat patrols kept any enemy off balance and brought subtle support and confidence to worried locals.

Chad, more specifically French interests in Chad, had come under threat by constant incursions by Libya for many years. Anti-government unrest there, supported by Libyan and Soviet agencies, had escalated into a serious rebellion in the mid-sixties. Fired by tribalism, religious conflict and a struggle for nationalism, rebels threatened to overrun the government and a plea for help was dispatched to France. The Legion's role then was to show active support for the government and to protect native tribes living in the south which had become vulnerable to attack from nomadic tribesmen in the north. They were to also assist a weak Chad army, who were trying to stem the incursions into Chad by Libya. Once again, it meant Legionnaires having to adapt quickly to new terrain, new conditions and different operational requirements. So for almost twenty years the Legion had been involved in an operation against rebel forces in Chad's rugged mountainous regions. The rebels were no longer relying on outdated firearms with which to hassle Legion patrols. The

Libyans had now armed them with an array of modern weapons including AK-47 rifles, 88 and 120mm mortars, rocket launchers and even twin-barrelled anti-aircraft guns.

By now, the late 1980s, Libya was less directly involved with incursions and raids by the rebels and this coincided with an increase in French air power, brought to the region to protect the Chad border. The Legion's presence this time was primarily to defend the air base at N'Djamena but there was little doubt we would be used by the President as combat troops in his battle with the rebels, should the need arise. There was a permanent staff of Legion personnel there and their experience provided invaluable advice.

I remember the desert in Northern Chad as being long, barren stretches of rock and dust, broken up by steep mountain ranges. It was inhospitable terrain. Fierce heat made day to day life difficult enough but it was the sudden sandstorms which were the most untenable problem. They would occur without warning, making movement almost impossible as basic breathing and vision were restricted. Seeking shelter was the only solution. We had to be covered up to avoid getting sunburnt and sunstroke, both potentially fatal. In some ways our kit was inspired by that of indigenous Arabs. It's always sensible to observe how the locals dress, wherever you are in the world: no matter how fashion or tourism might have traduced ethnic clothing, the basic kit has invariably been devised over centuries to enable human life to deal with the local natural elements. We were not to don T E Lawrence-style robes but as newly arrived Legionnaires, we were told by the experienced troops to continue to wear long trousers and to keep the sleeves on our shirts rolled down, however great the temptation to roll them up, and to keep our head-dress on at all times, be it beret or kepi. Strict self-discipline was paramount. Good personal hygiene, no alcohol (that alone caused some consternation) and good regulation of water supplies were other essentials. Obey these golden rules and you could survive here, not comfortably, but you could survive. This was a tough detachment.

After a couple of weeks of interminably boring sentry and guard duties, I went out on my first proper patrol. We mustered at 0430, the cool morning being a great time to check our kit: nothing could be left to chance out there in the desert. My illusions of a desert landscape were shattered. I had imagined long stretches of sand dunes with the odd wispy bush blown by a gentle breeze. The reality was long, barren beds of rock, and very little, if any, sand. It was a wilderness where nothing could grow. Blistering sun during the day gave way to icy conditions at night. The very sight of the landscape made a man thirsty. The purpose of our three-day patrol was made quite clear: a Legion presence will make any rebel think twice about either launching an attack or moving equipment and supplies across the desert. It is all about dominating the territory. And it was bloody good training for us.

We were dropped off some fifty to sixty kilometres away from the airfield. Within a minute of the truck heading back, the dust caused by the wheels had settled and we fifteen were on our own in this vast emptiness. The sky was perfectly clear and soon the sun would be scorching down. The plan was to move during the day and at night set up observation posts or an ambush, depending on local intelligence. Local men acting as guides and loyal to the Legion were a mine of information and had been cultivated over the years. They were our eyes and ears in some of the remote areas of this wasteland. That morning was silent, deadly quiet. No movement of birds or animals, nothing stirred. Kit was checked, a quick swig of water and off we went, a full section of Legionnaires. Now I did feel like Beau Geste, whose legend I had learned to dismiss.

Soon I became very hot: sweat was pouring off me, running down my back, seeping from my armpits. It was a horrible, sticky feeling but I couldn't whinge about it. The sergeant in charge navigated by compass. He had a map too, but that must have been useless as there were no features for him to determine our position by. We went off bearings, distance and time. We had been trained to know how many of our individual paces were in a kilometre, so the sergeant told two Legionnaires to count out paces as we patrolled. We would halt after every kilometre and average out the paces taken. It was painstakingly slow, but quite accurate and we never got lost. The occasional wadi – dried-up river bed – confirmed where we were.

As the baking day wore on, I prayed for the relief that night would bring. We had patrolled for nearly eight hours and hadn't seen anything of any importance. My morale was sinking – all this was obviously completely pointless. I must have pissed out litres of sweat and my feet were killing me. Walking on rock, with ankle-breaking boulders at every footfall, had turned them into a blistered mush of raw meat. I had a flashback to Castel and began talking to myself, encouraging myself somehow. The others must have thought I had lost my mind to the sun but I had to beast myself along, no matter what. Everyone had their own individual method of dealing with these desert marches so nobody took the piss.

We stopped for the night, having covered thirty kilometres, but if I thought I could relax, I was sadly mistaken. We halted in a wadi, small and easily defended in case of attack. Half the section went on guard, whilst the rest sorted their kit and themselves out. We swapped and when food was cooked we ate in shifts. There were always plenty of men on guard. Soldiers often do their combat work at night and in the dark, remaining under cover during daylight, like predatory beasts. Someone has to be awake and alert at all times. We rested in sleeping bags, no tents or bivouac cover and as darkness crept in it brought a bone-gnawing cold with it. The chill crept up on you, often too slowly for you to react – somehow you were already freezing by the time you realized that the discomfort had paralyzed you. It was a long, sleepless night.

235

We were up and off before the real heat of the sun began to burn. That morning, we came across a small range of hills. The main purpose of our patrol was at last explained. We were to search the hills, the caves and every bush for signs of rebels – equipment or debris left from camps. It was a back-breaking slog. All we had to show for it after ten hours searching was a cache of clothes, some shoes, food and water. Nothing to get excited about. We had hoped to find weapons, but at least it proved that we were in the right area. All I had to look forward to was another freezing night and four hours of guard duty, starting at midnight. The isolation on guard duty, coupled with correct alert tension always created fearful anticipation of your wily enemy's strategies. Mostly, however, nothing happened, except in one's own fevered imagination.

My feet were in such a bad way when we arrived back at the air base that I went straight to the infirmary to get them checked. The medic there shrugged his shoulders and said there was nothing he could do. Bathe your feet and if the blisters pop, wash and dress them in clean bandages, he advised. Brilliant, I didn't need a fucking doctor to tell me that. Basically sound health now seemed to me to be a curse. A broken limb, a wound that could not be treated here in the desert, would have been a blessing. How I longed to have something the matter which would have me sent back to the infirmary at Calvi. Thoughts of clean sheets briefly passed through my mind.

I was now beginning to have serious doubts about my future in the Legion. Whether this was all down to fatigue, I don't know but all I *did* know was I hated the jungle and I hated the desert, with its scorching heat and unforgiving terrain. Bearing in mind that such places were where I could expect to spend over two-thirds of my service, it didn't leave me a lot of room for manoeuvre. I had some serious thinking to do, for I only had a year of service left before I either signed up for more, or went home. Thinking of home, I fell asleep. After the claustrophobic hell of the jungle and the excitement of Rwanda, there had been a creeping sense of anti-climax for some time. My company was taken off 'spearhead' in order to let others be at the sharp end and we had settled into a routine of exercises, training and guard duty. From talking to older Legionnaires, I had to class myself as fortunate to have seen so much in a relatively short career. Some Legionnaires had never been off Calvi and the only action they had seen was in the bars of their adopted town. Raffali was far from being the only fit Legion base and men from other units could be called upon.

The section rested for a few days but before long, it was our turn to go out again. I had tried hard to raise my morale and not let my head drop too much. As it was in Rwanda, so it was in Chad and there was nothing I could do about it. The best and easiest way to get through was to put my head down and get on with the job as best I could.

The Legion is a fantastic leveller of men. Everyone starts off on the same footing. People take each other at face value; their personal history is of no consequence, hence the unwritten rule about not enquiring into a comrade's background. Because of the hardships endured along the way, such as this tortuous duty in Chad, a great sense of comradeship is generated. But once a man's time is up in the Legion, he goes on his way and any friendships developed fade into a distant memory. Contrarily, legend has it that if an ex-Legionnaire is in trouble, anywhere in the world, all he has to do is contact them and they will get him out of that trouble. Naturally I sincerely hoped I would never find myself in that situation but even thinking like this I suppose my mind must have already been half made up.

But another day, another duty and our next patrol differed slightly in that we were helicoptered out of the air base, straight to the northern mountain range of Tibesti and my first encounter with the battle-hardened warriors who inhabited this remote area. Although dropped in by helicopter, we still had a six hour march in terrible heat before we reached our target area. We found a cave and as we sorted ourselves out for the night, the sergeant and *caporal* went to introduce themselves to the tribal leaders, a hearts and minds exercise if you like. They returned later, excited by news they had learned from the tribesmen. A rebel group had been spotted ten kilometres up into the mountains. They had made camp and it looked like they were waiting for a supply drop from Libya. After frantic radio messages, we got our orders. Ambush the group away from their camp and preferably on their way to the drop. Then destroy them.

A great surge of my old adrenalin returned and when darkness fell we moved out and found our ambush area easily, even in deepest darkness. A sentry system was devised so at least some of us could get some sleep. Not me: a mixture of nerves and excitement kept me on edge. As dawn broke, everyone stood to, keen and alert. In the quiet, we could hear the sound of men moving stealthily across the ground. The ambush was going to be sprung. It sounded like they were heading straight for me. My mouth was dry and I was convinced they would hear my breathing above the soft sound of their own footsteps. I could clearly see their line of approach. My FAMAS was already cocked; all I had to do was squeeze the trigger. I was sweating again, despite the coolness of the dawn. Perhaps when you are primed to kill strangers before they kill you, you do tend to sweat a little. I whispered to the next man what I had seen and told him to be ready when this all kicked off. The killing zone was clear and once they had entered it, they did not leave it. Well, not walking anyway.

Slowly, agonizingly slowly, they crept closer. One minute seemed to drag on forever. Now, I was sure I could smell them, though I wasn't sure how many of them there were. They were that close I held my breath, fearing even that little noise would give me away. Then, I saw him. So clear. Only about five foot six tall, in traditional Arab dress, he had a thick black moustache and impossibly white teeth. His eyes opened fully the split second he saw me and realized his life was over. I opened up on automatic fire. He got the whole magazine. Thirty rounds fired in long bursts; not all of the rounds hit him, some went over, some to his side but enough hit the spot to end his days.

All hell seemed to break loose on that mountainside as the entire section opened up on the unsuspecting rebels. They never stood a chance and all five were killed instantly. It was over almost as soon as it had started. This was a great result for the section. Although we never saw any of the Libyan suppliers, I am convinced they heard the ambush kick off, and then hightailed it back to wherever they came from. We left the bodies where they had fallen as a message to the rebels and also to the tribesmen in the mountains – the Legion is here to protect you, you have nothing to fear if you are on our side.

We had an almost casual attitude towards death, difficult to explain. Maybe it was because we were permanently aware that we could die at any time. We were after all, expendable. The Legion and the French government didn't have to explain our loss to anyone. Money and possessions, anything external, can be replaced but life cannot. This made me think of the recent past and I began to think about my life a lot more clearly. Did I want to die in some remote and bleak wilderness? The answer was a definite 'No'. I had been confused for a long time about my life and what I wanted from it and it had taken this course of extreme action, a commitment to the Legion, to discover that this life wasn't for me any more. It is disturbing to realize that a complete stranger is driven to kill you. This successful killer will not be punished but will receive reward and honours from his fellow countrymen or 'patriots'.

It is no wonder that men who have fought in conflicts, wherever and for whatever reason, break down and suffer mental illness after obeying the extraordinary commands and demands of combat. How can an ordinary soldier make sense of seeing wounded friends nurse their shattered limbs? How can they ignore the anguished screams and looks of terror etched upon young faces as they attempt to stem the flow of blood from bodies destroyed? Few can. Those are sights and sounds that are carried forever in the minds of those that witness them. The only escape is death itself.

We returned to N'Djamena, where food and drink had been laid on for us once we had cleaned our weapons and returned all kit, including radios. Sadly the drink was Coca-Cola, not fucking Kronenbourg, but even that and some decent scoff was welcome. It was generally agreed that patrolling in the north was a lot tougher than the south. The terrain, the weather, the skirmishes with rebels all made duties in the northern sector an assignment to dread.

This three-month detachment passed reasonably quickly, all things considered. There was a steady round of patrols but no further contact was made with the enemy during my stay and guard duty at the camp meant I had no time to sit and think about how unhappy I really was. Maybe that was the Coke kicking in rather than dear old Mother Kronenbourg. There were reports of alleged Libyan incursions later, however, and these, plus the general unrest in the region and the threats to French interests and citizens, would ensure that the 2ème REP's tours of duty in Chad were certainly not finished yet.

But there would be no further tours of duty for me.

CHAPTER THIRTEEN

TIME TO GO HOME

BY THE TIME I RETURNED TO CAMP RAFFALI I'd decided that I'd had enough. I didn't want promotion and I didn't want to stay in the Legion. I had done my time.

I don't wish to make it sound like a prison sentence, because it wasn't and mostly I'd loved it. I just felt that I'd had enough. The things I saw in Rwanda had affected me deeply. I'd killed, nearly been killed and had seen my friends killed. When I told my company commander that I wished to leave he told me to go away, have a beer, talk to my comrades and think about it. I didn't really need to.

Steve was, as I had expected, shocked when I told him of my decision. I had done everything I had wanted to do. Even the bastard parachute jumps. My adventure had run its course and now it was over. I had not been properly prepared for Legion life, although I had convinced myself all those years ago that I was. That I now felt very well prepared to face any challenge that my new life would throw at me was down to the Legion and I am eternally grateful to it for that.

The two of us drank ourselves oblivious in the *Au Son des Guitares* that night. We solemnly promised to keep in touch but we haven't done so yet, although these days I find myself thinking about him more and more and reckon I might just try to trace him. Whatever, the memories are locked away in our minds for us both to remember. If I saw him in the street tomorrow, I would hug him, call him a fat bastard and bollock him rigid for not writing to me.

The music in the bar was booming, the place packed to the rafters with drunken Legionnaires. The beer and whisky flowed as did our tales and reminiscences. It was all great but I had had enough tales to last a lifetime and enough Kronenbourg to float a battleship. Some days of my service had been intolerable and I'd thought at times that I would never survive, neither training nor combat, but apart from hurting my parents, I did not regret any of it, not for one minute. My time in the Legion defined camaraderie. The people I met will remain with me forever in memories both good and bad. I cannot remember all their names, but the Legion – which takes away a man's real name, after all – had proved to me that it is not the name but the man behind the name that really counts.

The stories here are told as I remember them. Others who were there may have seen things differently. For that I offer no apologies. The names of Legionnaires are the names given to me by them. Their real identities may be known only to themselves, but they will know who they are.

Four months later I was back at Aubagne, my kit handed in and my old stuff returned to me. It was musty and stank from being in storage, which made me smile. The bastards give you stinking kit when you arrive and hand you back stinking kit when you leave. I stood on the parade square at Aubagne, along with ten other Legionnaires about to return to civilian life and received the certificate of good service. With my passport in my pocket and trying to remember my name, I saw beyond the square about two hundred scruffy young men, dressed in tracksuits and being hollered at quite loudly. I smiled to myself and hoped their journey would be as eventful as mine had been.

The Legion is full of good men, brave men. They perform dangerous chores for many governments all too willing to call on their professional services. When the shit hits the fan, they call on the Legion to clear it up. War is a stomach-churning reality, a constant threat. The Legion approaches difficult and dangerous situations with professionalism and without complaint. They are not mercenaries and they have a vital role to play in today's modern reaction forces called to deal with unrest throughout the world. The Legion sent three Regiments to assist the coalition forces in Operation Desert Storm, which liberated Kuwait from Iraqi aggression in 1991, as France's contribution to the operation. The 6ème REG, the REC and the 3ème REI played an important role in a massively political war. They were professional and performed their duties well. I am unsure of their exact role, but it is a clear example of the Legion being an important part of the Western alliance. France's reluctance to become involved in Operation Iraqi Freedom in 2003 will not have gone down well in any Legion unit but you can be assured that if France had sent troops, then it would have been the Legion who would have been called upon first.

I walked through the gates with little more in the way of possessions than when I had entered them. Sure, I now had money and plenty of it thanks to the Legion's system of conserving wages, but it was things you couldn't see that I took away with me – strength and loyalty. I passed a car containing the Interpol guys who were always stationed outside the gates on Fridays, discharge day. They didn't give me a second glance. I wanted them to ask me who I was. Where had I been? What had I been doing? I had tales that could have kept them enthralled for weeks. I wanted to say to them, 'I have served in the Legion for five years. I served with honour and fidelity.'

I sat on the ferry as it crossed the Channel and looked around at my fellow passengers. I wondered where they had travelled from and what they would tell their families about this holiday or business trip. I smiled as I recalled some of mine. Would anyone believe me? I looked just like any tourist in my new jeans and T-shirt together with training shoes. Would anyone even care about what I had seen and done? Probably not, because isn't the Legion just a Hollywood fantasy? Nobody actually serves in the Legion any more, do they? He must be just another fantasist or nutter...

I had a gut feeling that I would get stopped at Dover. I was a single, young skinhead. Where had I been? What had I been doing? How long was I there? The questions were fired at me by two of Her Majesty's Customs and Excise's best. I could tell they didn't believe me. Not until they emptied my bags and discovered a slew of Legion regalia and souvenirs did their attitude change. They left me in a plain, undecorated room and returned a few minutes later with another man. Without him even opening his mouth I knew he was a policeman. Why? I hadn't brought anything illegal into the country.

'Hello, nice holiday?'

I couldn't be bothered to go through the whole tale again, so I politely asked him why I was being held. The three of them looked at each other and smiled. 'Because you, my son, are AWOL.'

Absent without leave. No, there must be a mistake. I bought myself out. I'm not AWOL. I pleaded, scraped back in memory for details of those forms I'd completed so long ago when I applied for my early release, but to no avail. I was arrested and held while an escort was sent to take me back to camp. I hadn't waited for my PVR to be cleared before going to Paris – a serious mistake. I had been classed as AWOL since that first Monday. I was taken back to camp, interviewed and told I was being posted to another station to wait for my discharge papers. How ironic, I thought. If they had posted me when I first requested a move, then maybe none of this would ever have happened. Which might, of course, have been a pity.

I was sentenced to twenty-eight days detention at the Military

Corrective Training Centre at Colchester. After my time in the Legion this was a piece of piss. Upon my release I was informed that I was to be discharged for misconduct although, bafflingly, I was also issued with a good report for my time at the camp. The petty-minded bastards. It only went to prove that I had been right all along and I was hugely relieved when I was finally discharged. Although I still think fondly of most of the lads I have been honoured to serve with, I really couldn't give a toss about the hierarchy of either service at times like this. It is the comrade-ship, the respect and the esteem of your pals that is important.

I made my way home.

GLOSSARY

Accrochez! order to hook up static line in aircraft, prior to exit

Adjudant warrant officer

Ancien any ex-Legionnaire

Appel roll-call

Bidon water-bottle

Bleu volunteer who has passed initial selection at Aubagne and is waiting to go to Castelnaudary

Bordel (slang) shambles/cock-up (literally, brothel)

Boule à zero skinhead-type haircut, synonymous with the Legion

Brevet badge, or jump wings, normally worn on the chest

Brouillage issue webbing

Camerone famous Legion battle honour still celebrated today

Caporal chef senior NCO

Carfard (slang) the nervous disposition caused by Legion daily life

Carte d'identité identity card

Casse-croûte snack, usually taken mid-morning

Chants Legion songs, sung on the march or around camp fires, reinforcing camerarderie and sense of family

Civils civilians, meant as an insult

Corde rope climb using only the hands and arms

Corvée fatigues, usually consisting of litter picking throughout the quartier

CRAP (*Commandos de Recherche et d'Actions en le Profondeur*) Legion Special Forces

Debout! order given in the aircraft prior to *Accrochez!*: literally, Stand!

Deuxième Bureau Military Intelligence, used by the Legion as a vetting service

Engagé Volontaire Legion basic recruit

Permission Leave

Extinction des feux Lights-out

Fellagha (slang) rebel or enemy, dating back to the Algerian campaign

Foyer shop and beer hall, likened to a NAAFI

Francophone French speakers

Gardez-vous Attention!

GPS Global Positioning System, a satellite-based navigation system

Instruction basic training

Képi blanc sacred Legion head-dress, awarded after four weeks' training subject to passing certain tests

Mafia Anglaise English speakers who tend to stick together and look after each other

Matériel issued kit

Merde! (slang) Shit!

Nom de guerre volunteer's given Legion name

Pelle small US Army-type shovel for digging shell-scrapes and trenches

Petit déjeuner breakfast

Pinard Legion-made wine

Pitons sit-ups

Pompes press-ups

Promo jumps course

Quartier Legion barracks

Rangers issue boots

RCIR (*Ration de Combat Individuelle Rechauffable*) combat ration pack which can be reheated

Reassemblement parade

Reféctoire mess hall

REP (*Régiment Étranger des Parachutistes*) Legion parachute regiment

Rouge Red tag worn by volunteers waiting to go through selection at Aubagne

Sac à dos Bergen-type rucksack

Salle d'Honneur Legion museum, to which any visitor must be accompanied by a Legion officer

Sanglier wild boar, a Legion delicacy

Savon de Marseille block of soap issued for the hand washing of kit

Section platoon of men

Soupe evening meal

Soupe de midi lunch

Tenue de combat combat dress

Tenue de garde best dress, worn for guard duty

Tenue de sortie walking out dress

Transall C-160 transport aircraft

LE CODE D'HONNEUR

The Legion Code of Honour

1 You are a volunteer serving France faithfully and with honour.

2 Every Legionnaire is your brother in arms, irrespective of nationality, race or creed. You will prove this by according him the unwavering loyalty that will always bind members of the same family.

3 Respectful of the Legion's traditions and honouring your superiors, discipline and comradeship are your strengths, courage and loyalty your virtues.

4 Proud of your status as a Legionnaire, you will display this pride in your turn-out, always impeccable, in your behaviour, ever worthy and modest, and in your living quarters, always tidy.

5 As an elite soldier you will train vigorously. You will maintain your body at a peak of physical fitness and your weapon as if it were your most prized possession.

6 A mission, once given to you, becomes sacred. You will accomplish it at whatever cost.

7 In combat you will act dispassionately and without anger. You will respect the vanquished enemy. You will *never* abandon your dead, wounded or arms.

LEGION POEMS AND SONGS

A Legionnaire's Poem

I marched so proud –
a Legionnaire
my comrades by my side.
We fought our battles brave and well
whilst blood flowed like some raging tide.

Then with the battle fought and won
we'd turn our backs to leave
the families of our valiant foe
to crumple down and grieve.

And I cannot begin to think
within my tortured mind
'bout happy times –
when I last laughed,
for all I seem to find

Are moments when I'm carried back
into some battlefield,
where I have witnessed pain and death
and many fates were sealed.

I, too, have been a victim,
aggressor sometimes too,
but don't dare tell me what pain is
when you've no inkling what I've been through.

I've oft times thought why did I do
those things which I was taught,
but when you are a Legionnaire
you're a family that can't be bought.

The Paratrooper's Prayer

God, give me what you have left,
give me what no one ever requests.

I am not asking you for a rest,
nor tranquillity,
neither that of the soul nor the body.

I am not asking for wealth,
nor success, or even health.

You are asked for all these so often,
that you must have none left.

Give me God what you do have left,
give me what no one wants.

I seek insecurity and disquiet,
I seek torment and combat,
and God, give them to me indefinitely,
that I am sure to have them always,
because I won't always have the courage to ask you.

Give me God what you have left,
give me what others don't want,
but also give me courage, strength and faith.

Based on the original prayer by Andre Zirnheld, paratrooper, Free French Forces, killed in action 1942

Le Boudin

Tiens, voilà du boudin, voilà du boudin, voilà du boudin
pour les Alsaciens, les Suisses et les Lorrains.
Pour les Belges, y en a plus,
pour les Belges, y en a plus,
ces sont des tireurs au cul.

Au Tonkin, la Légion immortelle
à Tuyen-Quang a illustré notre drapeau.
Héros de Camerone et frères modèles,
dormez en paix dans vos tombeaux.

Well, there's sausage, there's sausage, there's sausage
for the Alsatians, the Swiss and the Lorrainers.
There's none left for the Belgians,
there's none left for the Belgians,
They are malingerers.

In Tonkin, the immortal Legion
shed lustre on our flag at Tuyen-Quang.
Heroes of Camerone and model brothers,
sleep in peace in your tombs.

CHANTES de 2ème REP

La Légion Marche

La Légion marche vers le front,
en chantant nous suivons,
héritiers de ses traditions,
nous sommes avec elle.

Nous sommes les hommes des troupes d'assaut,
soldats de la vieille Légion,
demain brandissant nos drapeaux,
en vainquers nous défilerons.

Nous n'avons pas seulement des armes,
mais le diable marche avec nous.
Ha! Ha! Ha! Ha! Ha Ha!
Car nos âinés de la Légion,
se battent là-bas, nous emboîtons le pas.

Pour ce destin de chevalier,
honneur, fidélité.
Nous sommes fiers d'appartenir
au deuxième REP.

The Legion marches towards the front,
singing we follow,
heirs to its traditions,
we are with her.

We are the men of the assault troops,
soldiers of the old Legion,
tomorrow brandishing our flags
as victors we will parade.

251

We do not only have weapons,
but the devil marches with us.
Ha! Ha! Ha! Ha! Ha! Ha!
Because our elders of the Legion
are fighting there, we follow in their footsteps.

For this destiny of knights,
honour, loyalty.
We are proud to belong
to the 2ème REP.

La Lune est Claire

La Lune est claire, la ville dort,
J'ai rendez-vous avec celle qui j'adore.
Mais la Légion s'en va, oui s'en va,
part au baroud, baroud.
Jeanine je reviendrai
sans aucun doute.

The Moon is clear, the town is sleeping,
I have a rendezvous with the one I love.
But the Legion is leaving, yes is leaving,
off to a gallant last fight, gallant last fight.
Jeanine I shall return
without any doubt.

INDEX

253